Christologies and Cultures

Religion and Reason 10

Method and Theory
in the Study and Interpretation of Religion

MOUTON · THE HAGUE · PARIS

Christologies and Cultures

Toward a Typology of Religious Worldviews

by
GEORGE RUPP
Harvard University

MOUTON · THE HAGUE · PARIS

ISBN: 90-279-7641-4
Jacket design by Jurriaan Schrofer
© 1974, Mouton & Co
Printed in Hungary

For Nancy

Acknowledgments

To acknowledge all those on whom this study depends is impossible. But I nonetheless want to register my gratitude to those who have most decisively influenced me.

Prominent in my own mind are the persons whose lives I have shared most intimately: first, my parents, who have encouraged me in all but a few of my interests and projects; and second, my wife Nancy and our daughters Kathy and Stephanie, with whom I continue to pursue changing interests and to undertake new projects. To Nancy especially I am grateful. She has not typed this manuscript. Nor has she refined my prose and corrected my spelling. She has instead contributed much more significantly in shaping all of our life together.

Though no detailed acknowledgment is even imaginable, I also owe a great debt to the tradition on which this study focuses. Perhaps a handful of figures whose influence on me is especially strong may represent this tradition: the writers of the New Testament, Calvin, Hegel, Ernst Troeltsch, H. Richard Niebuhr.

To institutions for their collective kindness and generosity, I too want to express my gratitude: to Princeton University for allowing me to receive full credit for a virtually unrestricted year studying literature and philosophy in Germany as an undergraduate; to the Danforth Foundation for its liberal support during my graduate studies; to Yale Divinity School for permitting me the luxury of a lover's quarrel with an able opponent; to Harvard's Divinity School, its Graduate School of Arts and Sciences, and its Center for the Study of World Religions, for providing me an intellectual and spiritual home that extended from Cambridge to Ceylon and back; to Johnston College in the University of Redlands for an informal yet provocative academic setting and congenial student and faculty colleagues; and finally to the University of Redlands as a whole together with the Ford Foundation for the faculty research grant during which final revisions and manuscript preparation of this study were completed.

Collective kindness and generosity are of course mediated through individuals. In my experience with institutions of higher education, those individuals have most frequently been my teachers and colleagues. As benevolent agents of the institutions they represent, as intellectual catalysts and models, as advisors and friends, my teachers and colleagues have in their various ways shaped my approach to issues like those examined in this study. So I want to thank those whose influence has been most decisive: E. D. H. Johnson at Princeton; David H. Kelsey and George A. Lindbeck at Yale; Daniel Day Williams of Union Theological Seminary in New York who taught at Yale in spring 1966; James S. N. Preus, formerly at Harvard and now at Indiana University; Wayne L. Proudfoot, formerly at Harvard and now at Columbia University; Herbert W. Richardson, formerly at Harvard and now at St. Michael's College in the University of Toronto; Nyanaponika Thera at the Forest Hermitage in Kandy, Ceylon; and especially Gordon D. Kaufman and Richard R. Niebuhr at Harvard and Wilfred Cantwell Smith, formerly at Harvard and now at Dalhousie University, Halifax, Nova Scotia.

I would also like to express my appreciation to Dr. Jacques D. J. Waardenburg, the general editor of the Mouton 'Religion and Reason' series, for his precise and helpful editorial suggestions.

For their skill and graciousness in typing and retyping the manuscript of this study, I want to thank Grace Friend Mullen of Cambridge, Massachusetts, and Doris M. Stockman and Angela C. Sanabia of Redlands, California.

Finally, I want to express my gratitude to the following institutions for permission to incorporate into the concluding chapter of this book portions of articles which originally appeared as indicated: to Temple University for several pages of my 'Reader Response', *Journal of Ecumenical Studies*, 7 (1970), pp. 547-551; to the University Press of Hawaii for extended passages from my article 'The Relationship between Nirvāṇa and Saṃsāra: An Essay on the Evolution of Buddhist Ethics', *Philosophy East and West*, 21 (1971), pp. 55-67; and to the President and Fellows of Harvard University for excerpts from my essay 'Religious Pluralism in the Context of an Emerging World Culture', *The Harvard Theological Review*, 66 (1973).

Redlands, California   George Rupp

Note on Abbreviated References

In those instances in which I refer in the text to a work in its entirety as representing a general tendency or line of interpretation, I indicate only the title in English and the date of initial publication. Since I call attention only to the work as a whole, I do not incorporate more detailed bibliographical data into the text or the footnotes. Whenever more specific reference is made to a work, the full information as to publication is given in the first footnote to that work in the chapter in question.

Note on Translations

All quotations appear in English. In those cases when there are standard translations of works originally published in a language other than English, I refer to the translations in the footnotes on the assumption that they will be more readily available to English-speaking readers. Except in those cases when identification by chapter and section or paragraph makes further guidance superfluous, I also note the corresponding page reference to the original between brackets; for both the translation and the non-English edition, I give bibliographical data only in the first appearance of a work in the chapter in question. Whenever I have modified the cited English translation, I indicate that in the appropriate note. In those cases when there is no translation, I refer to the non-English work and supply my own translation of any quoted passages.

Contents

Part Three: *Christology and Religious Pluralism*

Introduction

Two opposed dangers confront any attempt at elaborating a typology of religious worldviews. The first is that concern about comprehensiveness will result in only superficial treatment of any specific traditions. And the second is that a typology will remain confined in its relevance to a single tradition or complex of traditions. Of the two dangers, the first one seems to me to be the more serious; but contemporary man's pervasive awareness of multiple religious traditions also requires attention to the fact of religious pluralism.

To avoid the danger of superficiality, this study in the first instance focuses in detail on the Christian tradition. More specifically, I examine both historically and systematically Christian reflection on the significance of Jesus. My contention is that variables in Christology are correlative with differences in approaches to and interpretations of personal, social, and cultural life. Hence Christological controversies may be generalized into systematically opposed worldviews. I am persuaded that the resultant typology is also relevant to traditions in addition to the Christian and Western ones on which I concentrate. But I argue for that further relevance only after developing the typology (and advocating one of the opposed positions) with reference to illustrations from Western religious thought.

For the contemporary Christian or the religiously interested student of Christian faith, the question of the significance of Jesus and the fact of religious pluralism are of course already intimately related quite apart from the requirements of a cross-culturally usable typology of religious worldviews. As student of or committed participant in the Christian tradition, he or she cannot avoid the central concern of Christian theology with interpreting the significance of Jesus; and as a religiously interested person, he or she shares in the increasing awareness which religious traditions have of each other. This study is not, therefore, simply an academic exercise in describing religious worldviews. It is instead also an attempt to reflect constructively on the fact of religious pluralism and the figure of Jesus Christ as they meet in the contemporary religious consciousness of both the Christian and the student of Christian faith. Accordingly, this study may be viewed not only as phenomenology but also as theology. Indeed, it aspires to be both at the same time in its attempt to integrate descriptive and constructive approaches to interpreting religious life and thought.

ATONEMENT AND RELIGIOUS PLURALISM

The Christian tradition has with remarkable consistency seen the significance of Jesus in his action – even when that action has paradoxically been viewed as assuming the form of suffering. The church has, to be sure, also concerned itself with the question of who Jesus was. Indeed, it has promulgated a specific dogmatic formula on the person of Christ, not on his work. Yet every confession of who Jesus was has a preliminary character: it indicates what is deemed the necessary presupposition of his action. Doctrinal definition of the person of Christ is, in short, a specification of the church's conviction as to the nature which Jesus must have possessed if his action has the significance which Christians attribute to it.

One rubric under which the action of Jesus has traditionally been interpreted is Atonement. Frequently this term has been used to refer exclusively to the work of salvation effected in the death of Jesus. Any such strictly limited understanding of the term is, however, not adequate to the full spectrum of historical data. Consequently I include within the province of Atonement all interpretations of the significance of Jesus – of both the meaning and the effect of his action or his influence. This more inclusive perspective allows consideration not only of official formulations of the church and the positions of recognized theologians but also of influential interpretations of the significance of Jesus which have never attained general acceptance as orthodox.

In twentieth-century theology the Atonement as such has received little explicit attention. The *Systematic Theology* (1951–1963) of Paul Tillich may serve to epitomize a tendency to refrain from formal restatement of this doctrine: instead of expounding the Atonement he outlines six general principles to which any attempt at restatement should adhere. In the theological epoch beginning with World War I and continuing through the 1950s there have, to be sure, also been a number of substantial treatments of the Atonement. Probably the most influential ones are Emil Brunner's *The Mediator* (1927) and Karl Barth's fourth division of the *Church Dogmatics* (1953–1967). But despite a measure of willingness to adapt orthodox formulae to contemporary thought forms, such systematic expositions as those of Barth and Brunner have failed to forge an approach to the Atonement which is compelling or even intelligible to those not nurtured on and already committed to the dominant interpretations of the past.

In so far as it is accurate to generalize that the theologians addressing the question of Atonement most explicitly have tended to be those relatively more committed to traditional formulations, twentieth-century theology has perpetuated a pattern typical of Christian reflection since the late medieval period. That pattern is one of contrast between those who focus on the Atonement as a transaction of universal significance effected once and for all in the life and death of the Christ and those who concentrate more or less exclusively on the significance of the historical Jesus for the men whom he influences. The result of this polarization has been the impression that only two alternatives are open to the prospective interpreter of the Atonement: either an apparently orthodox explication which is dependent on unreasonable and morally offensive premises or a rational and humane approach which is not only unorthodox but also superficial. The reticence of most contemporary theologians in reference to the Atonement is, I think, in large measure derivative from their apprehension that this dichotomy exhausts the alternatives.

The history of controversy over the doctrine of the Atonement does unfortunately provide eloquent testimony to the ample representation of both species of deficiency. In this study I nonetheless explore yet once more the possibilities of overcoming the polarization characteristic of post-medieval discussions of the Atonement. First, I develop a typology for classifying interpretations of the Atonement so that both the similarities and differences among the various approaches may be evident in a systematic fashion. In the light of this typology I then examine the more immediate historical context of reflection on the significance of Jesus through a detailed study of the philosophy and the influence of the man who in my view has had a more profound impact on nineteenth and twentieth-century social and religious thought than has any other single individual: G. W. F. Hegel. Finally, I outline what I see as the most viable approach to a restatement of the doctrine of the Atonement.

The relationship between this extended consideration of interpretations of the significance of Jesus on the one hand and the fact of religious pluralism on the other is a highly dialectical one. The connection is perhaps most immediatly evident from the perspective of considering the Atonement. In that context the question of the Christian's attitude toward other religions traditions is in considerable measure answered as a corollary his of understanding of the significance of Jesus. To take the point at which the connection is most direct, the way in which a given interpreter of the Atonement treats the *eph hapax* – the once for all claim for the work of Christ – cannot but have implications for his approach to non-Christian religious traditions. The immediate relevance of a theology's interpretation of the Atonement for its understanding of religious pluralism should not, however, be allowed to obscure the degree to which there are implications in the other direction as well.

Those further implications concern not only the interpretation of the Atonement but also the very nature of the theological task. For a frank recognition of one's own tradition as one religious perspective among others raises unavoidable questions about theological method and the status of religious affirmations. Throughout the chapters devoted to a study of the Atonement this complex of questions is of course relevant in as much as my attempt to interpret a central Christian doctrine in the light of its historical development is itself an instance of theological enquiry conducted self-consciously in the context of religious pluralism. That general relevance becomes more specific when I consider the relationship between approaches to interpreting the significance of Jesus and attitudes toward other religious communities. Then, in the final chapter, I focus directly on the question of religious affirmation in the context of an emerging world culture which is radically pluralistic.

OVERVIEW OF THE ARGUMENT

This study develops a single line of argument. Because that argument concerns not only the whole history of Western philosophy and theology but also parallel developments in non-Western cultures, I define issues so as to maximize the internal coherence of the study itself. The most transparent example of this attempt to integrate the study into a coherent whole is my use of the same typological variables throughout. Consequently a cursory preview of the typology itself and the use to which it is put as an organizing principle may serve to summarize the line of argument which the study as a whole develops.

The typology used throughout the study employs two sets of variables. Each pair of contrasts is abstracted from the history of Western culture. They are Realist *vs.* Nominalist and Transactional *vs.* Processive.

My use of Realist and Nominalist as variables is derivative from the medieval debates between parties identified with those names. The disagreement was most concisely and comprehensively formulated as a philosophical issue: it is then the question of the status of universals. Whereas the Realists insisted that universal terms correspond to extramental reality, Nominalists maintained that only individuals exist and that, therefore, universals have no reality apart from them. There are, of course, positions which allow the affirmation of both Realist and Nominalist commitments in this statement of the contrast between them. But even this general statement of the issue does nonetheless focus a critical development in the post-classical West. That development is the emergence and the gradual institutionalization of an awareness which insists on the priority of the individual over against the corporate and the allegedly universal. There are examples of this tendency toward individualism in multiple dimensions of Western history from at least the eleventh century on: the founding of towns with increasing emphasis on private enterprise and rights of citizenship; the freeing of serfs over a period of centuries and the resulting change from membership in the organic society of the manor to existence as more or less independent entities; literary concern with the concrete and the particular in contrast to stylized representation and typological motifs; protest against the corporate authority and finally dissolution of unity in both the empire and the church. In maintaining that individuals alone exist,

Nominalism is not, then, simply challenging the dominant philosophical position of Platonic Realism. Instead it is correlative with and gives expression to social and other cultural tendencies which continue throughout the late middle ages and the become dominant in the modern period.

The medieval debates between Realists and Nominalists included Christological controversies. In this context the contrast is between those who affirmed that Christ in some sense assumed universal human nature and those who focused on the influence which Jesus exerted and his legacy continues to exert on individual believers. For the purpose of elaborating typological variables which are as comprehensive as possible, this Christological issue may be further generalized. Then the Realist alternative includes all positions which construe the work of Christ as in the first instance effecting an alteration in some universal state of affairs – in mankind or generic human nature, in the powers or structures governing the world, even in God himself. For in all such interpretations there is a definite contrast to the Nominalist emphasis on the changes which the historical Jesus or the church's images of Christ effect in particular believers.

Although it is not as overtly derived from a specific historical context as is the Realist-Nominalist contrast, the Transactional-Processive distinction may also be outlined with reference to the history of Western culture. In this case the critical development is the tendency throughout the modern period to place less and less emphasis on the possibility of a transhistorical fulfillment for human destiny and to concentrate instead on life in space and time. Symptomatic of this tendency is the decreasing power of such religious dualisms as heaven and earth or supernatural and natural – at least if they are interpreted in any literal sense. That no single force results in this movement toward self-conscious preoccupation with this world need scarcely be stressed. But among those forces is surely the conviction that the closed causal universe of modern science allows no such transhistorical fulfillment. The eighteenth century may serve to epitomize this connection between cosmic order and concern with historical development: begun with fervid praise for Newton's achievement in illumining the laws governing the universe, it ended with an ever more enthusiastic and exclusive emphasis on moral advance in the life of the individual and social progress in the history of the race. This concern of the Englightenment and its heirs with historical development illustrates the most generalized meaning of the term 'Processive' as I use it. My classification of a worldview as Processive indicates that in my judgment it construes change or development in spatio-temporal existence as ultimately significant. In contrast, for the typical Transactional position final religious value in some sense transcends historical life.

As with the Realist-Nominalist contrast, I use the Transactional-Processive distinction in the first instance to differentiate Christological commitments. In this context the Transactional position maintains that the work of Christ is effected in principle independently of its historical mediation. Examples include not only those traditional interpretations which insist that the Atonement is accomplished once and for all either in the first century or in God's eternal decree but also those characteristically modern approaches which focus on the individual's encounter with an ever-present Christ who is in principle not available to the modes of cognition applicable to phenomena in space and time. In contrast to this atemporal orientation, the Processive alternative confines its attention to changes in historical life. Hence it is concerned with the question of the mediation of Christ's influence through social and cultural forms; and it views the work of Christ as accomplished over time, either from the first century on or even through the whole course of history.

In Part One of this study I discuss the four Christological types which result from correlating the Realist-Nominalist and Transactional-Processive distinctions. I first specify the systematic issues to which the typology attends and then provide illustrations of the various positions from the history of Christian thought. That discussion closes with the contention that a consistently Processive interpretation offers the possibility of combining Realist and Nominalist commitments.

Part Two of the study in turn investigates in more detail the possibility of this Realist-Nominalist-Processive combination through an examination of Hegel's philosophy and a typological survey of its appropriation in the nineteenth century. In this connection I argue for a reading of Hegel which in effect accepts much of Marx's critique as a friendly amendment or even as simply a clarification of the original proposal. The result is an interpretation of Hegel's thought in which process and development are at the center of the system. In the course of the argument for this position I exhibit the intimate relationship between Hegel's metaphysics and his empirical studies in social and cultural history. At the same time I maintain that the issues addressed in Hegel's philosophical program as a whole parallel the Christological variables in the typology which I am proposing.

Part Three of the study first concludes my historical and systematic consideration of Christological commitments with a statement of what I see as the most promising line of interpretation and then correlates this complex of issues with the further questions implied in the fact of religious pluralism. Once again the Christological types inform the analysis throughout.

My constructive comments on interpreting the significance of Christ are an attempt to articulate what I see as an at least potential commonality between traditional Christian commitments and the Realist-Nominalist-Processive perspective which emerges in Part One and is advocated in Part Two. My procedure is first of all to describe the influence on the Christian consciousness of such traditional images of Christ as those expressed in the Biblical portrayal of Jesus and the sacramental life of the church. I then argue that this complex of images and rituals allows of an interpretation which construes individual transformation as ingredient in an ultimately universal process through which, to use the Biblical image, the rule or kingdom of God is established. This Realist-Nominalist-Processive position is not advanced as the only possible interpretation of the data. Nor do I claim that it is the most primitive or the most authoritative view. But in a tradition which is itself self-consciously developmental, such considerations are, I contend, in any case not the arbiters of final value. Instead, the tenability of any position can be adjudicated only with reference to the criteria of coherence and adequacy to total experience – that is, with reference to the criteria which in practice do in fact determine the viability of any worldview. My argument in the first chapter of Part Three is, therefore, simply that the Realist-Nominalist-Processive position represents one possible approach to the traditional portrayal of Christ. Once that contention is granted, the claim for greater adequacy than the alternatives rests not on a claim for unsurpassable fidelity to the most primitive data in the Biblical tradition but rather on the line of argument developed through out the study and expressed most explicitly in the final chapter.

As is the case with my constructive comments on interpreting the significance of Christ, my examination of the questions implied in the fact of religious pluralism presupposes the Christological types elaborated in Part One and Part Two. Because Christian attitudes toward or judgments about other religious traditions may be viewed as correlative with Christological commitments, it is possible to differentiate theological interpretations of the fact of religious pluralism with reference to variables in Christology. Hence I begin my analysis of the relationship between Christianity and other religious traditions with an explication of what the different Christological types systematically imply about those other traditions. I then examine the positions of two contemporary theologians – Karl Rahner and Schubert Ogden – to document with some specificity my contention that interpretations of religious pluralism are inadequate in so far as they presuppose either a Realist-Transactional or a Nominalist-Transactional Christology. This critical examination of the thought of Rahner and Ogden along with an exposition of Ernst Troeltsch's contrasting formulation of the issues in turn provides the context for my constructive attempt to outline an approach to the fact of religious pluralism which is consistent with the Realist-Nominalist-Processive perspective advocated throughout this study.

This constructive statement constitutes the final chapter of the study. It incorporates considerable ranges of new data; but this information is used to concretize and integrate conclusions which emerge from the line of argument developed in the study as a whole. For example, the analyses of religious history which Arend Theodoor van Leeuwen and Robert N. Bellah advance are examined not only for their intrinsic interest but also because they illustrate contemporary approaches significantly analogus to that of Hegel. Similarly, I survey Buddhist commitments in some detail because attention to the particularity of the various traditions is precisely what in my view renders Processive interpretations of the fact of religious pluralism more adequate than Transactional ones.

In any case, the argument which reference to these varied data is intended to support follows two lines. Negatively, I maintain that the Realist-Nominalist-Processive perspective has no compelling theological reason to deny the existence of genuine spirituality in non-Christian traditions. Positively, I scrutinize the process of interaction between traditions and exhibit the parallels between that process and the integration of the particular into the universal which is central to Christian reconciliation as it is described in the first chapter of Part Three. As a result, I suggest that dialogue with adherents of other tradition may be as much an implicate of a Realist-Nominalist-Processive Christology as evangelization with the aim of conversion is for traditional orthodoxy.

PART ONE

Interpretations of the Significance of Christ:
A Typology

2

The Need for a New Typology

There are at least two reasons for developing a new typology to classify interpretations of the significance of Christ. The first is that such a typology can be useful in understanding the central commitments which Christologies in their various forms have sought to affirm; and the second is that presently available typologies are either inadequate to the historical data or deficient in systematic control.

TYPOLOGY AND TRADITION

Both the usefulness and the limitation of typological analysis are perhaps most evident in its function as a tool for historical understanding. The development of a typology requires the isolation of a restricted number of variables so that comparison becomes feasible. Any such exercise in systematic classification is, of course, least questionable when the only variables are those under comparison. Hence an exhaustive catalogue of a finite number of logical possibilities offers the ideal of typological precision. In the case of historical enquiry that ideal is, however, unattainable simply because the number of variables is virtually unlimited. Consequently the application of typological schemes to historical data is unavoidably problematical. Yet precisely this inherent limitation of historical typologies also indicates their potential power; for the very profusion of variables makes any systematic discernment of patterns all the more valuable.

Frequently typologies used to organize historical data advance no claim to be exhaustive in principle. Instead the types are simply descriptive. That such typologies can be illuminating in the historical and sociological scrutiny of religious traditions is already amply illustrated in the seminal studies of Max Weber and Ernst Troeltsch. And the continuing fruitfulness of descriptive types particularly in specifying comparative patterns is evident in the work of twentieth century phenomenologists of religion from van der

Leeuw on. Even the most determinedly descriptive approach cannot, however, prescind from the process of systematization inherent in the very conception of a typology. Although the contingencies in the data are not intrinsically limited, the typology must itself consistently focus on specified variables. In reference to those selected variables, the logical model of exhaustively classifying the possible systematic relations is not inappropriate. The crucial issue is, of course, whether or not the variables on which the typology focuses are the significant ones; and that issue can be adjudicated only through attention to the ability of the typology in question to illumine the historical data which it interprets. But the aim at systematic completeness is in itself legitimate. It is, moreover, potentially useful in at least two ways.

The first is that the systematic implications of the typology may themselves call attention to historical data which would otherwise be ignored. There is, to be sure, the correlative danger that available data will be distorted so as to conform to the requirements of the typology. But the possibility of such distortion should not obscure the contribution that a perceptive and accurate typology can make in illumining parallels which are not at first self-evident.

A second service which careful attention to the systematic dimension of a typology can perform is more a constructive than a strictly historical one. In so far as a typology seeks to understand commitments which are integral to a living tradition, it at the same time delineates the systematic considerations which any appropriation of those commitments in the present must take into account. This function is particularly important if the tradition is viewed as in principle susceptible of development – a view which a typology of the various historical interpretations cannot but tend to support. For then a systematic classification of the various typical (orthodox and heterodox) positions can provide valuable guidance in any attempt to overcome inadequacies in past interpretations.

GUSTAF AULÉN'S TYPOLOGY

The best known twentieth–century typology of interpretations of the work of Christ is the one Gustaf Aulén develops in his influential series of lectures entitled *Christus Victor*. Whatever its intrinsic merits, Aulén's book cannot be ignored if only because it has become one of the most frequently cited theological typologies ever developed. One reason for the attention which *Christus Victor* has received is that in presenting his own analysis Aulén argues vigorously against 'the generally accepted view' of 'the history of the idea of the Atonement'. Characteristic of this view is the development of a fundamental contrast between 'objective' and 'subjective' understandings of the significance of Christ. In Aulén's own description of the line of interpretation which he opposes, the figures of Anselm and Abélard are the paradigms for the objective and subjective positions respectively. The two types are then traced through the further history of Western theology with medieval scholasticism, the Reformation, and Protestant orthodoxy continuing the Anselmic line while much of eighteenth and nineteenth-century religious thought revives the Abélardian approach, which had received little attention prior to the Enlightenment.

In outlining the interpretation of the historical data which he challenges, Aulén focuses on Ritschl's *Christian Doctrine of Justification and Reconciliation* in particular. But there can be no disputing his contention that the general interpretation which he opposes has been a very influential one not only in histories of doctrine but also in the development of controversies over interpreting the work of Christ. The interest in Aulén's alternative classification of the historical data has, then, been considerable because he offers the prospect of avoiding the polarization characteristic of post-Reformation debates on the Atonement in favor of a third position which can acknowledge inadequacies on both sides of the traditional controversy.

Aulén's claim is that the contrast between the approaches which Anselm and Abélard represent leaves out of consideration a third historical position which in fact is more adequate than either of the other two. This third position Aulén terms 'the classic idea of the Atonement'. Its central theme is that of conflict with evil and ultimate victory over the 'tyrants' under whom man is in bondage and suffering. Aulén insists that this idea of the Atonement has a 'clear and distinct character of its own, quite different from the other two types'.[1] Differentiation from the subjective view is

1. Gustaf Aulén, *Christus Victor: An Historical Study of the Three Main Types of the Idea of Antonement*, A. G. Herbert, trans. (New York: MacMillan, 1967), p. 4 [*Den Kristna Försoningstanken: Huvudtyper och Brytningar* (Stockholm: Svenska Kyrkans Diakonistyrelses Bokförlag, 1940), p. 10].

emphatic. Aulén uses this term 'to describe a doctrine which explains the Atonement as consisting essentially in a change taking place in men rather than a changed attitude on the part of God'.[2] In contrast, the classic idea is held to portray 'a complete change in the situation, a change also in God's own attitude'.[3] Though the distinction between the classic idea and the remaining type is more subtle, Aulén is no less emphatic in maintaining a difference in principle between the two interpretations. This Latin or Anselmic type is objective in a very strong sense. Hence Aulén sees no contrast between the Latin and the classic or dramatic types on this issue. Instead he focuses on the question of the agent of reconciliation:

> The most marked difference between the 'dramatic' type and the so-called 'objective' type lies in the fact that it represents the work of Atonement or reconciliation as from first to last a work of God Himself, a *continuous* Divine work; while according to the other view, the act of Atonement has indeed its origins in God's will, but is, in its carrying-out, an offering made to God by Christ as man and on man's behalf, and may therefore be called a *discontinuous* Divine work.[4]

Aulén not infrequently refers to further differences between the classic and the other two types. But because he apparently considers the distinction between the Latin and the classic types on the one hand and subjective views on the other as self-evident, he concentrates his argument on establishing the distinction he sees between the two objective interpretations. One recurrent comparison, which Aulén terms 'formal' and hence applicable on innumerable specific issues, is that the classic idea rejects the ideal of 'rational systematization' characteristic of the Latin and the subjective types. Instead it accepts 'a whole series of contrasts of opposites' and declines 'to find rational solutions of the antinomies along theological or psychological lines'.[5] In addition to this formal comparison and to what he terms the structural difference between continuous and discontinuous divine work, Aulén elaborates a total of four further contrasts when he offers a concluding summary of the salient features of the three types. Each of the

2. *Christus Victor*, p. 2 [7].
3. *Christus Victor*, p. 6 [12].
4. *Christus Victor*, p. 5 [11].
5. *Christus Victor*, pp. 154–155 [260–261]. Pp. 154–158 [260–266] gives Aulen's summary statement of this position.

further contrasts which he enumerates advances his argument for the greater adequacy of the classic idea as compared to the Latin type. Thus he maintais it has a more comprehensive conception of evil than does the Latin type – with the correlative effect that its view of salvation is more positive than the 'mere remission of punishment' characteristic of that type.[6] Similarly, he holds that for the classic idea 'Justification is simply the Atonement brought into the present' while for the Latin theory, Atonement, Justification, and Sanctification are 'a series of acts standing in relatively loose connection'.[7] The Latin type is also charged with losing sight of the close connection between the Incarnation and the Atonement.[8] And finally, the Latin interpretation is said to fail to develop fully the intense personal conflict not only between God and evil in history but also between the divine love and the divine wrath.[9]

CRITIQUE OF AULÉN'S TYPOLOGY

In evaluating a book like *Christus Victor* it would be possible simply to dismiss the work as little more than an ingenious compilation of historical inaccuracies. For at virtually every turn in the argument, Aulén indulges in highly dubious interpretations of the historical data. At the least he offers only partial descriptions of views which he purports to outline in a balanced and comprehensive way. This failure to take seriously emphases which do not readily conform to his typology is evident even in Aulén's treatment of the Fathers. The thought of Irenaeus, for instance, is delineated in considerable detail; but what Aulén himself terms 'his most comprehensive theological idea', namely that of recapitulation, is mentioned only in passing and in a context which inaccurately implies a central connection to the motif of victory over the devil.[10] Even more cavalierly, Augustine is numbered among those adhering to the classic view simply because the idea of God's love is central to his view of God's work.[11] In the case of

6. *Christus Victor*, pp. 147–150 [246–151].
7. *Christus Victor*, pp. 150–151 [251–253].
8. *Christus Victor*, pp. 151–153 [254–257].
9. *Christus Victor*, pp. 153–154 [257–260].
10. *Christus Victor*, pp. 21–22 [46–47].
11. *Christus Victor*, pp. 39–40, 45–46 [75–77, 85–86].

Gregory of Nyssa, Aulén quite correctly notes his considerable attention to the motif of deceiving the devil. But he virtually ignores the implications present even in the passages he quotes that the very act of God's Incarnation itself purfies man and restores him from his state of defilement.[12] Similarly, Aulén observes that Athanasius speaks of Christ's rendering satisfaction by 'paying the debt for all by His death' – a death also described as 'His vicarious sacrifice'. Yet he dismisses any attempt to see continuity between such formulations and Anselm's interpretation.[13]

The pattern revealed in Aulén's examination of the Fathers continues throughout the lectures. That his procedure represents a consistently applied method is evident from a consideration of those pivotal passages in which Aulén classifies individual theologians or theological schools as belonging either to the Latin or to the classic type. The criterion used to adjudicate such cases is always the same: Is the work of Christ treated as the work of God himself from start to finish?[14] With the application of this criterion a theologian or even a theological school is indelibly typed. Hence other qualities of the theological position in question can be used to characterize the type itself. The result is that instead of seeing multiple influences at work in a thinker or a tradition, the types themselves are elaborated. This process of amplification is epitomized in Aulén's concluding comments on the differences between the Latin and the classic types. Whereas the only contrast stated explicitly in his initial presentation of the types is that of continuous *vs.* discontinuous divine action, this structural criterion is only one of six contrasts in the concluding summary.

There is, of course, no reason to exclude as illegitimate the development of Aulén's types through the addition of concrete detail apparent in the empirical data which they classify. It is, however, imperative that some control be exercised as to which details are integrally related to the type as such and which ones only coincidentally occur in the thought of figures who are classified as included in the type on other grounds. And on this question of control Aulén is at best careless. It does not, for example, follow without

12. *Christus Victor*, pp. 46–49 [86–89].
13. *Christus Victor*, pp. 56–57 [101–102].
14. See *Christus Victor*, pp. 33, 45–46, 56–57 72–73, 76–77, 86, 88–89, 91, 114, 116 and 131 [66, 85–86, 101–102, 128–129, 135–136, 148, 142–153, 157, 194–196 and 220] for Aulén's classification of Irenaeus, Augustine, Athanasius, Paul, the Epistle to the Hebrews, Anselm, Luther, and Protestant orthodoxy.

further argument that Luther's intensely personal view of sin is dependent on what Aulén sees as his adherence to the classic idea of the Atonement. Yet Aulén draws conclusions about the type from the particular case of Luther: 'The conclusion, then, is that the view which most fully objectivises sin ends by giving us the deepest and most personal idea of sin.'[15] Similarly, the fact that some of those whom Aulén specifies as belonging to the classic type speak of tension between God's love and his wrath does not demonstrate that such language is integral to the type itself.[16] What in fact happens in the course of Aulén's lectures is that his advocacy of the classic motif leads him to identify with it emphases which are more characteristic of originally discrete interpretations. That patently is the case with Luther's intensely personal view of sin. But even in the case of conflict between God's wrath and his love, Aulén appropriates for the classic idea a theme which is, to be sure, adumbrated in the Fathers but which is nonetheless developed in much greater depth in the Latin theory than in any other.

Aulén's procedure of beginning with a highly schematic definition of the classic idea and then elaborating it in the course of his study to include other motifs which appear in thinkers whom he classifies as belonging to this type has at least three unfortunate consequences. The first is that the Latin type becomes little more than a caricature. That result is scarcely surprising, since Aulén defines this view in contrast to the classic idea – after including much of what is powerful in the thought of Anselm and his successors in at least some of his descriptions of that idea. Aulén offers his own summary in his analysis of Anselm's *Why the Godman?*:

Here, then, the contrast between Anselm and the Fathers is as plain as daylight. They show how God became incarnate that he might redeem; he teaches a human work of satisfaction, accomplished by Christ.[17]

Hence the Latin type becomes a view which fails to see God as fully involved in the work of reconciliation, which fails in its attempt to emphasize the gravity of sin, which fails to relate the Atonement integrally to an understanding of justification and sanctification, which even fails to take seriously

15. *Christus Victor*, p. 148 [248].
16. *Christus Victor*, pp. 153–154 [257–260].
17. *Christus Victor*, p. 88 [151].

the personal conflict in God between love and wrath – which fails, in short, in everything at which the classic idea is said to succeed.

The second consequence of Aulén's procedure is the converse of this first result. Because the classic idea is elaborated in the course of the lectures to include all the strengths of the positions classified as examples of this type, one of its distinctive features becomes obscured. That feature is the understanding of the purpose and the effect of the work of Christ as a transformation of human nature, of mankind as a whole. This understanding stands in contrast both to the Anselmic focus on resolving conflict in God himself and to the subjective type's preoccupation with change in individual men. Aulén occasionally alludes to this concern with the human race in its entirety as characteristic of the classic idea. He indicates it in a straightforward way when he contrasts the classic idea with his subjective type; for there he emphasizes the commitment of the classic motif to an objective change in the situation of all men. In contending that the classic motif entails deliverance from sin and death and not simply individual remission of punishment, he also is aware of the concern of the patristics for the human race as a whole. But because Aulén first focuses on the issue of continuous *vs.* discontinuous divine action and then expands the classic idea to include emphases also evident in the Latin and even the subjective types, he never develops this characteristically patristic problematic. Failure to attend to a significant feature of patristic thought on the Atonement is, of course, unfortunate in itself; but it also has the correlative effect of obscuring an area of continuity between the classic idea and the subjective type. In both cases attention is concentrated directly on the need to transform men – rather than in the first instance on the need for resolving a conflict in the divine nature, as in the Latin type. There are, to be sure, important differences between the patristic and the modern approaches to this question. But in any case Aulén's preoccupation with differentiating the classic idea from the Latin type while avoiding any possible suggestion of compromising the objectivity of the Atonement precludes his exploring possible areas of common ground with the subjective type.

This specific instance of failure to examine the implications of similarities and differences between the classic and the subjective types indicates the third and, I think, the most serious of the unfortunate consequences of Aulén's procedure. Because his central concern is to establish the classic

motif as a discrete type which is no less objective than the Anselmic interpretation, Aulén's consideration of the subjective type is perfunctory at
best. The fact that he frequently refers to it simply as 'the third type' epitomizes his approach: in his lectures this type has no discernible identity.
His discussion of 'the "subjective" or humanistic doctrine' in its own right
encompasses all of three pages – with another closely related six pages on
the nineteenth century. In the process of comparing the Latin theory unfavorably with the classic idea Aulén does, to be sure, occasionally insert
a paragraph to assert the even greater bankruptcy of the third type. But
there is no attempt to understand the genesis of Enlightenment and nineteenth-century views on the Atonement in their own cultural context.
Instead they are presented simply as the obviously unacceptable only
alternative to Latin orthodoxy – the only alternative, that is, for those who
have neglected to see the classic idea as a discrete interpetation.

Aulén's working premise here is that doctrines or interpretations of the
Atonement are only incidentally related to the social and cultural context
in which they arise. He does, to be sure, grant that some of the more bizarre
imagery associated with the classic motif in particular is dispensable. But
the underlying conceptions or ideas transcend any such conditioned forms.
Aulén offers his own concluding summary:

> It is therefore of the first importance to distinguish between the classic idea itself
> and the forms in which it has been expressed... The images are but popular helps
> for the understanding of the idea. It is the idea itself that is primary.[18]

Aulén's typology reflects his belief in the ready separability of images and
ideas – of apparently superficial trappings and an unchanging conceptual
core. As a result he never explores the possibility that definite cultural and
social presuppositions may be necessary for the comprehension of even
an apparently rational structure as schematic as that to which he at first
reduces the classic idea. Similarly, he does not investigate the extent to
which his third type may reflect cultural and social developments which
cannot simply be ignored if a contemporary restatement of the doctrine
of the Atonement is to be intelligible. Yet precisely such issues cannot be
overlooked if a typology of interpretations of the Atonement is to be
adequate historically and useful systematically.

18. *Christus Victor*, pp. 157–158 [266].

SHAILER MATHEWS' APPROACH

One of the few books self-consciously to raise this complex of issues in specific reference to interpretations of the Atonement is Shailer Mathews' *The Atonement and the Social Process*. Like *Christus Victor* it first appeared in published form in 1930. But there the similarity stops.

Mathews is emphatic in maintaining the crucial role of social context in the development of religious beliefs. His book is in fact an attempt to discern the various social metaphors informing traditional doctrines of the Atonement – and then to elaborate a new interpretation viable in the contemporary situation. Central to Mathews' argument is his conception of the function of what he terms 'patterns':

A pattern is a social institution or practice used to give content and intelligibility to otherwise unrationalized beliefs. What the axiom is to mathematics, a pattern is to thought. [19]

A pattern is, then, in the first instance an institution or form of social action; but for thought in that social context, it also functions as an unquestioned metaphor – unquestioned because it conforms to accepted social norms. The task of theology is, in Mathews' view, the creation of such patterns:

Speaking generally, orthodox theology is the use of political experience to set forth the reasonableness of Christian confidence in salvation. [20]

All Christian doctrines are patterns. They originated in the impulse to make something intelligible by discovering a likeness to something unquestioned.[21]

In the course of *The Atonement and the Social Process* Mathews elaborates the patterns which he sees as underlying the various interpretations of the Atonement. In each case the aim of the doctrine is the same; it is 'to make clear that God's forgiveness does not contravene his moral order'.[22] Mathews

19. Shailer Mathews, *The Atonement and the Social Process* (New York: MacMillan, 1930), p. 31.
20. *The Atonement...*, p. 33.
21. *The Atonement...*, p. 31.
22. *The Atonement...*, p. 165.

finds the impetus for developing interpretations of the Atonement in the Christian community's experience of 'new life through faith in Jesus'. Doctrines of the Atonement are, he maintains, simply attempts to explain and even to justify this experience. Mathews provides a characteristically terse summary:

If conscious of salvation, they may be assured of forgiveness – the conclusion which Paul so urgently argued in Galatians and Romans. But when one thinks of forgiveness he at once recalls preconditions of forgiveness in social practice. Not only that, but he begins to query whether those preconditions have been met in the forgiveness of God which he enjoys. Unless they have been met, such forgiveness must appear morally unjustifiable. Each and every doctrine of the Atonement is an answer to the need for such moral justification of God's gracious act.[23]

Mathews' exposition of the varied historical intepretationsof the Atonement consistently follows this approach. Each doctrine or motif reflects prevailing social conventions as to the conditions governing the granting of forgiveness. In the course of his book Mathews pursues his line of argument from the New Testament data through to the modern period. Jesus simply appeals to the parental analogy in explaining or 'justifying' belief in the forgiveness which his followers experienced. But other analogies or metaphors also appear in the New Testament. The pattern of sacrifice emerges because among both Jews and Greeks God's forgiveness was conditioned upon sacrifice. Similarly, the motif of ransom reflects the social practice of releasing captives through payment of a ransom. In Latin Christianity social practice is also employed as a means to understand the relations between God and man. Anselm, for example, appeals to the unquestioned feudal convention that violation of a lord's honor requires either satisfaction or punishment. That is the prevailing social condition of forgiveness. As the national replaces the feudal order, the legitimacy of the sovereign is conceived of as depending on his ability to enforce the laws of the state. Punishment for violations of law becomes essential to the maintenance of governmental authority. Hence the pattern of Jesus as satisfying the need for punishment emerges as a dominant interpretation of the Atonement. With the ascendency of the bourgeois class in the eighteenth century unques-

23. *The Atonement . . .*, pp. 165–166.

tioned commercial patterns complement the political pattern of absolute sovereignty as accepted norms for the relations between creditors and debtors also provide a social metaphor for understanding the Atonement. In this way arise the political, juridical, and commercial motifs which still remain dominant in Western theology.

What vitiates most modern treatments of the Atonement, argues Mathews, is the failure to recognize that discrete patterns cannot simply be combined. He singles out in particular the tendency to interchange the conceptions of punishment and suffering resulting from sin. Instead of attempting to soften the implications of the conception of punishment for sin, in the way that he terms 'romanticized orthodoxy' does, Mathews calls for a frank realization that a new pattern is required for interpreting the significance of Christ – a pattern which can replace the entire complex of conceptions based on the political and juridical practices associated with the absolute monarchy. To meet the need which he sees Mathews outlines his own constructive proposal for understanding the Atonement. Calling his interpretation 'the pattern of process' he draws on the knowledge of the natural sciences and views man as a participant in the development of the cosmos rather than simply as subject or citizen. With the abandonment of divine sovereignty and of the human guilt which Mathews sees as its correlative, the formulation of the critical issue which the doctrine of the Atonement addresses is changed. The question is no longer: How can God's forgiveness be justified? Instead it is, in Mathews' words:

Can one think of any reason or beneficent purpose in the cosmic process, and is love rather than coercion a basis upon which to build human society and organize one's own individual life?[24]

Mathews' constructive proposal is, then, not only the appropriation of a new pattern but also a reformulation of the underlying question which is being addressed. As a result its connection to the previous interpretations which he outlines is only a very tenuous one.

The strength of Mathews' book as a typology of doctrines of the Atonement is its success in describing a number of interpretations in reference to their own social and cultural presuppositions. Although he does frequently

24. *The Atonement...*, p. 181.

oversimplify matters in seeing a single explanation of the power of a doctrine as exhaustive, Mathews nonetheless performs a service in emphasizing the social matrix of theological reflection. But while his descriptive types are useful in their attention to variations resulting from modification in histor‐ ical context, the systematic power of his analysis is less than satisfactory. The difficulty is that his approach has at the same time both too much and too little system. In attempting to reduce all doctrines of the Atonement to the formula of justifying the forgiveness of God which believers experi‐ ence, Mathews universalizes a problematic which has been immensely influential particularly in Western Christianity but which has not been the only approach to the work or even the death of Christ. That Mathews' own constructive proposal does not readily conform to his formulation of the issue which every doctrine of the Atonement allegedly addresses is one indication of the difficulty which his typology poses. But many other post-Enlightenment and at least some patristic and medieval interpretations of the Atonement would also not approach the question in the way Mathews formulates it. The failure of all interpretations to conform to the Anselmic problematic which Mathews' formula echoes in turn means that his typology has too little system. For the result is a series of more or less closely related descriptive patterns which have no systematic connection either to each other or to additional possible patterns – such as Mathews' 'pattern of process', for example. There is, in short, no axis which gives structure to the typology as a whole.

The Aim of a New Typology

The efforts of Aulén and Mathews do not, of course, exhaust the typological approaches to the doctrine of the Atonement which have been proffered in the past. But they do represent the spectrum of attempts and hence they may serve to epitomize the two dominant varieties of inadequacy in typolo‐ gies of the work of Christ. In contrast to the studies of Aulén and Mathews, what is needed is an interpretation which begins with the historical data and thus avoids forcing thinkers into a pre-established scheme while none‐ theless attending to the systematic questions which underlie every under‐ standing of the significance of Christ. Both Aulén and Mathews do, to be sure, propose to meet this dual requirement. But Aulén's preoccupation with formal structure results in distortion of the historical material; and Mathews' attention to historical variations is not matched with commensurate care in examining the question of systematic relations between types.

3

The Two Crucial Variables

Even a cursory examination of the limitations evident in the typologies of Aulén and Mathews underscores the need to begin with the variety of the historical data rather than with a selected interpretation which assumes a normative status. One approach which may hope to minimize the potential for distortion is to focus on those questions which as a matter of historical fact have been the critical issues between opposing interpretations of the significance of Christ. Using this criterion, the traditional and admittedly often abused distinction between predominantly objective and predominantly subjective theories must be said to call attention to a significant contrast. The issue involved certainly requires more precise specification; but the distinction nonetheless discriminates between positions which are in more or less self-conscious opposition throughout at least the post-medieval period. Among patristic and medieval thinkers the subjective-objective contrast may also be employed with some success as an analytical tool. That the distinction is not prominent in the pre-modern data itself is, however, an important difference. Indeed, this difference suggests the possibility of an approach which may avoid the oversimplifications to which use of a subjective-objective dichotomy almost invariably leads.

A word about procedure may serve to anticipate the objection that in spite of its announced interest in the variety of historical data, the discussion in this chapter is more systematic and general than historical and particular. This chapter does focus on what have emerged historically as critical issues between opposing interpretations of the significance of Christ. It is, however, an attempt to formulate those issues systematically through an isolation of the variables which opposing views either state explicitly or imply. That procedure of course presupposes the variety of the historical data which it in turn organizes. But the question of whether or not a typology illumines the positions of particular thinkers can arise only after the outlines of the typology itself are specified. Consequently I first address the more systematic question in this chapter before turning to more detailed historical illustrations of the typology in the following chapter.

The debate as to where the medieval period ends and the modern era begins is an interminable and inconclusive one. But the discussion has nonetheless produced something of a consensus that it is inaccurate to view all characteristically modern tendencies as completely novel creations of the Renaissance. This result has been, in short, the increased awareness that modernity has medieval as well as classical roots. Since the relative self-consciousness about the subjective-objective issue in Christological debates constitutes a marked contrast between typical modern and typical pre-modern interpretations, it seems reasonable to explore the medieval developments continuous with characteristic Renaissance-Reformation-Enlightenment commitments in order to locate possible causes of the increase in explicit attention to this central question.

In specifying the issues underlying controversies between positions which consider themselves objective and those which they in turn term subjective, it is important to note that the designation 'objective' is a derivative one. The characterization of a view as subjective is, to be sure, invariably the work of an opposing interpretation which presents itself as objective in contrast. But the very consciousness of one's own position as objective presupposes the existence of other approaches which are rejected as merely subjective. Hence the crucial development for the emergence of self-conscious attention to the subjective *vs.* objective issue is the appearance of interpretations which may plausibly be construed as exclusively subjective.

As a generalization based on the historical controversies surrounding the doctrine of the Atonement, it may be said that an interpretation incurs the censure of being merely subjective in so far as it focuses its attention exclusively on the question of the way in which the work of Christ effects change in the concrete individuals who appropriate its benefits. The contrast is to those views which do not in the first instance concentrate on this question of change in individuals but rather see such change as derivative from a more fundamental transaction or result of Christ's work. The issue is, then, whether the change or transformation of individuals is the fundamental or a derivative fact about the Atonement. That this issue emerges as central only in the modern period is one indication of the social and cultural fact that preoccupation with man as a more or less autonomous individual is a relatively recent development in the history of Western Christendom. But the marked increase in attention to this issue from the Renaissance on should not obscure the extent to which medieval social and cultural history provides the context in which the underlying questions are formulated.

In the evolution of late medieval social patterns there are numerous pressures in the direction of a primary focus on individuals as increasingly autonomous entities. Correlative with the gradual breakdown of feudalism as an organic structure integrally relating the full spectrum of status groups was the emergence of new social forms which are more atomistic in their organization. The most dramatic evidence of this tendency is the commutation of serfs to tenants over a period of several centuries and the not unrelated development of medieval towns to offer a strong alternative to declining manoral life.

Dating at least from the economic recovery of the eleventh century, this process is already evident simply in the physical growth of towns. After centuries of occupying only a fraction of the walled enclosure comprising the municipal limits prior to the fall of Rome, city after city (for example, Cologne, Ghent, Bruges and of course the Italian port cities) expanded to include considerable areas outside the Roman walls.[1] Attendant on the expansion of existing towns was the formation of guilds and then the organization of commercial fairs to promote trade. But already in the twelfth century and still more in the thirteenth whole new towns were founded so that areas which were not traditionally centers of trade could also engage in commercial enterprises. What is especially significant in this organizing of new towns is the fact that they were frequently established on the basis

1. For statistical details, see, for example, Carl Stephenson, *Medieval History: Europe from the Second to the Sixteenth Century* (New York: Harper & Brothers, 1943), pp. 303–326, esp. 307–310. For a more general survey of the revival of urban life, see, for example, Sidney Painter, *A History of the Middle Ages: 584–1500* (New York: Alfred A. Knopf, 1953), pp. 220–247.

of charters which declared the inhabitants to possess certain fundamental rights as citizens. Perhaps the most revolutionary guarantee as far as subverting the surrounding feudal structure is concerned was the frequent provision that anyone living within the municipal limits for a period of one year was a free man. But other rights were also often specified – the right to be tried by municipal courts, for example. In the Italian cities of Venice, Genoa and Pisa, moreover, still greater freedoms obtained, since they were based simply on a sworn association of citizens rather than on charters granted by accepted political authority.

That feudal lords made substantive concessions of their authority in order to attract the benefits of commercial activity which founding new towns offered is one index of the changing structure of late medieval society. Another is the gradual abolition of serfdom. The commutation of the status of serf to that of tenant was well under way by the thirteenth century – though it was not completed until some three hundred years later. Through this change in status, men who had been integral units within an organic social system became independent laborers with an increasing measure of autonomy. They too came more and more to claim for themselves the rights which the town citizenry enjoyed. As a result rural as well as urban society moved toward a structure of discrete individuals voluntarily related to each other on the basis of recognized rights and not simply traditional responsibilities.

This modification in social and economic relations has its counterpart in the cultural sphere. Perhaps the most significant development is the increasing use of the vernacular in literature especially from the twelfth century on. That vernacular literature did not always focus exclusively or even primarily on the poor and the newly self-conscious townsfolk is evident from the writings of Dante and Chaucer, to name only the most illustrious figures. But there is nonetheless a movement toward sympathetic treatment of ordinary laborers and craftsmen – a movement which may be epitomized by one of its mature products, the comparatively late 'Vision of Piers Plowman' (ca. 1360), with its caustic critique of corrupt wealth and its glorification of the common worker. The growth of ecclesiastical drama from the mass to more elaborate sketches on the occasion of prominent feasts and finally to full cycles of plays indicates the same tendency. In contrast to the elaborately stylized quality of courtly verse and the tortured allegorizing of medieval Biblical exegesis, the mystery and miracle plays are often rich in concrete detail. There are, to be sure, an Everyman and numerous type characters including personified virtues and vices in the later (fourteenth century) morality plays. But in the miracle and mystery plays there are also Noah and his quarrelsome wife, a perplexed Abraham and his trusting son, the Christmas shepherd portrayed carefully to fit into the conditions of medieval Europe, and innumerable other humble and realistically portrayed characters.

Like vernacular literature and church drama, religious art and devotion also reveal a tendency toward increased concentration on the human and the particular. No less an authority than Henry Osborn Taylor speaks of the tenth and the eleventh centuries as a formative period for 'the emotional humanizing of Latin Christianity'.[2] Veneration of Mary as the *Mater dolorosa* was elaborated in tremendous detail and Joseph also became an important figure for the popular imagination. The saints were portrayed with increasing frequency in contemporary dress. And, most significantly, piety came to focus increasingly on the details of Jesus' humanity. In addition to the elaborate portrayals of his life in church art, the stations of the cross became an important pattern for devotion during the twelfth century. Finally, reenforcing the attention to Jesus' concrete humanity evident in drama, art, and devotion, the Crusades brought thousands of believers into contact with the Palestine which was his home.

That cultural movements were not always simply a passive reflection of changing social and economic relations is evident from the numerous religious reform and sectarian groups which emerged during the closing centuries of the medieval period.[3] Relatively early groups like the Cathari

2. *The Medieval Mind* (Cambridge: Harvard University Press, 1949), vol. 1, p. 361. For a survey of this tendency up to its mature expression in the fourteenth and fifteenth centuries, see J. Huizinga, *The Waning of the Middle Ages* (London: Edward Arnold, 1955), pp. 136–159 [*Herfsttij der Middeleeuwen* (Haarlem: H. D. Tjeenk Willink & Zoon, 1919), pp. 242–287].

3. For details and helpful notes including extensive bibliographical references on the origins and development of medieval sects, see Ernst Troeltsch, *The Social Teachings of the Christian Churches*, O. Wyon, trans. (New York: Harper & Brothers–Torchbooks, 1960), vol. 1, pp. 328–382, 431–445 [*Die Soziallehren der christlichen Kirchen und Gruppen* (Tübingen: J. C. B. Mohr–Paul Siebeck, 1912), pp. 358–426 [*bibliographical notes included with the text*)]. For a study which takes into account more recent scholarship, see Norman Cohn, *The Pursuit of the Millenium*(New York: Oxford University Press, 1970). Especially

were ascetic and elitist fellowships of ethical perfectionists who rejected established ecclesiastical policies of accumulating wealth and institutional power. Despite their radically otherworldly orientation, the Cathari and those under their influence are, however, indicative of the direction in which reform and sectarian groups were to move. Significant are their call for a return to the apostolic church and the historical Jesus, their championing of the poor, and their emphasis on lay participation. Later reform movements – from the Waldensians beginning in the twelfth century to Wyclif and the Lollards, the radical Hussite Taborites, and the *Devotio moderna* – continued the emphases on returning to historical origins, lay involvement, and supporting the poor, but they also came increasingly to formulate their concerns in reference to contemporary social and economic inequities. Thus they not only reflected and interpreted but also at least marginally shaped the growing consciousness that particular individuals in their specific circumstances were worthy of attention in their own right.

THE REALIST-NOMINALIST DEBATES AND LATE MEDIEVAL NOMINALISM

The question of the status of universals is generally recognized as one of the dominant intellectual issues in the medieval period from the end of the eleventh century on. But because the controversies surrounding this question are almost invariably interpreted as exclusively philosophical disagreements, little or no attention is directed to the social and cultural context within which the discussion proceeds. Perhaps the relevance of contemporary cultural and social developments would be more patent if the philosophical question at issue were characterized as the problem of individuals instead of as the problem of universals. At least then the parallels between this philosophical question on the one hand and changes in other cultural and social patterns on the other could not as readily be ignored.

The discussions which in time took the form of controversy between those who called themselves Realists and those who came to be known as

---

provocative are Cohn's observations on the significance of voluntary poverty as a sociological correlate of dissent. See pp. 156–162 in particular. Specifically on the Cathari, see Jeffrey Burton Russel, *Dissent and Reform in the Early Middle Ages* (Berkeley: University of California Press, 1965), pp. 188–229.

Nominalists had their origin in speculation about the ontological status of generic terms. The immediate occasion for the discussions was Boethius' commentary on the *Isagoge* of Porphyry, in which this question is raised. The range of issues on which the early debates focused is illustrated in the career of an apparently self-proclaimed Nominalist dialectician named Roscelin.[4] Although his works have been lost, extant critiques of his thought ascribe to Roscelin a straightforward denial that general conceptions have any reference to extra-mental reality. In maintaining that such general terms are only names and that only individuals have real existence, Roscelin affirmed a position which threatened accepted theological commitments on a number of points. On the evidence of Anselm's criticism of Roscelin, one position to which he took exception is the not uncommon medieval view that mankind as a whole is a single unified reality of which individual men are only properties. During the time of Roscelin's prominence as a spokesman for the Nominalist position the monk Odo of Tournai formulated this Realist interpretation of the unity of all men very explicitly as a way of understanding the dogma of original sin. Anselm's criticism is that if someone cannot conceive of how numerous individual men can be a single reality, neither can he accept the dogma of the Trinity with its affirmation that three persons are one God.[5] Unfortunately for Roscelin, the Council at Soissons agreed; condemned in 1092 for adhering to a position of tritheism, Roscelin retracted the offending views.

Roscelin was condemned for subscribing to tritheism. But his views posed an obvious threat not only to the church's beliefs but also to its liturgy and its institutions. The doctrine of transsubstantiation, to take the most transparent example, all but requires a Realist metaphysic if its

4. Summaries of what little is known about Roscelin are available in Meyrick H. Carré, *Realists and Nominalists* (Oxford: Oxford University Press, 1946), pp. 41–42 and Frederick Copleston, *A History of Philosophy II/1* (Garden City, N. Y.: Doubleday-Image Books, 1962), pp. 164–166.

5. Anselm, *On the Incarnation of the Word* in *Theological Treatises II*, J. Hopkins and H. Richardson, eds. (Cambridge: Harvard Divinity School Library, 1966), pp. 75–80, esp. 75–76 [*Epistola de incarnatione verbi* in *Opera omnia*, F. S. Schmitt, ed. (Stuttgart: Friedrich Frommann Verlag–Günther Holzboog, 1968), vol. 2, pp. 10–14, esp. 10–11]. This reference is to paragraph 2, but the paragraph divisions of different editions of Anselm's works do not always agree. In the *Patrologia Latina CLVIII* (Paris: J. P. Migne, 1863), columns 259–248, this letter appears with slightly different paragraph divisions under the title *De fide Trinitatis et de incarnatione verbi*.

commitment to a substantial change in which all the accidents remain unaltered is to be rendered conceivable. Similarly, the corporate and hierarchical structure of ecclesiastical institutions at all levels is very readily legitimated if the possibility of a unity of many components in a single reality is presupposed. This priority of corporate persons over particular individuals is perhaps most crucial in interpreting the institution of the Papacy as the personified unity of the corporate church as a whole. Though alternative defenses of such traditional commitments are possible even on Nominalist premises, it is scarcely surprising that this process of rethinking would generate vigorous resistance.

There were, then, significant theological and ecclesiastical issues at stake in the debates between the Realists and the Nominalists. That should not, however, obscure the continuities between the immediate doctrinal focus of the controversies and the broader cultural and social developments of the period. Early critics of those extreme forms of Realism which hypostasized ideas were, to be sure, for the most part dialecticians who focused on the intellectual absurdities which they thought this position entailed. But with the further development of Nominalism as a constructive position the systematic continuities with the social and cultural movement toward greater individual autonomy become more evident. The thought of William of Ockham may serve to illustrate this parallelism.

On the specific question of the status of universals Ockham agrees with his Nominalist predecessors that only individuals exist, that there is no common reality or substance existing in individuals of the same species, that universals are only mental concepts. But Ockham disagrees with extreme Nominalists like Roscelin in so far as they at least appear to have held that a universal is a mere sound or word (*flatus vocis*) with no referent whatever. Instead he maintains that universals stand for real qualities which the mind abstracts from individual things. Hence Ockham's position bears a considerable resemblance to the moderate realism of Thomas or to the somewhat unsystematic conceptualism which Abélard espouses. In all three cases, an empiricist epistemology combines with the affirmation that only individuals exist. What distinguishes Ockham is his systematic application of Nominalist commitments to more specifically theological and anthropological issues.

Whereas both Abélard and Thomas retain the Platonic-Augustinian tradition of the divine ideas as exemplars, Ockham rejects all attempts to retain the *universale ante rem*. When he does nonetheless use the traditional Augustinian language, he indicates that God's 'ideas' are the actually existent individuals or creatures which he knows and which, as known eternally, may in turn be considered the exemplars of themselves.[6] Ockham's reasons for denying the *universale ante rem* are at least twofold. The first is simply his criterion of economy; for in his view it is unnecessary to postulate anything other than the human mind and individual entities to explain the origin and function of universals. The second is the specifically theological argument that the existence of any such divine ideas would in principle infringe on God's absolute sovereignty. Hence Ockham denies that there is any metaphysical reason for existent matters of fact. They are simply and directly the result of God's arbitrary will.

From what would on the face of it seem to be this unpromising theological starting point, Ockham moves to an anthropology which lays heavy stress on man's freedom and responsibility. Indeed, the most salient characteristic of his view of man is its strong voluntarism. Just as in his doctrine of God the divine ideas yield any claim to intrinsic rational structure in favor of the arbitrary act of creation, so in his anthropology man's reason is subordinate to his will. As a result the discipline of theology becomes a practical task heavily dependent on authority and faith rather than a speculative rational enterprise. Because God's action is not in principle dependent on the requirements of any rationality, neither his nature nor his future action can be deduced from any past events. Acutely aware of the limits which this theological conception places on human knowledge of God, Ockham insists that the scholastic proofs can at best be probable arguments. What is finally needed is faith as a willed decision, not rational conclusions based on proofs.

If this insistence on the limits of human reason and on the need for faith as a volitional act were the whole of Ockham's view, the claim that

---

6. For a lucid exposition of this complex issue see Frederick Copleston, *A History of Philosophy III/1* (Garden City, N. Y.: Doubleday-Image Books, 1963), pp. 69–71, 100–103. My summary characterization of Ockham's position relies heavily on Copleston's treatment. For more details, including references to primary sources, see his pp. 65–164. Also helpful is Paul Vignaux, *Philosophy in tne Middle Ages:An Introduction*, E. C. Hall, trans. (Cleveland: World Publishing–Meridian Books, 1959), pp. 165–179 [*Philosophie au moyen age* (Paris: Librarie Armand Colin, 1958), pp. 170–186].

his Nominalism represents the *via modern* over against the Realist *via antiqua* would have to be severely circumscribed. But using the distinction between *potentia absoluta* and *potentia ordinata* which also is operative in the thought of John Duns Scotus, Ockham in effect creates a very considerable sphere of action in which man is in fact not simply the faithful vassal of his totally arbitrary lord. Despite his unfaltering affirmation that God is omnipotent without qualification (*potentia absoluta*), Ockham nonetheless in practice places great emphasis on the fact that this all powerful Lord has willed to order the exercise of his might (*potentia ordinata*) in ways that are reliable and that give definite responsibilities to man. Ockham's criticism of the deterministic implications in the thought of Thomas and Duns Scotus on predestination and his argument for equating predestination and fore-knowledge provide what is perhaps the most direct indication of his affir-mation of human freedom and responsibility. But this emphasis is evident throughout his work – ranging from his Mariology, which focuses on the willingness of Mary to be God's instrument, to his political writings, which protest papal absolutism and defend fellow Franciscans under papal con-demnation.

More important than Ockham's particular views is, however, the fact that he represents a pattern of thought which had become a significant force by the fourteenth century. That he protested papal absolutism, for example, is important not only in its own right but also because it indicates his participation in a larger cultural and social process which shared his criticism. Even those political supporters who saw in this process only an opportunity to increase their own sphere of sovereignty still represent a movement away from the universal focus of the medieval synthesis to the more provincial and the particular, from any claims on the eternal to the concrete problems of temporal existence. And in the case of Ockham and his fellow Nominalist Marsilius of Padua, the movement entails more than this shift; for Ockham's political writings and Marsilius' *Defensor pacis* (ca. 1324) do not, at least ideally, envision the exchange of one absolutism for another, but rather the establishment of social structures in which authority derives in at least some measure from the exercise of indivi-dual choices on the part of the citizenry.[7]

7. For a concise discussion of late medieval developments in political theory with

As in the political, so also in the religious and the more broadly cultural realms, Ockham's position reflects and in turn shapes broader historical developments. In the life of piety, there are, of course, general continuities between the Franciscan Ockham's voluntarism and the practical, ethical orientation of the Franciscans from St. Francis on. In a figure like Jean Gerson it is even possible to see a type of Nominalist mysticism which replaces absorption into the Godhead with an ethical communion in which the will displaces the primacy of the intellect and in which the individual personality is preserved.[8] Finally, in the Brethren of the Common Life or the so-called *Devotio moderna* one can see strong Nominalist influences on a practical piety which affirms the possibility of communion with God expressed in the concerns of everyday life.[9] In a broader cultural context there are, moreover, important parallels between the commitments of late medieval Nominalists like Ockham and humanists of the Italian Renaissance like Marsilio Ficino and Giovanni Pico della Mirandola.[10] Both Ficino and Pico were, to be sure, central to the revival of Platonism in the fifteenth century. But both men also studied the medieval scholastic tradition and admitted its influence on them. Even in Pico's strongly Platonic *Oration on the Dignity of Man* (1486) with its image of man as the head of creation having the freedom to move either up or down the hierarchy of being, the self is centered not in reason but in the will; and ultimate union with God is attained through a love which is a function of the will.

---

particular reference to the question of popular consent, see J. W. Gough, *The Social Contract: A Critical Study of its Developments* (Oxford: Clyrendon Press, 1963), pp. 36–48. For more detailed consideration of the contribution of Marsilius in particular to political thought, see Alexander Passerin D'Entréves, *The Medieval Contribution to Political Thought* (Oxford: Oxford University Press, 1939), pp. 44–87.

8. Heiko A. Oberman, *The Harvest of Medieval Theology: Gabriel Biel and Late Medieval Nominalism* (Cambridge: Harvard University Press, 1963), pp. 323–360, argues that men like Gerson illustrate a distinctively Nominalist form of mysticism.

9. J. Haller, *Pabsttum und Kirchenreform* (Berlin: Weidmannische Buchhandlung, 1903), vol. I. pp. 78–83 stresses the continuities between Ockham and the anti-clericalism of the poor laity in particular.

10. For a consideration of this question, see Heiko A. Oberman, 'Some Notes on the Theology of Nominalism with Attention to its Relation to the Renaissance', *Harvard Theological Review*, LIII (1960), 47–76.

REALIST AND NOMINALIST AS CHRISTOLOGICAL TYPES

The controversies between the Realist and the Nominalists do not, then, center only on esoteric philosophical disagreements but rather formulate critical metaphysical issues with significant social and cultural ramifications. It is, moreover, in this context of broader social and cultural developments that the relevance of the controversies to the history of the doctrine of the Atonement must be seen. Nonetheless, the specific usefulness of the distinction between Realists and Nominalists for discriminating between interpretations of the significance of Christ is suggested in a central issue raised directly in the debates themselves: the question of the relation between the individual person and human nature as such.

That there is a generic human nature is presupposed as the connection between Christ's work and mankind in the characteristic patristic Christologies. That connection must, to be sure, be actualized. Hence baptism in particular assumes a central role in the appropriation of salvation; it finally actualizes incorporation into Christ. But the connection in principle between Christ's work and other men is never in question. Whatever specific interpretation a thinker offers in attempting to understand the Atonement – whether it is paying the debt of death to gain immortality or defeating the devil or reversing Adam's disobedience through obedience or offering sacrificial expiation for sin – the question of the efficacy of that action for all men poses no difficulties as long as Christ is seen as possessing generic human nature. That Christ's manhood is a universal in the technical Platonic sense of the term need not of course always be explicitly stated. In the ecclesiastically normative formulation of Chalcedon, for example, the affirmation that Christ is consubstantial with men in his humanity assumes a Realist ontology only implicitly. But the conception of universal or generic human nature in any case functions more or less consciously as a cultural presupposition in the patristic and early medieval period to facilitate comprehension of the connection between Christ's work and successive generations of believers.

The systematic elaboration of the Nominalist position is critical for the history of the interpretation of the Atonement precisely because it calls into question this presupposition of a fundamental metaphysical connection between Christ's work and other human individuals. In insisting that individuals alone are real, Nominalism in effect focuses attention on the very issue which Realist approaches to the work of Christ considered self-explanatory and therefore never analyzed systematically. There are of course Fathers who explore the ways in which Christ's life and death move or influence believers separated from him in time quite apart from the question of an underlying unity of nature between him and all men. Augustine is a particularly powerful case in point. But even in Augustine there is no systematic presentation of an interpretation along psychological and ethical lines as a discrete alternative which raises fundamental questions about the premises underlying other theories also appearing in his writings. Only with the emergence of a self-conscious Nominalism during and after the medieval period does this systematic and polemical approach become evident.

That there was as a matter of historical fact specific and repeated disagreement over the existence of a generic human nature does not of course restrict the Nominalist challenge to this particular question. If that were the only point at issue a number of patristic views and certainly a theory like that of Anselm could still be propounded after the elimination of references to the universal character of Christ's manhood. But the consistent Nominalist position equally excludes interpretations which locate the effect of the Atonement in any other universal. Stated in its most general form the distinction between Realist and Nominalist as I use it in classifying interpretations of the significance of Christ is, therefore, a distinction in reference to the locus of the result which his work is said to accomplish.

The Realist position affirms an effect of the Atonement distinguishable from the change finally realized in historical believers and their communities – an effect from which the change in believers and their communities is derivative. Those patristic views which construe all of mankind as involved in the work of Christ because the Logos assumed generic or universal human nature are of course Realist in this sense. So too are those similarly Platonic interpretations in the nineteenth century, for example, which see in Jesus the archetypal man either as inclusive of mankind or, in an attempt to modify the physical connotations of the patristic view, as the designated representative of all men. This emphasis on Christ's universal humanity is, however, only one illustration of the Realist type. Further examples include all views which construe the Atonement as effecting a change either in God or in the cosmic process, a change which in turn makes possible healing in man.

In contrast to this Realist approach, the Nominalist type locates the result of Christ's work exclusively in the changes effected in those individuals (and their communities) who appropriate its benefits. This Nominalist perspective is evident in interpretations which view the life and death of Christ as illustrating or teaching immutable truths about man's existence or as exerting a salutary moral influence on believers or as initiating a powerful historical influence through the church.

THE QUESTION OF TIME AND THE STATUS OF HISTORICAL DEVELOPMENT

Although the Realist-Nominalist distinction does parallel one of the differences suggested in the frequently used contrast between objective and subjective theories of the Atonement, it is more adequate because it avoids the tendency of the objective-subjective dichotomy to conflate two sets of issues which can and should at least provisionally be differentiated. In addition to distinguishing between those positions which attend exclusively to the influence of Christ on individuals and those which instead maintain that change in individuals is derivative from a more fundamental effect of the Atonement, the objective-subjective contrast also is frequently construed as addressing the question of the temporal duration of the work of Christ. This second question is most directly in evidence when the *eph hapax* – the once for all claim for the Atonement – is under discussion. The designation of a position as objective then indicates that it assents to the once for all character of the Atonement in contrast to the varius subjective views which are portrayed as unable to make this affirmation.

This correlation of the time question with the universal-individual contrast is both historically accurate and systematically illuminating. It is, however, important to recognize that two sets of variables are being correlated rather than to suppose that only a single distinction is involved. The question of time and the Realist-Nominalist distinction are, to be sure, very closely related. A literal affirmation of the *eph hapax* does require conceiving of the Atonement as at least in principle accomplished in a single transaction which is universal in scope; and questioning that affirmation is the unavoidable correlate of focusing on change in discrete individuals in their particular historical contexts. But to maintain that the temporal question is simply an implicate of this Realist-Nominalist contrast and therefore to restrict the alternatives to the same two fundamental positions is to oversimplify the complexities which the temporal variable introduces. One indication of the extent to which the temporal question involves a second set of issues is the fact that a number of the systematic alternatives with reference to this question are advanced self-consciously as alternatives in a period of Western social and cultural development subsequent to that of explicit and systematically elaborated opposition between Realists and Nominalists. The movement of post-medieval history is not, of course, independent of the contrasting tendencies which underlie the Realist-Nominalist debates. But continuing development nonetheless has the cumulative result of in effect introducing significantly novel forces.

For the formulation of the question of time as a religious issue, perhaps the most important of such at least relatively new social and cultural forces is a product of the revolution in the natural sciences which the figure of Newton epitomizes. As Newton's own writings illustrate, two complementary tendencies find expression in the scientific advance which his thought represents. On the one hand, there is the Newton of the *Optiks* (1704) engaging in careful experimentation and observation of particular data. On the other hand, there is the Newton of the *Principia* (1687) formulating universal laws which govern the patterns perceivable in the wealth of phenomena which the scientist organizes. The Newtonian enterprise as a whole is, to be sure, dependent on scrupulous attention to the particular data from which universal laws are generalized. In this sense the foundations of the empirical science which he epitomizes are Nominalist. But Newton's own speculative interests and his synthesizing or generalizing power also testify to the Realist concern for universal regularities. This latter capacity is perhaps the more compelling tendency for the cultural imagination of Newton's own generation and its immediate successors. As is his habit, Alexander Pope expresses the common judgment of the age in an uncommonly memorable fashion:

NATURE and Nature's laws lay hid in Night:
God said, Let NEWTON *be*! and all was Light![11]

11. 'Intended for Isaac Newton' in *The Complete Poetical Works of Alexander Pope – Cambridge Edition*, H. W. Boynton, ed. (Boston: Houghton Mifflin – Riverside Press,

For the Enlightenment Newton is, then, the foremost examplar of the power of human reason to illumine the world through understanding it as a cosmos ordered in accordance with universal causal laws.

As do many of his late seventeenth and eighteenth-century admirers and advocates, Newton himself presents his discoveries as testifying to the divine providence ruling the world. Indeed, as the preoccupation of the age with the problem of theodicy indicates, the hypotheses of the new science can be combined with the philosophical resources of the Platonic tradition in particular to argue that the cosmos is the best of all possible worlds. For representative Enlightenment Deists, acceptance of Newtonian science is, moreover, compatible with a continued belief in immortalyty and in future rewards and punishments. The result is, in short, a position which attempts to affirm what are construed as the essential tenets of traditional Christianity without violating the canons of scientific rationality.[12] But as materialists like La Mettrie in his *Man a Machine* (1748) and

1903), p. 135. Not surprisingly in view of the imagery implicit in the very term 'Enlightenment', examples of this conviction of a new dawn could be multiplied indefinitely from the literature and art of the age. Another particularly striking example is provided in the frontispieces which that prototypically Enlightenment figure Christiaan Wolff had affixed to his books. The dominant motif repeatedly is that of the sun breaking through clouds to illumine a pastoral landscape. See, for example, the frontispieces in *Vernünftige Gedanken von Gott, der Welt und der Seele des Menschen* (Halle: Regnerische Buchhandlung, 1751) and *Vernünftige Gedanken von der Menschen Thun und Lassen* (Halle: Regnerische Buchhandlung, 1743).

12. For a discussion of Newton's own position as still affirming as much as possible of traditional beliefs while at the same time unavoidably facilitating movement toward conceiving of the universe as infinite and godless, see Alexandre Koyré, *From the Closed World to the Infinite Universe* (New York: Harper & Row–Torchbooks, 1958), esp, pp. 206–276. The classic discussion of attempts to correlate the new physics with traditional Platonic commitments is Arthur O. Lovejoy, *The Great Chain of Being: A Study of the History of an Idea* (New York: Harper & Row–Torchbooks, 1960). See esp, pp. 91–241. For a detailed description of the religious beliefs of English Deists, German *Neologen*, and French *philosophes*, see Emanuel Hirsch, *Geschichte der neuern evangelischen Theologie* (Gütersloh: C. Bertelsmann Verlag, 1949–1954), vol. 1, pp. 147–152, 244–252, 271–344, vol. 2, pp. 48–91, 370–390, 417–432, vol. 3, pp. 58–143, vol. 4, pp. 1–165. For a very much more concise discussion of the English Deists, see Frank E. Manuel, *The Eighteenth Century Confronts the Gods* (New York: Atheneum, 1967), pp. 55–81. For further elaboration of the multiple tendencies included under the rubrics 'deism' and 'natural religion', see Paul Hazard, *European Thought in the Eighteenth Century: From Montesquieu to Lessing*, J. L. May, trans. (Cleveland: World Publishing–Meridian Books, 1963), pp. 44–92, 113–129, 393–434 [*La Pensée Européenne au XVIIIéme Siécle: De Montesquieu á Lessing* (Paris: Boivin, 1946), pp. 58–123, 151–173, 163–220].

d'Holbach in *The System of Nature* (1770) argue programmatically, Newtonian science also allows of a very different line of inference. Their consistently materialist and mechanist reading of the new physics denies both the existence of God and the possibility of any form of existence beyond this life. Enlightenment Christendom is not, of course, itself explicitly atheistic. Nor is there evidence that very many Christian thinkers accepted the conclusion that man's existence is ended completely with his death. Even a late eighteenth-century materialist like Joseph Priestley still subscribes to belief in a general resurrection and last judgment as integral to Christian faith. Yet despite the continued affirmation both of a Creator who established the cosmic order and of an immortality which transcends earthly existence, the attack on traditional dualism is far more pervasive in its influence on Christian reflection than the relatively infrequent acceptance of its alternative positions suggests.[13]

This broader influence is evident in increasingly exclusive attention to the implications which traditional beliefs have for shaping human life in this world. The tendency to focus unambiguously on man's earthly existence most frequently assumes the form of an interpretation of Christian faith as supporting and promoting morality. Matthew Tindal's *Christianity as Old as the Creation* (1730), the 'Creed of a Priest of Savoy' which appears in Rousseau's *Emile* (1762), and Kant's *Religion within the Limits of Reason Alone* (1793) may serve to epitomize this pervasive and influential Enlightenment tradition. As is most systematically argued in Kant's writings, this line of interpretation in effect construes all beliefs about a suprahistorical God or transmundane human existence as derivative from the requirements of man's moral life.

Although this understanding of religion as serving morality is no doubt the most common pattern, it is not the only form in which the attack on traditional dualism finds indirect expression in religious thought. A closely

13. See Basil Willey's discussion of Priestley's views in *The Eighteenth Century Background* (Boston: Beacon Press, 1961), pp.1 68–204, esp. 181–194. Willey also offers a convenient summary of d'Holbach's thought. See pp. 155–167. For a forceful, almost vehement, argument that materialists like d'Holbach and La Mettrie are the exception rather than the rule even among the French *philosophes*, see Ernst Cassirer, *The Philosophy of the Enlightenment*, F. C. A. Koelln and J. P. Pettegrove, trans. (Boston: Beacon Press, 1955), pp. 50–73 [*Die Philosophie der Aufklärung* (Tübingen: J. C. B. Mohr–Paul Siebeck, 1932), pp. 65–98].

related and in time perhaps even more influential tendency is an increasing interest in more comprehensive historical development. Here too the perspective of a thoroughly secularized atheism represent one consistent extreme; it programmatically repudiates the traditional religious commitment to heavenly fulfillment for the faithful in favor of an aggressively this-worldly appraisal of man's potential for achieving progressive self-realization. Condorcet's *Outlines of an Historical View of the Progress of the Human Mind* (1793) is an exuberant illustration of this position. Consideration of historical development is not, however, restricted to those who adopt this approach of totally secularizing traditional religious themes. Instead there is also a renewed interest in Christian motifs which allow interpretation with reference to historical development even if they finally affirm a transhistorical goal. Perhaps the most striking illustration of this tendency is Lessing's 'The Education of the Human Race' (1777). Similarly under the influence of theological motifs are Herder's *Another Philosophy on the Education of Mankind* (1774) and his *Ideas on the History of Mankind* (1784–1787). But despite the considerable differences between the aggressively secular and the broadly theological approaches, the common concern with the dynamics of history testifies to a highly significant development in the second half of the eighteenth century. Confronted with what can at least readily be construed as a causally closed cosmic order and the consequent implausibility of a transhistorical fulfillment for human life, Western thought turns increasingly toward an unambiguous focus on the possibility of realizing ideals in the future through development within the historical process itself. The pattern of moralized Christian faith is, in short, again in evidence: even when the transhistorical culmination of human history is affirmed, it is interpreted so as to support the possibility of development toward that goal within time. Concern with natural and cultural development is of course even more pronounced in the nineteenth century than in the Enlightenment. But that fact serves only to underscore the significance of the increasing preoccupation with historical studies and with the philosophy of history in the course of the eighteenth century.[14]

14. For an incisive polemic against the stereotype of the Enlightenment as 'unhistorical', see Cassirer, *Philosophy of the Enlightenment*, pp. 197–233 (263–312). See also: Carl L. Becker, *The Heavenly City of Eighteenth-Century Philosophers* (New Haven: Yale University Press, 1959), pp. 71–118; Karl Löwith, *Meaning in History* (Chicago: University

TRANSACTIONAL AND PROCESSIVE AS CHRISTOLOGICAL TYPES

Attention to historical development as religiously significant is not, of course, the unprecedented discovery of the eighteenth century. Much of the Old Testament counts against any such generalization. So too does the thought of such theologians as Augustine, Joachim of Flores, and Calvin, to name only the most dramatic illustrations. With reference to more specifically Christological issues, consideration of the question of the historical mediation of the benefits of Christ's work is, moreover, evidenced in Christian theology of all periods. In spite of parallel concerns in earlier ages, attention to historical process in the modern period is, however, novel in so far as that emphasis is viewed as an alternative to affirming any form of trans-temporal efficacy to the Atonement. The most extreme form of this alternative is the contention not only that there is no trans-temporal efficacy of the work of Christ but also that there are no grounds at all for believing in or hoping for a suprahistorical goal of the religious life. But even when that extreme position is eschewed, interpretation of the significance of Christ with reference to the course of the historical process may be seen as a systematic alternative to any literal affirmation of the *eph hapax*.

To systematize this contrast as an ideal typical distinction is, then, to focus on the relation between time and the change which the work of Christ is said to effect as a second variable for classifying interpretations of the significance of Christ. The designations which I use to differentiate alternatives on this issue are Transactional and Processive. In isolating this temporal question as a second variable I in no way deny its intimate relation to the Realist-Nominalist distinction. Indeed, I recognize that the elaboration of the historically-focused Processive type as a self-conscious alternative to the trans-temporal tendencies of the Transactional position is in the first instance a further development of Nominalist concerns. But despite the original community of interest between the Nominalist and the Processive alternatives, there are also instances of Nominalist interpretations which are a-temporal or Transactional and Realist positions which are Processive. It is, therefore, useful at least initially to distinguish the two variables.

---

of Chicago Press – Phoenix Books, 1964), pp. 91–136; Lovejoy, *The Great Chain of Being*, pp. 242–287.

The paradigm for the Transactional type is the interpretation which unambiguously and literally affirms the once for all character of the Atonement: it understands the work of Christ as effecting a total transformation in the situation of the creation as a whole at the particular historical time of the crucifixion. This view has traditionally been very widespread in popular conceptions of Jesus' death; but it also not infrequently contributes rhetorical force to elaborately reasoned theological interpretations. Because of its at least in principle universalistic understanding of the significance of Christ, this view is correlative with the Realist type. In addition to this paradigmatically Transactional interpretation, I use the type to designate two closely related variations. One is theories which identify the effect of Christ's work with an eternal decision or action. Although it is strictly improper to classify such interpretations on a temporal axis, they undoubtedly do deal with the question of time and at least metaphorically construe the work of Atonement as 'already completed' or as effected without temporal duration. The second somewhat extended use of the Transactional type is to designate interpretations which reject any result of the Atonement other than its effect on individuals – which are, that is, Nominalist in reference to the other variable of the typology which I am advocating – but which conceive of the change as the result of a decision or action in some sense outside time and therefore not available to ordinary empirical inspection and not subject to the causal laws governing historical existence. Like the most programmatically Processive views, this variant of the Nominalist-Transactional type is a peculiarly modern position. But while the Processive approach focuses on historical development once modern science renders any trans-historical existence highly problematical, the Nominalist-Transactional perspective attempts to extract man as a moral and religious being from the closed causal nexus which it accepts as encompassing all of temporal existence.

In contrast to the Transactional position the Processive type conceives of the Atonement as an inherently temporal process – that is, as effecting change exclusively in spatio-temporal existence. In so far as the *eph hapax* is construed to imply that the work of Christ is efficacious in principle apart from the question of its historical mediation, the Processive perspective qualifies that traditional affirmation. Hence attention to the question of appropriating the benefits of the work of Christ does not in itself indicate that the interpretation in question is to be classified as Processive. Transactional theories also consider the appropriation question. Instead those views which I designate as Processive see the entire action of Atonement as transpiring over time – typically over the whole course of history at least from the first century on. As a result, Processive interpretations often emphasize the fact of development and a belief in increase in being and/or value in individual selves, in the cosmic process, or even in God.

THE QUESTION OF SYSTEMATIC COMPLETENESS

Although I am content to let the case for the adequacy of this typology rest with its ability to analyze and illumine the central concerns of the various interpretations of the significance of Christ, my selection of the two particular variables which I employ does not reflect a simply inductive procedure. Instead it also represents an attempt to isolate and then to generalize questions which any systematic interpretation of the work of Christ confronts. If they agree on nothing else, all interpretations of the Atonement at least implicitly give their assent to the general proposition that the work of Christ effects a change of some kind. Stated formally, the two variables which I am using in classifying views of the significance of Christ simply differentiate interpretations on the basis of how they locate that change in space and time. In asking whether the effect of the work of Christ occurs in the first instance in some universal – in God, the total situation of the world, or mankind as a whole, for example – or whether it in the last analysis is simply the cumulative change which particular individuals and their communities experience, the Realist-Nominalist distinction is in effect addressing the question of spatial location. Similarly, if more obviously and directly, the contrast between Transactional and Processive is a contrast in the relation between the change which the Atonement is said to effect and time.

As is perhaps already evident, I am persuaded that Christological commitments have systematic ethical and metaphysical implications or correlates. One reason why I find both the Realist-Nominalist and the Transactional-Processive distinctions useful in classifying views of the work of Christ is that they are able to relate this theological doctrine not only to broader cultural and social questions but also to the finally metaphysical issues which underlie them. In so far as this premise of a close relation between interpretations of the significance of Christ and basic metaphysical issues is accepted, it is, therefore, reassuring as to the systematic completeness of the typology I have outlined to find that it also serves to classify alternative positions on fundamental metaphysical problems.[15] That the Transactional-Processive contrast corresponds closely to the traditional categories of eternal and temporal has already been adumbrated; and the Realist-Nominalist distinction may readily be viewed as a reformulation of the traditional philosophical problem of the one and the many.

In classifying a thinker's approach to interpreting the significance of Christ one is, then, also describing his at least implicit metaphysics. Thus a consistent thinker with a Nominalist-Transactional Christology would also have a pluralistic ontology and would not emphasize the fact of temporal process. His philosophical colleague would be Descartes, for example. In contrast, the Nominalist-Processive type would be correlative with a pluralistic and teleological metaphysics. Dewey would be a good example. The Realist-Transactional view would correspond to a monistic or at least wholistic ontology combined with a placing of final authority in the timeless or eternal over against the temporal. The philosophical counterpart of this position would be a thinker like Spinoza. Finally, the Realistic-Processive type would have its parallel in a monistic or wholistic metaphysics which emphasizes the temporal character of all reality. Hegel illustrates this position, though his Realism attempts to incorporate the concerns of Nominalism as well – an attempt which requires detailed examination in its own right and receives that examination in the second part of this study.

15. On the question of parallelism between theories of the Atonement and fundamental metaphysical options, my views are deeply indebted to Wayne Proudfoot. Proudfoot's 1972 Ph.D. dissertation for Harvard (entitled *Types of Finite-Infinite Relation and conceptions of the Unity of the Self*) is on ideal-typical conceptions of the relation between the finite and the infinite. In innumerable discussions over the last several years I have benefited immensely from his thinking on this set of issues.

4

Historical Illustration of the Typology

There are at least two correctible deficiencies in the foregoing outline of the typology which I am advocating. The first is that any such schematic presentation of a typology is unavoidably abstract; and the second is that the correlation between the two variables in the typology is obscured because each distinction is developed in its own right. In an attempt to mitigate both deficiencies, this chapter offers historical illustrations of the typology, taking in turn the points at which the two variables intersect.

THE REALIST-TRANSACTIONAL TYPE

There are a number of Fathers who illustrate the Realist-Transactional type in paradigmatic form in that they explicitly develop the conception of the flesh which the Logos is said to have assumed as generic or universal human nature. Cyril of Alexandria and Gregory of Nyssa are examples among the Greek Fathers and Hilary of Poitiers among the Latins.[1] In each case further explanations of the mode of efficacy of Christ's life and death are offered. Gregory, for example, develops his interpretation of Christ's work as his deceiving the Devil and thus successfully paying the price or ransom necessary to free man from the dominion of evil – an interpretation which he elaborates in colorful imagery when he compares the divinity of Christ disguised in his humanity to the bait concealing the hook on which the 'greedy fish' is caught.[2] Similarly, Cyril and Hilary present a number of explanations of the transaction which Christ accomplishes; notable is Cyril's

1. George S. Hendry, *The Gospel of the Incarnation* (Philadelphia: Westminster Press, 1958), pp. 48–54 offers a summary collection of passages on this point from the treatises, letters, and Biblical commentaries of the Fathers.

2. *An Address on Religious Instruction* in *Christology of the Later Fathers*, E. R. Hardy, ed. (Philadelphia: Westminster Press, 1954), paragraphs 20–33, esp. 23–24 [*The Catechetical Oration of Gregory of Nyssa – The Greek Text*, J. H. Srawley, ed. (Cambridge: University Press, 1903), same paragraph divisions].

reference to the Biblical motifs of sacrifice and ransom and Hilary's comments on the cross as satisfying penal obligation.[3] But such further explanations or interpretations still presuppose the human nature which Christ assumed as the connection between the transaction in question and believers.

This presupposition is frequently operative even when it is not explicitly expressed. Athanasius' *On the Incarnation of the Word* is a case in point. The systematic problem which Athanasius sees the work of Christ as addressing is the fact of human corruption and death. To renew the image of God in man, to restore him from corruption and grant him immortality, it is necessary that the Savior satisfy the debt which all men owe – the debt of death.[4] But for Athanasius, too, the fact that Christ's death pays the debt for all men derives from his having the very substance of human nature. Although Athanasius does not speak of Christ as possessing universal human nature, he nonetheless indicates that the connection between the Word's victory over death and the incorruptibility available to all men is the common humanity which they share. Athanasius illustrates his position with a parable about a king who brings honor and deliverance to a whole city simply by living in a single house:

So too has it been with the monarch of us all. For now that he has come to our realm, and taken up his abode in one body among his peers, henceforth the whole conspiracy of the enemy against mankind is checked, and the corruption of death which before was prevailing against them is done away. For the race of men had gone to ruin, had not the Lord and Savior of all, the Son of God, come among us to meet the end of death.[5]

3. For details, see Robert S. Franks, *The Work of Christ: A Historical Study of Christian Doctrine* (London: Thomas Nelson and Sons, 1962), pp. 63–64, 81–82.

4. *On the Incarnation of the Word* in *Christology of the Later Fathers*, E. R. Hardy, ed. (Philadelphia: Westminster Press, 1954), paragraphs 9 and 20 [*St. Athanasius on the Incarnation: the Greek Text*, A. Robertson, ed. (London: David Nutt, 1901), same paragraph divisions]. See also paragraph 16 which describes Christ's work as his 'putting away death and renewing us again' and paragraph 13 which speaks at length of the Word's renewing or creating afresh the image of God in man.

5. *On the Incarnation...*, paragraph 9. This parable is particularly striking in the context of Athanasius' treatise because its political imagery stands in contrast to his more characteristic ontological conceptuality with its focus on the metaphor of renewing the image of God in man and its use of such motifs as life displacing death, incorruption overcoming corruption, and divinization transforming humanity. Even this political or

Though Christ appeared in only a single body, that body is instrumental in the salvation of mankind because there is a single human nature uniting all men.

The thought of Anselm of Canterbury illustrates the influence which the patristic preoccupation with Christ's human nature as the bond between the work of redemption and all men continued to have for centuries; at the same time, however, the treatise *Why the Godman?* in particular presents a systematically argued interpretation of the Atonement which is Realist-Transactional even apart from its commitment to the position that universal humanity was present in Christ. There can be no doubt that Anselm views the humanity of Jesus as a universal. Not only is there the negative evidence of his criticism of Roscelin on precisely this point; he also explicitly affirms this position in the letter on the Incarnation in which he criticizes Roscelin.[6] Nonetheless, the argument of *Why the Godman?* does not require Anselm's affirmation that Christ possessed universal human nature. Christ is not paying the debt of death which all men owe or a ransom to the devil equivalent to the lives of all men. Instead in Anselm's interpretation he is restoring the infinite damage done to God's honor through man's disobedience. This task must, to be sure, be performed by a man; but it is given its infinite value by the divinity united to man. What is needed, in short, is not a quantitative sum equivalent to the whole of humanity but an infinite value which can derive only from God himself.[7] Once this satisfaction has been rendered, the condition for universal forgiveness is met. Perhaps because of the strong sacramental tradition of being incorporated into the body of Christ, Anselm himself continues to affirm the universality of Christ's human nature. There

---

'Nominalist' imagery is, however, used to portray the unity of all men with Christ – an indication that Athanasius' systematic position is not simply a function of the metaphors he employs.

6. *On the Incarnation of the Word* in *Theological Treatises II*, J. Hopkins and H. Richardson, eds. (Cambridge: Harvard Divinity School Library, 1966), pp. 90–92, 94–95 [*Epistola de incarnatione verbi* in *Opera omnia*, F. S. Schmitt, ed. (Stuttgart: Friedrich Frommann Verlag-Günther Holzboog, 1968), vol. 2, pp. 23–25, 26–28]. The passages are in the somewhat lengthy chapters IX and X. It is noteworthy that Anselm discusses redemption as redemption from the devil in this context.

7. *Cur Deus Homo* in *Saint Anselm: Basic Writings*, S. Deane, trans, (La Salle, Ill.: Open Court, 1962), II/6, 7 [*Cur deus homo* in *Opera omnia*, vol. 2, same book and chapter divisions].

is, however, no integral or necessary connection between his own constructive theory and this particular expression of Realism.

Both the patristic and the Anselmic varieties of the Realist-Transactional
type have had an enormous influence on the subsequent history of Christian
thought. Indeed, virtually all of those theologians whom the major Christian
churches have recognized as orthodox – Thomas, Luther, and Calvin, for
example – have accepted the traditional structure of thought on the significance of Christ exemplified in Anselm and the Fathers. Among such
orthodox theologians there have also, to be sure, been new insights and
emphases; but they are invariably presented with a self-conscious attempt
to integrate them into this already accepted framework for reflection on
the work of Christ. To trace the details of the influence which the patristic
and the Anselmic varieties of the Realist-Transactional type have exercised
is, therefore, not possible in any such summary characterization as this
one. As an alternative to what would have to be a very cursory historical
survey, consideration of two twentieth-century theologians – E. L. Mascall
and Karl Barth – may serve to epitomize the continued influence of the
Realist-Transactional perspective. Both men are self-consciously thinkers of
and for the church and hence may not unjustly be taken as representative
of their innumerable predecessors who shared this view of the theological
task. That Mascall and Barth stand in the Anglo-Catholic and Reformed
traditions respectively may, moreover, serve to indicate the ecumenicity
of the company of thinkers whom they represent.

Mascall's discussion of the Atonement in his *Christ, the Christian and
the Church* is a particularly interesting illustration of the Realist-Transactional type because he himself explicitly addresses the question of the
status of universals. Mascall does not 'discuss in detail the various elements
that are involved in the doctrine of the Atonement'. Instead he contents
himself with observing that 'it is impossible to dispense with either of the
two great strands that go to form the Catholic tradition' – namely, 'in the
language of traditional theology' that Christ 'both paid man's debt to God
and destroyed the power of the devil'.[8] The question Mascall does focus
on is 'What is the bond between us and him?' In the course of his response
to this question Mascall argues that 'on a purely nominalistic view of human

---

8. *Christ, the Christian and the Church* (London: Longmans, Green, 1946), p. 75.

nature ... there can be no real connection between what happens in Christ's human nature and what happens in mine'.[9] That Christ is not simply an individual man, that his manhood is 'impersonal', that 'he is the "universal" ' – is for Mascall a 'great mystery' which he does not claim to have 'solved'.[10] Nonetheless he affirms it and as a result stands in the Realist-Transactional tradition of the Fathers. His own summary demonstrates the parallelism concisely:

The death of Christ on the cross was the recreation of man, and not merely its antecedent condition. Since Christ is the universal man, his payment of our debt and his victory over our foes were in actual fact our re-creation, even though the fruits of that re-creation can be produced only as, by grace, we live in him.[11]

Karl Barth does not offer a similarly concise summation of his position. His voluminous interpretation of the work of Christ is, however, also Realist and Transactional. To make any such generalization about a position as comprehensive and as varied in its multiple perspectives as is Barth's is no doubt to indulge in over-simplification. Consequently, certain qualifications would be necessary in a detailed characterization of Barth's interpretation. Any study focused exclusively on Barth's views would, for example, have to explore the not inconsiderable historical influence of late medieval Nominalism on Barth's formulation of the doctrine of election. But in spite of the need to allow for the fact of divergent influences and commitments, Barth's understanding of the work of Christ is in its underlying structure both Realist and Transactional.

Unlike Mascall, Barth does not espouse the view that the Word assumed universal humanity. He does appropriate the categories *enhypostasis* and *anhypostasis* from the Greek Fathers. But his interpretation of these terms rejects the rendering of *anhypostasis* in particular as referring to impersonal or universal human nature.[12] Despite his rejection of a physical unity between the Word and all men, Barth does, however, insist that 'Jesus Christ ...

9. *Christ* ..., pp. 70–71.
10. *Christ* ..., p. 74.
11. *Christ* ..., p. 76.
12. *Church Dogmatics I/2* (Edinburgh: T. & T. Clark, 1956), pp. 163–165 [*Kirchliche Dogmatik I/2* (Zürich: E. V. Z. Verlag, 1938), pp. 178–180]. Though the point is only tangential to a discussion of Barth's own position, his interpretation of *anhypostasis* is not without its difficulties. In any case, the term does imply that Christ's human nature

is not merely one man side by side with many others'. Rather he is '*the* One, whose existence necessarily touches that of all other men'; he is 'their Head from all eternity'.[13] Consequently Barth can speak of an 'ontological connection between the man Jesus on the one side and all other men on the other' – a connection which is, significantly, said to be based on the fact that 'objectively they are His, they belong to Him, and they can be claimed as his *de jure*'.[14]

The affirmation that all men are Christ's *de jure* is the heart of Barth's doctrine of reconciliation. In the context of the doctrine of election, it means that Jesus Christ is the elected man – that in him man as such is elected and that the election of individuals is derivative from his election.[15] And in reference specifically to the doctrine of reconciliation, the affirmation that all men are Christ's means they are 'already' objectively (though *de jure* as opposed to *de facto*) justified and even sanctified and called. Emphasis is, to be sure, in the first instance placed on justification: Christ is 'the judge judged in our place'.[16] But Barth insists that sanctification and vocation

---

is not fully individualized. *Enhypostasis* is used with a similar effect, for the first time in the thought of Leontius of Byzantium. For a concise discussion of the issues, see Friedrich Loofs, *Leitfaden zum Studium der Dogmengeschichte* (Halle: Verlag von Max Niemeyer, 1906), pp. 291–295, 304–309.

13. *Church Dogmatics IV/2* (Edinburgh: T. & T. Clark, 1958), p. 36 [*Kirchliche Dogmatik IV/2* (Zürich: E. V. Z. Verlag, 1964), p. 38]. For a rejection of all 'purely "nominalistic"' interpretations of Jesus, see *Church Dogmatics IV/1* (Edinburgh: T. & T. Clark, 1956), pp. 122–123 [*Kirchliche Dogmatik IV/1* (Zürich: E. V. Z. Verlag, 1960), p. 134]. For a summary statement of 'the Being of Man in Jesus Christ', which entails God's 'coming together with all men', see *Church Dogmatics IV/6*, pp. 92–122 [98–133].

14. *Church Dogmatics IV/2*, p. 275 [305].

15. *Church Dogmatics II/2* (Edinburgh: T. & T. Clark, 1957), pp. 94–145, 195–205, 306–506 [*Kirchliche Dogmatik II/2* (Zürich: E. V. Z. Verlag, 1942), pp. 101–157, 215–226, 336–563]. For a much more concise summary, see *Church Dogmatics IV/2*, pp. 31–36 [32–38]. In his doctrine of election as well as in his ethics Barth's very pronounced voluntarism (with reference both to God and man) is of course under the influence of Nominalism. In designating his interpretation of the significance of Christ as Realist, I do not deny the existence of strong Nominalist tendencies in his thought as a whole. Instead I contend only that the systematic universalism of his Christology exemplifies the Realist position and that his voluntarism either expresses this universalism (as in the case of his interpretation of election) or at least presupposes it and attempts to avoid denying it (as in the case of his ethics).

16. See especially *Church Dogmatics IV/1*, pp. 211–357, 514–642 [231-394, 573–718]. Also relevant in this connection is his conversation with Rudolf Bultmann, whom Barth

are not later processes but rather are integral to the one act of reconciliation effected in the action of justification.[17] Hence *de jure* sin and evil have been overcome and have continued power only as 'an impossible possibility', as indeed 'that which is not' or 'the not-ish' or 'the nothing', to attempt to paraphrase Barth's invented term, *das Nichtige*.[18]

In interpreting his commitment to an objective work of justification in particular, Barth favors the use of the forensic imagery of, for example, Romans 3 and Anselm – though he explicitly argues that other imagery is also possible.[19] The emphasis which he places on the concept of covenant in his initial survey of the doctrine of reconciliation and his extensive treatment of the theme of *Christus victor* further illustrate the comprehensiveness of his approach to the work of Christ.[20] Although Barth on occasion uses very Anselmian language in referring to the need to satisfy God's wrath or righteousness in the earlier volumes of the *Church Dogmatics*, in his treatment of the Doctrine of Reconciliation he rejects as unbiblical all theories of the Atonement which focus on satisfying God's wrath. Instead he reinterprets the concept of satisfaction in the direction of doing what is 'sufficient' for total victory over sin.[21] In this way he is able to combine the language of Anselm and the Reformers with that of covenantal theology and the early Fathers. In each case, the work of Christ is the doing of that which suffices for engaging and finally annihilating sin and evil so that God's love and faithfulness may be reciprocated; in each case, moreover, this work of Christ is sufficient for total victory, for the final redemption of all men.[22]

---

charges with focusing exclusively on sanctification. See *Church Dogmatics IV/1*, p. ix [i–ii] and *IV/2*, pp. 503–505 [569–571].

17. *Church Dogmatics IV/1*, pp. 101, 108 [190, 116–117]; *IV/2*, pp. 499–553 [565–626]; *IV/3-1* (Edinburgh: T. & T. Clark, 1961), pp. 3–38 [*Kirchliche Dogmatik IV/3-1* (Zürich: E. V. Z. Verlag, 1959), pp. 1–40]; *IV/3-2* (Edinburgh: T & T. Clark, 1962), pp. 481–554 [*Kirchliche Dogmatik IV/3-2* (Zürich: E. V. Z. Verlag, 1959), pp. 553–636].

18. *Church Dogmatics III/3* (Edinburgh: T. & T. Clark, 1960), pp. 289–368 [*Kirchliche Dogmatik* (Zürich: E. V. Z. Verlag, 1950), pp. 327–425]; *IV/1*, pp. 138–145, 407–413 [151–159, 451–458]; *IV/6-1*, pp. 173–180 [198–206].

19. *Church Dogmatics IV/1*, pp. 273–283 [300–311].

20. *Church Dogmatics IV/1*, pp. 22–78 [22–83] and *IV/3-1*, pp. 165–274 [188–317].

21. *Church Dogmatics IV/1*, pp. 253–255 [278–280].

22. Barth insists that in view of the freedom of God's grace, the question of whether or not all will at last escape condemnation must remain an open one. See *Church Dogmatics II/2*, pp. 417–419 [461–464] and *IV/3-1*, pp. 477–478 [549–551]. But that reconciliation is in principle or objectively universal in Barth's thought is always maintained.

Barth's interpretation of the Atonement is not only Realist but also Transactional. The work of Christ is both an eternal reality – based on God's eternal decree – and also a temporal event, indeed that event which defines true temporality. Hence Barth can speak in very strong terms about Jesus' historicity as distinguishing him from other dying and rising gods and about the Atonement as a specific historical act.[23] But as he indicates in the same contexts, it is a very special history. Asserting that 'general human time and history' are 'the veil concealing revelation' and rejecting the universality and relativity of such history, Barth maintains 'quite concretely' that 'the years 1–30' are 'real, fulfilled time' as opposed to 'fallen time'. It is here that the temporal and the eternal meet to produce the genuinely and normatively temporal.[24] Hence the federal theologians are criticized for bifurcating the eternal decrees from their actualization in history; instead, Barth insists on seeing 'the eternal and therefore the only basis of the divine work in the work itself, in its temporal occurrence'.[25] And in this eternal-temporal transaction, Atonement is effected once for all.

THE NOMINALIST-TRANSACTIONAL TYPE

Those interpretations of the significance of Christ which I classify as Nominalist-Transactional fall into two distinct groups. One includes the approaches which are, in effect, an attempt to combine the central commitments of the Realist-Transactional type with various Nominalist emphases which are more consistently expressed in the Nominalist-Processive type. The interpretations in this group are either transitional ones in a historical sense or unstable if not incoherent from the systematic point of view. The thought of the fifteenth-century Nominalist Gabriel Biel may serve to illustrate the process of historical transition, while Emil Brunner's views on the work of Christ are an example of the systematic problem. The second group includes interpretations which I consider distinctively Nominalist

23. See, for examples of Barth's emphatic statements on this point, *Church Dogmatics* *IV/1*, pp. 157, 251, 283–284, 288 [171, 276–277, 311–312, 316–317].
24. *Church Dogmatics* *I/2*, pp. 45–70 [50–77], esp. 56–59 [62–64].
25. *Church Dogmatics* *IV/1*, pp. 54–66 [57–70], esp. p. 66 [70].

and Transactional – that is, interpretations which are not simply transitional or problematical combinations of Realist-Transactional and Nominalist-Processive commitments. Included in this group are interpretations which speak in transactional language but interpret the transaction(s) which the work of Christ effects either as a-temporal or trans-temporal transformation in the individual or exclusively as a historical turning point in man's social-cultural history. The focus on a transaction in the life of the individual construed as in some significant sense extracted from the spatial-temporal process is illustrated in a powerful tradition of religious and ethical thought stretching at least from Kant to twentieth-century existentialists like Bultmann. The interpretation of the work of Christ as effecting a crucial breakthrough in man's religious development is illustrated in a tradition of Enlightenment and nineteenth-century thinkers ranging from some Deist theologians to a poet like Novalis and a philosopher like Fichte.

To understand the place of Nominalist theologians like Gabriel Biel in the historical evolution of interpretations of the work of Christ, it is instructive to note the points of both continuity and discontinuity with the thought of Anselm. Both theologians conceive of Christ's life and preeminently his death as producing merit then available to the believer through the sacraments in particular. They also agree in focusing attention on the sacrament of penance together with the eucharist.[26] Granted this area of agreement, there are, however, significant contrasts between Biel and Anselm. One

26. On this point it is, I think, possible to see Anselm as also reflecting the tendencies finding expression in the Nominalism which he opposed. As George H. Williams has maintained in detail in his *Anselm: Communion and Atonement* (St. Louis: Concordia Publishing House, 1950), esp. pp. 5–13, 39–42, 44–46, 51–52, 62–67, Anselm shifts the sacramental focus of the Atonement from the patristic preoccupation with baptism to a more central concern with penance and the eucharist. One reason for this shift is that by the eleventh century infant baptism had displaced adult believer's baptism as the ordinary procedure. But one can also see in his concentration on penance and the eucharist an attempt to do justice to the question of the relation between Christ's death and the particular sins of individual Christians. Williams' demonstration that Anselm distinguishes between 'natural sin' (which derives from the individual's genetic presence in Adam and which is removed in baptism) and 'personal sin' (which the individual commits and which requires penance) lends support to this line of conjecture. It is interesting that R. W. Southern also focuses on Anselm as a transitional figure who still adheres to inherited patterns while nonetheless incipiently giving expression to new cultural currents. See his concluding comments in *The Making of the Middle Ages* (New Haven: Yale University Press, ca. 1952), pp. 222–228, 234–238.

frequently noted criticism of Anselm, which Thomas and Duns Scotus also voice but which nonetheless is characteristic of Biel's Nominalism, is a rejection of any rational necessity in the work of Christ apart from God's willing it so. Still more revealing of Biel's soteriological Nominalism in particular is his insistence that the merit of Christ is in the first instance finite because it accrues from the suffering of his particular human nature, not from the infinite dignity of his divinity, as Anselm holds.[27] This merit is, moreover, only for those who obey him – that is, for the elect, not for all men.[28]

That Biel interprets the efficacy of the Atonement in reference to the elect alone epitomizes the contrast between him and Anselm. Biel still speaks of the cross as an objective work of sacrifice and as victory over the devil. But the focus of his attention has shifted to the question of change in the individual believer. *De potentia absoluta* justification is through God's grace alone, since he in his complete freedom wills to grant man salvation according to a definite plan. The result is, however, that *de potentia ordinata* God has committed himself to grant the healing infusion of grace, divine forgiveness or acceptation and ultimately beatification to those who do their best – *facere quod in se est*. Hence the whole emphasis in practice falls on man's realizing that genuine contrition and love of God from which follow (according to the divinely willed order of savation) both stages of justification – the granting of infused grace and divine acceptation – as well as, ultimately, beatification. Christ is, to be sure, *victor*: but he is also *dux*, the leader or example whose teaching and suffering as a particular man inspire the believer's faith and trust in God and whose institution of the sacraments provide concrete help to the believer as he seeks to obey God.[29]

It is, I think, accurate to see Biel's position historically as a transitional

27. This merit is only in the first instance finite because Biel says God nonetheless wills to accept it as sufficient for an infinite posterity of believers if there be such. See, for example, *Epitome et collectorium ex Occamo circa quatuor cententiarum libros* (Frankfurt/ Main: Miverva, 1965), book III, distinction 19, question 1, article 2, conclusion 3 and conclusion 5.

28. *Epitome et collectorium . . .*, book III, distinction 19, question 1, article 2, conclusion 4 and answer to doubt 2.

29. For detailed documentation of this understanding of Biel, see Heiko A. Oberman, *The Harvest of Medieval Theology: Gabriel Biel and Late Medieval Nominalism* (Cambridge: Harvard University Press, 1963), esp. pp. 147–148, 154–157, 164–165, 169–178, 181–184, 224–235, 249–251, 260–261, 266–275.

one because once attention is directed toward changes in the present in believers, there is a definite tendency to move away from construing Christ's life and death as a transaction creating merit or effecting salvation in principle independently of those believers. This judgment does not, however, imply that Nominalist-Transactional interpretations structurally parallel to Biel's cease to be historically significant. In the debates of seventeenth-century Protestant scholasticism, for example, one systematic distinction which can be drawn between the Reformed and the Lutheran positions on the Atonement is that the former follow the Nominalist approach in maintaining that Christ died for the elect only, while the latter insist on the Anselmic conception of a universal satisfaction sufficient for mankind as a whole. Quenstedt illustrates the Lutheran view and Heidegger the Reformed one.[30] The influential *Defence...* of Hugo Grotius may also be seen as structurally parallel to Biel's positions. For it is an attempt to formulate a Transactional interpretation on Nominalist premises. The result is that the death of Christ is viewed not as propitiation of God's wrath but rather as a 'weighty example against the great crimes of all of us' to the end that God is able to forgive without undermining the authority of the law through which he rules.[31] One indication of the appeal of Grotius' position to eighteenth and even nineteenth-century Calvinists in particular is its influence among New England theologians over a period of a number of generations: Joseph Bellamy's *The Atonement* (1750), Samuel Hopkins' treatment of the work of Christ in his *System of Doctrines Contained in Revelation* (1793), and Nathaniel W. Taylor's *Moral Government* (1859) all echo the view of their seventeenth-century Dutch predecessor.[32]

The program of combining Nominalist commitments with a Transactional interpretation of the significance of Christ patterned on the view of Realist orthodoxy does not end with the influence of Grotius. Indeed, the attempt to ethicize the approach of orthodoxy may be said to be characteristic of even self-consciously Realist post-Enlightenment thinkers, as is

30. For details see Franks, *The Work of Christ...*, pp. 410–447.

31. *A Defence of the Catholic Faith concerning the Satisfaction of Christ against Faustus Socinus*, F. H. Foster, trans. (Andover, Mass: Warren F. Draper, 1889), pp. 100–101 [*Defensio fidei Catholicae de satisfactione Christi adversus Faustum Socinum* (Lugduni Batavorum (Leyden): J. Patius, 1617), pp. 64–65].

32. See Frank Hugh Foster, *Genetic History of New England Theology* (Chicago: University of Chicago Press, 1907), pp. 113–117, 177–182, 392–400.

illustrated in a whole tradition of British reflection including such figures as Samuel Taylor Coleridge, F. D. Maurice, and P. T. Forsyth. [33] In addition to such self-consciously Realist approaches which appropriate ethical categories there are, however, also theologians whose commitment to an objective forensic justification leads to an occasional use of Realist language but who nonetheless attempt to focus their interpretations on the relation of the Atonement to men as discrete individuals. Emil Brunner may serve to epitomize this approach.

Like Biel, Brunner attempts to affirm the Anselmic understanding of the Atonement with as few alterations as possible. In his early work *The Mediator* Brunner accepts a kind of Realism in order to counter what he sees as the excessive individualism of moderns; hence he maintains that in Christ, 'God deals with humanity as a whole'. But he immediately qualifies this assertion with an affirmation of the centrality of human decision:

It is thus a personal transaction between the Divine Person and the person of the human being who believes. The chief point is always that of decision.[34]

Brunner does not, however, allow that the Atonement is simply the cumu-

33. All these men not only stress the central need for man's ethical response but also interpret Christ's own life and work in predominantly ethical categories. Nonetheless the emphasis of Coleridge on the role of the universal Logos as the mediator between God an man, of Maurice on Christ as the Lord and Head of mankind through his role in creation, and of Forsyth on Christ as 'supernal man' and 'a universal personality' provides an underlying Realist structure to each of their interpretations of the Atonement. For details, see: Coleridge, *Aids to Reflection, The Complete Works*, Shedd, ed. (New York: Harper & Brothers, 1853), vol. I, pp. 110–367, esp. 204–367 and 'Essay on Faith' in *The Complete Works*, vol. V, pp. 557–565; Maurice, 'On the Atonement' in *Theological Essays* (New York: Redfield, 1854), pp. 99–113; Forsyth, 'The Moral Poignancy of the Cross' in *Positive Preaching and the Modern Mind* (Grand Rapids, Mich.: Wm. B. Eerdmans, 1864), pp. 232–254, *The Person and Place of Jesus Christ* (London: Independent Press, 1961), and *The Work of Christ* (London: Independent Press, 1938).

34. *The Mediator*, O. Wyon, trans. (Philadelphia: Westminster Press, 1947), p. 321 [*Der Mittler* (Zürich: Zwingli-Verlag, 1947), pp. 286–287]. The contrast which he himself sees between his position and that of Barth on this issue is neatly summarized in Brunner's article 'Der neue Barth: Bemerkungen zu Karl Barths Lehre vom Menschen', *Zeitschrift für Theologie und Kirche*, XLVIII (1951), esp. pp. 97–100. Brunner criticizes Barth for maintaining that all men participate in God's plan of salvation simply in view of their creation in Christ. In contrast Brunner himself insists that man's 'participation in the covenant of God is lost and perverted through sin and is *re*stored (*wieder*hergestellt) only through the second Word of God, the Word of Reconciliation, *in so far as he believes* (*sofern er glaubt*)' (p. 99).

lative product of such individual transactions. Instead he insists on an objective alteration in the relation between God and mankind through a 'divine transaction' in the death of Christ, a transaction for which the language of expiatory sacrifice and vicarious suffering is not inappropriate.[35] Brunner's entire exposition and in particular his polemic against those who argue for forgiveness *sans phrase*, without further ado, reflects Grotius' position that God had to demonstrate the seriousness of sin. So also does his refusal to see Jesus' death as effecting a change in God.[36] But he nonetheless seeks to interpret the cross as the necessary presupposition for forgiveness itself in as much as guilt is an objective reality between God and man – that is, an obstacle from God's point of view as well as from man's.[37] The discussion of the work of Christ in the later *Christian Doctrine of Creation and Redemption* reveals the same ambivalence.[38] Here Brunner offers a concise criticism of Anselm's *a priori* argument for the necessity of the Atonement. As an alternative explanation of the seeming 'necessity' of the cross, he refers to the Christian believer's *a posteriori* conviction: 'Looking back, the believer knows that there was no other way for him, in order to attain the renewal of fellowship with God.' In the same context he interprets God's wrath as 'His relation to the sinner so long as the sinner does not believe'. Yet in the very next sentence he describes that divine wrath as 'something real, which can only be removed by the real event of the death of Christ on the cross, and by faith in Him.' Brunner himself describes his position as dependent on seeing God's wrath as '"subjective-objective", a reality of "encounter"'. But his specific explanation refers only to a change in the consciousness of the individual believer. He continues to affirm the dependence of this change on the 'real event' of the cross; he does not, however, formulate with any precision the nature of that dependence.

The ambivalence in Brunner's position derives from his attempt to

---

35. *The Mediator*, pp. 464, 468–471, 473, 481–486, 488–489, 524 [419, 423–426, 428, 436–440, 442–443, 475].

36. *The Mediator*, pp. 470–471 [425–426].

37. *The Mediator*, pp. 443–444 [399–401].

38. *The Christian Doctrine of Creation and Redemption, Dogmatics II*, O. Wyon, trans. (Philadelphia: Westminster Press, n. d.); all of the following quotations are from pp. 296–297 [*Die christliche Lehre von Schöpfung und Erlösung, Dogmatik II* (Zürich: Zwingli Verlag, 1950), pp. 350–352]. See also pp. 286–287 [336–338].

combine a Nominalist approach with the commitment of orthodoxy to an objective once for all Transaction either in the first century or in eternity. His position is very close to one of the two lines of interpretation which I consider distinctively Nominalist-Transactional – although the ambivalence in Brunner's position results from his attempt to deny the similarity. This line of interpretation simply rejects what Brunner tries so vigorously to retain: an objective or supra-individual Transaction related integrally to Christ's life and death. Rejection of any such universal Transaction in favor of a focus on change in individuals and their communities is characteristically Nominalist. It is, in addition, Transactional in those interpretations which construe the transformation of individual selves as the result of acts or decisions which are construed as not confined within space and time.

For modern Western thought this position receives classic formulation in Kant's *Religion within the Limits of Reason Alone*. Kant offers an elaborate explanation of the Atonement as a description of the moral transformation of the inividual. In something of a *tour de force* he appropriates traditional Christian imagery, identifying man's moral disposition with the Son of God as the archetype of the good:

And this moral disposition which in all its purity (like unto the purity of the Son of God) the man has made his own – or (if we personify this idea) this Son of God, Himself – bears as *vicarious substitute* the guilt of sin for him, and indeed for all who believe (practically) in Him; as *savior* He renders satisfaction to supreme justice by His sufferings and death; and as *advocate* He makes it possible to hope to appear before their judge as justified. Only it must be remembered that (in this mode of representation) the suffering which the new man, in becoming dead to the *old*, must accept throughout life is pictured as a death endured once for all by the representative of mankind.[39]

Atonement is, then, the 'rebirth' of the self whereby man's moral constitution, which is in Kant's view by nature radically evil, is restructured so that morally right maxims or policies have precedence over immoral in-

_____

39. *Religion within the Limits of Reason Alone*, T. M. Greene and H. H. Hudson, trans. (New York: Harper & Row–Torchbooks, 1960), p. 69 [*Die Religion innerhalb der Grenzen der blossen Vernunft* in *Kant's gesammelte Schriften*, edition of the Königliche Preussische Akademie der Wissenschaften (Berlin: Verlag von Georg Reimer, 1914), vol. 6, pp. 74–75]. Kant offers a parallel interpretation of the Incarnation on pp. 54–55 [60–62].

clinations or propensities. For this change in the individual a total transformation or 'revolution' is necessary; Kant explicitly rules out the possibility of 'reformation' because the change is one of kind, not of degree.
To use the metaphor which he borrows, the contrast is between heaven
and hell, not heaven and earth. Either one in principle subordinates all
inclinations to the moral law or one's every action is immoral.[40] The achievement of that subordination is the aim of all ethics and religion. Like the
origin of the condition of radical evil which it reverses, the transaction
effecting the victory of the moral law in the individual is not, however, in
time and is therefore not susceptible of empirical investigation. Using the
vocabulary which he systematically defines in the first *Critique*, Kant refers
both the origin of evil and the transaction overcoming it to that noumenal
reality unavailable to man's cognitive processes because they require the
sense data of spatial-temporal existence.[41]

As he states explicitly in the preface to the second edition of the first
Critique and as is evident in particular throughout the discussion of the
Antinomy of Reason in the first *Critique* and of the postulates of freedom,
God, and immortality in the second *Critique*, Kant is persuaded that his
displacement of ultimate moral decisions into timelessness is the only
way to protect the necessary presuppositions of ethical and religious life
from the critical threat of empirical science. That both this analysis of the
problem and this line of solution continue to exercise an appeal may be
epitomized in the thought of Rudolf Bultmann.

Like Kant, Bultmann interprets such doctrines as that of the Atonement
as symbolic representations of man's personal religious and moral experience.[42] The Atonement in particular does not refer to a unique historical
transaction. Instead the event of Jesus Christ is and must be contemporary
with the believer: 'The eschatological event which is Jesus Christ happens
here and now as the Word is being preached'. The meaning of 'once for all'

40. *Religion...*, pp. 17–20, 42–43, 53 [22–24, 46–47, 60]. Kant of course develops the
ethical theory underlying these assertions in detail in *The Critique of Practical Reason,
The Foundations of the Metaphysics of Morals*, and *The Metaphysics of Morals;* but nowhere does he formulate his position as succinctly and as dramatically as in the *Religion....*
41. *Religion...*, pp. 17–18, 20–21, 25–27, 32, 34–39, 42–43, 60–61 [22–23, 24–25, 29–32,
36–37, 39–44, 46–47, 66–67].
42. *Jesus Christ and Mythology* (London: S. C. M. Press, 1960), pp. 68–70 offers
Bultmann's most concise statement of this position.

of Romans 6:10 is precisely that this event is eschatological – that it is always present.[43] Hence the transaction effected in the event of Jesus Christ is God's bestowal of a new self-understanding to the believer, a self-understanding entailing utter freedom from himself and his past and total openness to future.[44] Despite the temporal reference, this transformation of the individual self is not, however, a simply temporal one. Indeed, the model for Bultmann's eschatological event is the eternal now, not temporal duration. In the conclusion of his *Gifford Lectures*, Bultmann is explicit on this point:

It is the paradox of Christian being that the believer is taken out of the world and exists, so to speak, as unworldly and that at the same time he remains within the world, within his historicity. To be historical means to live from the future. The believer too lives from the future; first because his faith and his freedom can never be a possession; as belonging to the eschatological event they can never become facts of past time but are reality only over and over again as event; secondly because the believer remains within history.[45]

Bultmann does not of course deny that man is a historical being. On the contrary, he affirms it repeatedly and emphatically. But the effects of the eschatological encounter with God which constitutes the event of Jesus Christ must not be interpreted as ingredient in that historical process available to empirical historiography. Bultmann's perspective is evident throughout his *Gifford Lectures*. Hegel is criticized because in his thought 'the history of salvation is projected on to the level of world-history'; and belief in historical progress is rejected as opposed to the Christian faith.[46]

43. *Jesus Christ...*, pp. 78–83.
44. *Jesus Christ...*, pp. 73–77.
45. *History and Eschatology: the Presence of Eternity* (New York: Harper & Row–Torchbooks, 1957), p. 152. If this passage and the subtitle of the lectures are not enough, see the immediately following words of Erich Frank which Bultmann quotes with approval: 'History comes to an end in the religious experience of any Christian "who is in Christ". In his faith he is above time and history.... In his faith the Christian is a contemporary of Christ, and time and the world's history are overcome. The advent of Christ is an event in the realm of eternity which is incommensurable with historical time. ... History and the world do not change, but man's attitude to the world changes' (p. 153). See also *Glauben und Verstehen* (Tübingen: J. C. B. Mohr-Paul Siebeck, 1933), vol. I, pp. 106–107, 206–213, 227–228, where Bultmann emphasizes the eschatological character of Jesus' presence through the preached word.
46 *History and Eschatology*, pp. 67, 70.

Vico, Herder, and Spengler are censured for interpreting history on the model of nature or for construing man as part of natural evolution.[47] The literary realism of Stendhal, Balzac, Flaubert, and Hauptmann is charged with having no concept of a 'genuine self' in as much as it views man as totally 'imbedded in the whole of the political and social reality which is constantly in process of development'.[48] Conversely, Jaspers is praised over against Croce and Dilthey for attempting to conceptualize 'for the individual a stand-point beyond history in what he calls "Transzendenz"'.[49] Consistent with this evaluation of other thinkers is Bultmann's insistence that eschatological encounter with God effects change not in the empirically observable world, but in that *existentiell* self-understanding which is in principle unavailable to objectifying knowledge and which must, moreover, be renewed ever again since it does not have temporal duration.

A final variant of the Nominalist-Transactional type is the position which sees the central achievement of Christ in his critical reformulation of accepted religious conceptions. This line of interpretation very readily combines with other views. It is after all already present in the Pauline conviction of deliverance from the Jewish law. But it assumes a new importance as the Nominalist critique of the Realist-Transactional position becomes a commonplace in the eighteenth and nineteenth centuries. The tendency to see Christ's significance pre-eminently in his role as a critic of pre-Christian religious ideas and a creator of a new religious perspective is perhaps most pronounced among German theologians in the latter part of the eighteenth century. Examples include J. J. Spalding, J. Salomo Semler, J. A. Eberhard, J. F. C. Löffler, and Gotthelf S. Steinbart.[50] This approach is Nominalist in that it construes Jesus' work in reference to the particular historical influence which he exercised; and it is Transactional in so far as attention

47. *History and Eschatology*, pp. 78–83.
48. *History and Eschatology*, pp. 106–109. It is noteworthy that in discussing speech about God as Father in *Jesus Christ and Mythology*, p. 69, Bultmann observes: 'As applied to God the physical import of the term father has disappeared completely; it expresses a purely personal relationship.' The disjunction between 'personal' and 'physical' suggests the ethereal (I am tempted to say noumenal) quality of the personal encounters about which Bultmann speaks.
49. *History and Eschatology*, pp. 129–130.
50. The best detailed discussion of these figures is Emanuel Hirsch's consideration of the *Neologen* in his *Geschichte der neueren evangelischen Theologie* (Gütersloh: C. Bertelsmann Verlag, 1949–54), vol. 4, pp. 1–119.

is focused on the historical breakthrough which he achieved rather than on the continuing influence either of his ideas or of the religious consciousness which he communicated.

THE NOMINALIST-PROCESSIVE TYPE

The distinction between 'historical breakthrough' and 'continuing influence' is one indication of the continuity between the Nominalist-Transactional and the Nominalist-Processive types. Continuity is also evident between some thinkers whom I classify as Nominalist-Processive and the position which Kant and Bultmann illustrate; for the distinction in this case depends on a judgment as to whether or not a given figure construes the change which encounter with Christ is said to effect on the individual as genuinely temporal instead of as a transaction in principle isolated from the flux of ordinary events. Finally, continuity is simply a matter of definition in so far as it is justified to view a theologian like Biel as a transitional figure. Despite the difficulties which such continuities on occasion pose when it comes to adjudicating the classification of specific cases, the differentiation between Transactional and Processive approaches among Nominalists does, however, illumine significant contrasts both in the interpretation of Christ's work itself and in the understanding of the cultural and social questions to which the interpretation is responding.

It is appropriate that the dialectician who was perhaps the most prominent early critic of extreme Realism should also be a central figure in the development of a Nominalist approach to the significance of Christ. That figure is Abélard. Abélard apparently avoided embracing the extreme Nominalism of his teacher Roscelin; instead, he combined his criticism of ultra-Realism with a form of conceptualism, holding that while a universal is only a word (*sermo*), it nonetheless corresponds to a reality in the individual to which it is predicated and is not, therefore, a mere sound (*flatus vocis*) with no referent whatever – the position at least attributed to Roscelin. When he develops his interpretation of Christ's work in his *Commentary on St. Paul's Epistle to the Romans*, Abélard is similarly moderate. He does reject the doctrine of redemption from the Devil, even as Anselm does; but he continues to use such traditional formulations as, for instance, that Christ is a sacrifice for sin or bears men's sins. Nonetheless, as in the dispute over universals so also in his interpretation of the significance of Christ, Abélard decisively shifts the focus of his attention to the individual.

Abélard's approach is not without precedence among the Fathers. Augustine in particular not infrequently attends to the psychological dynamics of Christ's influence on believers.[51] But in contrast even to Augustine, Abélard makes the effective revelation of God's love the central theme of his understanding of the work of Christ. He sums up his own position:

It seems to us, however, that we are justified by the blood of Christ and reconciled to God, in this, that by this singular grace shown us, that his son took our nature and persevered in instructing us both in word and deed even unto death, he more largely bound us to himself by love, so that kindled as we are by so great a benefit of the Divine grace, true charity should henceforth fear nothing at all... And so our redemption is that supreme love manifested in our case by the passion of Christ, who not merely delivers us from the bondage of sin, but also acquires for us the liberty of the sons of God, so that we fulfill all things from love rather than from fear of him, who, as he himself bears witness, showed us grace so great that no greater is possible.[52]

Abélard names deliverance from the bondage of sin as one of the benefits of Christ's work. But he does not specify how it follows from the death of Christ except to indicate a close connection to the kindling of charity in the believer. That this suggested connection is not accidental is evident from the immediately preceding commentary where Abélard again relates remission of sins and charity, this time quoting Jesus' words, 'Her sins are forgiven because she loved much'.[53]

51. See: *The Trinity*, S. McKenna, trans. (Washington, D. C.: Catholic University of America Press, 1963), XIII. 10. 13 and XIII. 17. 12 [*De Trinitate* in *Corpus Christianorum L-A* (Turnholti: Typographi Brepols Editores Pontificii, 1968), same book, chapter, and paragraph divisions]; *De catechizandis rudibus* in *Corpus Christianorum XLVI* (Turnholti: Typographi Brepols Editores Pontiffcii, 1969), IV. 7 and XXII. 39. But despite this tendency in Augustine, his systematic interpretations of the Atonement invariably focus on the theme of sacrifice. See, for example, *Enchiridion on Faith, Hope, and Love* in *Augustine: Confessions and Enchiridion*, A. Outler, Trans. (Philadelphia: Westminster Press, 1955), paragraphs 33, 41, 108 [*Enchiridion ad Laurentium de fide et spe et caritate* in *Corpus Christianorum XLVI*, same paragraph divisions].
52. *Commentariorum super S. Pauli epistolam ad Romanos* in *Patrologia Latina CLXXVIII* (Paris: J. P. Migne, 1855), column 836.
53. *Commentariorum...*, column 833.

In Abélard's view the work of Christ is, then, the awaking of love in men. That Abélard's interpretation is more than simply a minor shift in emphasis from earlier treatments is suggested in his understanding of the relation between election and Atonement; for he is the first theologian formally to subordinate the doctrine of the work of Christ to the doctrine of predestination.[54] The result is that the elect alone are the objects of Christ's redeeming work. It is a result singularly appropriate to an approach which in any case sees the work of Christ in its actual kindling of love in believers and one which, therefore, became characteristic not only for late medieval Nominalists but also for their successors in the tradition of soteriological Nominalism.

In spite of the Nominalist influences on Luther in particular, the moderate Reformers carefully combine attention to the moral and psychological effect of the image of the suffering Christ on believers with explicit affirmation of several varieties of Realist-Transactional interpretations of the Atonement. A similar concern for orthodoxy is evident in the Counter-reformation. Consequently the Nominalist-Processive approach which Abélard represents is mediated to the modern period in its most emphatic form through the left or radical wing of the Reformation. Two tendencies are evident, both of which continue to be significant. The first is rationalistic and the second is pietistic or spiritualistic.

The figure of Faustus Socinus illustrates the rationalistic tendency. Socinus in effect takes the Nominalist critique of Anselm's argument for the necessity of the Godman to one of its possible conclusions. The Nominalists argue that there is no necessity for the Incarnation except God's arbitrary will and that, consequently, God could have saved mankind in other ways – through a mere man, for example; Socinus simply affirms this hypothetical possibility as fact. Hence Jesus was a mortal man, though one miraculously conceived and finally exalted to immortality and granted divine power and wisdom.[55] Correlative with this view of the person of Christ, Socinus maintains that Jesus does not procure salvation but rather makes known the forgiveness a loving God willingly offers. Jesus' teaching and his example therefore become central as the means whereby God draws men from their

54. Franks makes this point in *The Work of Christ...*, pp. 144, 149.
55. *De Christi natura* in *Bibliotheca Fratrum Polonorum quos Unitarios vocant* (Irenepoli: no publisher indicated, 1956), vol. 1, pp. 781–789.

sins[56]; and the orthodox conceptions of God's justice and the need for satisfaction are severely criticized.[57]

The rationalist approach which Socinus illustrates asserts itself in full force only in the Enlightenment. Then it becomes a very concerted force over against traditional orthodoxy. With the more radical of the French *philosophes* it takes the form of a total attack on Christianity. But there are also trenchant critiques from those who still consider themselves Christian, although they reject all authoritarian ecclesiastical structure and such seemingly irrational doctrine as the orthodox theories of the Atonement. The English Deists John Toland, Anthony Collins, and Matthew Tindal are examples of this perspective. Finally, there are those who share the critical approach of Socinus but who also display his concern to understand the positive role which Jesus exercises on believers as an imposing religious teacher and as a powerful example of active love and obedience to the moral law. Moderate Deists like John Locke and Thomas Chubb and German *Neologen* like J. Gottlieb Töllner illustrate this position.

Also representative of the Nominalist-Processive type are certain expressions of pietism or spiritualism. Again, the left or radical wing of the Reformation is important in mediating and developing this perspective because it is less concerned with continuing the orthodox ecclesiastical tradition than are the Romans and the non-sectarian Reformers – although in this case Calvin is also very influential because of the centrality which the question of sanctification has in the *Institutes* (1559). Nonetheless the sectarian Reformation offers the most emphatic illustration of preoccupation with the need for achieving sanctification – for realizing the effects of Christ's work in the here and now. In the extreme case of spiritualists like Müntzer and Carlstadt this quest for sanctification assumed the form of an apocalypticism which looked to the imminent transformation of all of life. But also among the Anabaptists, the realization of holiness in the present is the overriding concern. Typically, an objective justification of all men in the death of Christ is affirmed; but this belief is functionally equivalent to Socinus' insistence that God is in any case forgiving, since for the Anabaptists also the immediately relevant work of God through Christ is his sanctifying individuals in the present. In some cases, moreover, justification

56. *De Jesu Christo servatore* in *Bibliotheca Fratrum* . . ., vol. 2, pp. 124–130.
57. *De Jesu* . . ., pp. 121–124, 186–246.

is itself understood as sanctification – as when Balthasar Hubmeier sub-stitutes 'making just' (*Gerechtmachung*) for justification (*Rechtfertigung*) which is usually, in his view, misunderstood as a forensic declaration (*Gerechterklärung*).[58]

In the modern period, pietists of course continue the concern of the sectarian Reformation with realizing the work of Christ in the present temporal lives of believers. Moreover, as Emanuel Hirsch demonstrates through a detailed study of the University of Halle from the end of the seventeenth to the middle of the eighteenth centuries, the influence of pietistic circles contributed at least in Germany to undermining established orthodoxy and in that way indirectly prepared for the Enlightenment rationalism which it later opposed.[59] But the role of pietism in the development of reflection on the Atonement in the modern period has nonetheless been at least a double one. In figures like John Wesley the Nominalist-Processive emphasis on sanctification in the present is still central. Among radical pietists like J. Konrad Dippel there is, moreover, an explicit rejection of orthodoxy's interpretations of the need for satisfaction of the divine wrath and of Christ's vicarious suffering in favor of a strongly Processive interpretation centering on the goal of becoming ever more fully reborn as children of God.[60] Other tendencies are, however, also in evidence. Already with Spener at the very outset of distinctively modern pietism on the Continent and much more emphatically with his successors from Franke on, a focusing of attention on the crucified Christ in preaching and devotion combines in the course of the first half of the eighteenth century with opposition to rationalistic Enlightenment theologians to make German pietism in particular a bulwark of a strongly Realist and Transactional understanding of the Atonement. The history of the Moravians from Zinzendorf on is one case in point; but

58. For details on Hubmaier and other leading Anabaptists of the sixteenth century, see George H. Williams, 'Sanctification in the Testimony of Several so-called *Schwärmer*', *Mennonite Quarterly Review*, XLII (1968), 5–25, esp. 15–17, 19–22.

59. *Geschichte...*, II, pp. 48–438, esp. 391–399.

60. See, for example, the extended polemical passages in *Vera demonstratio evangelica: ...Beweiss der Lehre und des Mittler–Amts Jesu Christi* (Frankfurt and Leipzig: no publisher indicated, 1729), pp. 153–200, 218–234, 264–337. For brief confessional statements of Dippel's own position see *Vera demonstratio...*, pp. 101–108 and 'Summarische und aufrichtige Glaubensbekenntnis' in *Sämtliche Schriften* (published under the super-scription *Eröffneter Weg zum Frieden mit Gott und allen Kreaturen*) (Berleburg: J. J. Haug, 1747), vol. 1, pp. 494–504.

pietistic movements from the mid-eighteenth on through the nineteenth century on the whole display the same tendency.

There is a final characteristic of some Nominalist-Processive interpretations of the significance of Christ which is evident in sectarian groups like the Anabaptists but which is much less pronounced in modern pietism. That is an emphasis on the corporate nature of the experience in the present of the benefits of Christ's work. Although this emphasis is also present in the earlier history of doctrine – in Augustine's *City of God* (ca. 413–426), for example – it again assumes increasing importance in the nineteenth century in particular. Especially among those theologians under the influence of Schleiermacher, the effecting of Christ's work in the believer through the medium of the church receives considerable attention. In contrast to much of the sacramentalism of the Roman and Anglican traditions, this interpretation of Christ's continuing work as effected through the historical community of believers is, moreover, predominantly ethical and psychological in the categories it uses. It may, therefore, appropriately be classified as Nominalist and Processive.

The thought of Albrecht Ritschl may be taken as representative of this social or communal line of interpretation. That Ritschl is a Nominalist is perhaps most apparent in the systematic contrast which he draws between the human and the natural world or, to be precise, between redeemed personal selves and all other existence. Hence eternal life is lordship over the world and the kingdom of God is, in the last analysis, the final or supramundane end of human history and as such is not simply to be identified with the church as a historical institution.[61] Similarly, the problem which the doctrines of justification and reconciliation address is human sin, which is to be sharply distinguished from natural evil.[62] Despite the strong Kantian influence which such formulations reflect, Ritschl's view is, however, Processive, not Transactional. His position is emphatically not Transactional in the Realist sense: justification is systematically interpreted to exclude any need for satisfying the divine justice or any place for a once

61. *The Christian Doctrine of Justification and Reconciliation: The Positive Development of the Doctrine*, H. R. Mackintosh and A. B. Macaulay, trans. (Edinburgh: T. & T. Clark, 1900), pp. 17–25, 305–306, 483, 533–535, 609–614 [*Die christliche Lehre von der Rechtfertigung und Versöhnung* (Bonn: Adolph Marcus, 1888–1889), vol. III, pp. 17–26, 289–290, 454, 502–504, 575–580].

62. ...*Justification and Reconciliation* ..., pp. 327–384 [310–363].

for all defeat of the powers of evil. But his interpretation is also not Transactional in the Nominalist sense of focusing on individual encounters having no temporal continuity or historical embodiment.

For Ritschl the work of Christ is preeminently that of founding the Kingdom of God on earth. To establish the Kingdom includes both justification and reconciliation: for justification or forgiveness of sins is the 'religious expression of that operation of God upon men which... is the acceptance of sinners into that fellowship with God in which their salvation is to be realized'; and reconciliation is justification in so far as it is effective, with the result that 'the place of mistrust towards God is taken by the positive assent of the will to God and His saving purpose'.[63] Echoing Töllner and other Enlightenment theologians, Ritschl maintains that this teleological view eliminates any possible problem in seeing God as always forgiving, since the divine pardon is an effective means toward the end of realizing the Kingdom.[64] Ritschl does insist that the Kingdom of God may not simply be identified with the institutional church. But members of the church nonetheless are said to comprise the Kingdom in so far as they carry out in history moral action devoted to their fellow men and to God.[65] Ritschl emphasizes again and again that the very possibility of fellowship with God is, moreover, dependent on the existence of a concrete community of believers derivative from Jesus' historical activity and antecedent to the adherence of particular individuals to it. It is of course true that Bultmann, for instance, also recognizes the dependence of the preached Word on the historical church. But Ritschl's view is Processive in a way that Bultmann's is not because in seeing the Kingdom of God as the final end of human history he affirms a continuity between developments within time and the divine goal for the world. His Nominalism may lead Ritschl to share with Bultmann a rejection of 'cosmic eschatology'; but in his view God's relation to history is nonetheless to public and observable history, not only to that personal history which Bultmann protects from scrutiny under the rubric of *Geschichte* as opposed to *Historie*.

63. ...*Justification and Reconciliation*..., p. 85 [83].

64. ...*Justification and Reconciliation*..., pp. 91–93, 318–321, 478–484, 495–496, 607–608 [89–90, 301–304, 450–455, 465–467, 573–574].

65. ...*Justification and Reconciliation*..., pp. 280–282 [266–268].

THE REALIST-PROCESSIVE TYPE

Because Nominalism focuses on the individual to the exclusion of the universal, it tends to set man over against the cosmos as a whole. One result is that a position like that of Ritschl confines itself to development in the human world. There are, however, also interpretations which are Processive and Realist. In this case the change which the work of Christ effects is seen as a process operative not only in human individuals and their communities but also in the cosmos and/or in God himself. The Realist-Processive type is characteristic of the modern era – and of the nineteenth century in particular; but it is also not without instances in the earlier tradition of the church.

The writings of Irenaeus are perhaps the most elaborate example of the Realist-Processive type in the ancient church. Whether his own thought as a whole is to be so classified admittedly involves questions in dispute among historians of doctrine. On the one hand, Adolf Harnack, Friedrich Loofs and André Benoit have argued forcefully that Irenaeus' major work, *Against Heresies*, is a compilation of disparate sources and contradictory commitments.[66] In the case of Loofs in particular, only an inferior and relatively inconsequential residue remains as 'Irenaeus himself'. On the other hand, Gottlieb N. Bonwetsch, Alfred Bengsch, and Gustaf Wingren have maintained that although Irenaeus may well have appropriated other sources, he nonetheless forges the materials he uses into a synthesis having a considerable measure of coherence.[67] I find the latter position more persuasive because the appraisals of Harnack and Loofs in particular fail, I think, to take sufficient cognizance of the polemical context in which Irenaeus wrote; as a result they see contradictory themes when instead not incoherent commitments receive varying degrees of emphasis depending

66. Harnack, *History of Dogma* (New York: Dover, 1961), vol. II, pp. 230–318 [*Lehrbuch der Dogmengeschichte* (Türbingen: J. C. B. Mohr–Paul Siebeck, 1909), vol. I, pp. 550–637]; Loofs, *Theophilus von Antiochen adversus Marcionem und die anderen theologischen Quellen bei Irenäus* (Leipzig: J. C. Hinrichs, 1930); Benoit, *Saint Irénée: Introduction a l'Ètude de sa Théologie* (Paris: Presses Universitaires, 1960).

67. Bonwetsch, *Die Theologie des Irenäus* (Gütersloh: C. Bertelsmann, 1925); Bengsch, *Heilsgeschichte und Heilswissen: eine Untersuchung zur Struktur und Entfaltung des theologischen Denkens des hl. Irenäus von Lyon* (Leipzig: St. Benno Verlag, 1957); Wingren, *Man and the Incarnation: a Study in the Biblical Theology of Irenaeus*, R. MacKenzie, trans. (Edinburgh: Oliver and Boyd, 1959) [*Människan och Inkarnationen enligt Irenaeus* (Lund: C. W. K. Gleerup, 1947)].

on the opponent in view. But even if one is disposed to accept the radical conclusions of Loofs, it is at the very least still the case that Irenaeus' works in their extant form combine – certainly somewhat unsystematically and perhaps not completely coherently – both Realist and Processive tendencies.

The Realist and Processive approach of Irenaeus to the work of Christ is illustrated in the interaction of two themes in his works. One centers on the conception of recapitulation and the other on the complex of concerns expressed through both literal and metaphorical references to growth or increase.

There has been considerable attention to the etymology of the word rendered as recapitulation (ἀνακεφαλαίωσις).[68] The most likely derivation is from the technical term in classical rhetoric for the chief point or summary (κεφαλαιον). But other less defensible connotations linguistically also are operative in Irenaeus' writings. At least three additional ones are important: first, restoration or renewal (reading ἀνά as 'back' and κεφαλή as the equivalent of αρχή, 'beginning'); second, consummation or perfection (reading ἀνά as ἄνω, 'from above', and κεφαλή as the equivalent of τέλος, 'end'); third, uniting or summing up under one head (κεφαλή). Those scholars who maintain that *Against Heresies* is a compilation of mutually contradictory sources and that the themes of recapitulation and growth in particular are incompatible fail to do justice to the multiple connotations which recapitulation bears in Irenaeus' thought. Harnack, for example, simply equates recapitulation with restoration and then sees a 'complete contradiction' between it and the 'apologetic and moralistic train of thought' which the conception of growth represents.[69] Even more remarkably, Loofs contends specifically that the conception of uniting or summing up under one head (*das Unter-ein-Haupt-fassen*) of the epistle to the Ephesians plays no role whatever in Irenaeus.[70] In contrast to this tendency to focus on a single narrow meaning of recapitulation, consideration of these passages

68. See, for example: Gustav Molwitz, *De 'ανακεφαλαίωσις* in *Irenaei Theologia Potestate* (Dresden: B. G. Teubner, 1874); Emmeran Scharl, 'Der Rekapitulationsbegriff des heiligen Irenäus', *Orientalia Christiana Periodica*, VI (1940), 376–416.

69. *History of Dogma*, vol. II, pp. 267–275 [vol. I, pp. 588–596].

70. *Theophilus...*, p. 368. But compare Irenaeus, *Against Heresies* in *Writings*, W. H. Rambant and A. Roberts, eds., 2 vols. (Edinburgh: T. & T. Clark, 1910–11), III. 16.6; III. 19.3; V. 18.2; V. 20.2; only fragments of the Greek text are available, but see *Contra omnes haereses libri quinque*, A. Stieren, ed., 2 vols. (Lipsiae: Weigel, 1848), same book,

which seem to require a reading like 'bringing to perfection' or 'finally uniting under one head' suggests Irenaeus' attempt to relate those themes which otherwise appear as contradictory.

The passages which most readily support an understanding of recapitulation simply as a repetition which restores man's original state are the very frequent instances of comparison between Adam and Christ. The central theme is that Christ 'recapitulates' in perfect obedience Adam's history of disobedience. The parallels include comparisons between their births (virgin soil, virgin), the two sets of temptations, the tree in the garden and the cross, as well as ancillary comparisons between Eve and Mary.[71] But even the numerous passages which deal with parallels between Christ and Adam can be read as evidence that recapitulation means to restore man to his state before the Fall only if they are isolated from the context of Irenaeus' writings as a whole. That Irenaeus consistently portrays Adam and Eve before the Fall as innocent and childlike and still requiring maturation and growth in itself counsels against any interpretation of recapitulation simply as restoration to that condition prior to corruption.[72] There are, moreover, positive indications that Irenaeus does not see the result of the work of Christ as a return to original innocence and the opportunity to begin again. He refers frequently, for example, to the positive value of the knowledge of moral discipline which the Fall makes possible, even

---

chapter and paragraph divisions. In these passages a deliberate play on the connection between head and recapitulation is evident. See also III. 11.8; III. 22.3; V. 18.3; V. 21.1; V. 23.2 and *Proof of the Apostolic Preaching*, J. P. Smith, trans. (Westminster, Md.: Newman Press, 1952), 6; 37; and 99 [the Greek text has been lost, but an Armenian translation of the Greek has been discovered; see *Des heiligen Irenäus Schrift zum Erweise der apostolischen Verkündung*, A. Harnack, K. Ter-mekerttschian, and E. Ter-Minassiantz, eds. (Leipzig: J. C. Hinrichs, 1907)]. All of these passages either quote or echo Ephesians 1.10. Even if the issue is defined as Irenaeus himself *vs.* other sources, it is difficult to see how all such references can be attributed to non-Irenaean sources in view of Loofs' own attribution of the teaching on recapitulation for the most part to Irenaeus himself.

71. On two births, see: *Against Heresies* III. 18.7; III. 23.7; IV. 21.10; IV. 40.3; V. 1.3; V. 21;1. On the temptations, see: *Against Heresies* III. 23.7; IV. 40.3; V. 21.2–3; V. 32.1. On the parallelism between the two trees, see: *Proof of the Apostolic Preaching* 34; *Against Heresies* IV. 2.7; V. 16.3; V. 17.3; V. 18.3; V. 19.1. Irenaeus also advances an elaborate argument to the effect that Adam and Christ died on the same day; see *Against Heresies* V. 23.2. Finally, he presents parallels between Eve and Mary in *Against Heresies* III. 18.7; III. 22.4; V. 19.1 and in *Proof of the Apostolic Preaching* 33.

72. *Proof of the Apostolic Preaching* 12; 14. *Against Heresies* III. 22.4; IV. 38–39

praising the function of the law in this context.[73] Similarly, he places a high valuation on the role of the patriarchs and prophets. Specifically, he sees them as accustoming mankind to bear the Spirit.[74] This description of their role presupposes Irenaeus' complex and not always consistent anthropology in which man at creation possesses flesh and soul but grows into his full maturity only when he becomes imbued with Spirit as well.[75] Hence Irenaeus sees mankind as progressing toward that final destiny even under the old covenant.

In this context, then, Christ's work of recapitulation is not only a rectification of Adam's disobedience but also the decisive point in the divine plan or process (economy) of salvation through which man develops toward that eschatological destiny for which he is intended. For Christ, too, enables the Spirit to become 'accustomed in fellowship with Him to dwell in the human race'.[76] Continuous with the past preparation of the patriarchs and prophets, Christ's work continues to the end of time as well:

He took up man into Himself... summing up (*recapitulans*) all things in Himself: so that ... as well as constituting Himself Head (*caput*) of the church, He might draw all things to Himself at the proper time.[77]

Believers 'between the times' continue to mature toward their destiny. They 'now receive a certain portion of His Spirit, tending towards perfection, and preparing... for incorruption, being little by little accustomed to receive and bear God'.[78] 'Watered' and 'nourished' through the Holy Spirit and through the sacraments in particular, they are able 'to be fruitful, counting out the increase to the Lord' as they 'become imitators of His

73. *Against Heresies* III. 20.2; IV. 12.5; IV. 13.2; IV 16.5; IV. 37.7; IV. 38.4; IV. 39.1.
74. *Against Heresies* VI. 5.4; IV. 13.4; IV. 2; IV. 16.2,3; IV. 21.1,3; IV. 25.1,3. See also IV. 9.3 where Irenaeus describes God's purpose as that men 'might always make progress through believing in him, and by means of the covenants, should gradually attain to (*maturescere*) perfect salvation'.
75. *Against Heresies* V. 6.1; V. 7.1; V. 9.1; V. 10.2; V. 12.2.
76. *Against Heresies* III. 17.1. See also III. 16.3; III. 18.3; III. 19.1; III. 20.2; IV. 33.4; V. 1.1; V. 20.2.
77. *Against Heresies* III. 16.6. Cf. III. 19.3; V. 31.1–2; *Proof of the Apostolic Preaching* 6; 39.
78. *Against Heresies* V. 8.1. See also: II. 28.3; IV. 9.2; IV. 12.2.; IV. 37.7; IV. 38.4; V. 8.1; V. 32.1.

works as well as doers of His words'.[79] Yet even this present maturing of believers is only a foretaste of that end when the cosmos shall finally be united in Christ and when 'the whole creation shall, according to God's will, obtain a vast increase, that it may bring forth and sustain fruits'.[80]

The tradition of a coming cosmic redemption adumbrated in the New Testament, most notably in Colossians and Ephesians, and reflected if not developed further in Irenaeus' works is not a central theme in the history of Western thought. Even in patristic and early medieval reflection, Processive perspectives characteristically confine themselves to development in man's communities, as is illustrated in Augustine's *City of God* (ca. 413–426) and the periodizing of history into the three dispensations of the Father, the Son and finally the Spirit in the thought of the twelfth-century Italian abbot Joachim of Flores. The tendency to isolate nature from the question of redemption receives systematic expression in the Aristotelianism of Thomas. Even though nature participates in the teleological structure of all reality, redemption as such entails a supernatural destiny for man. With the development of a fully autonomous natural science in the Renaissance and the Enlightenment – a development correlative with the full emergence of Nominalism – the restriction of redemption to the human or the spiritual becomes a generally accepted pattern.

Even in wholistic theological systems – those under the influence of Spinoza, for instance – process which is significant for the enhancement of value is restricted to the human world. Lessing's 'The Education of the Human Race' (1777) and Schleiermacher's *Christian Faith* (1821–1822) illustrate this tendency. In both cases a Realist or wholistic metaphysics is combined with a view of the work of redemption which remains Nominalist, though very much Processive. The step from this position to one which incorporates genuine temporal development toward the goal of redemption into the underlying metaphysics itself is, to be sure, a short one; but that step is not very frequently taken before the nineteenth century. Two events in the Western intellectual history of the nineteenth century mark a return to the Realist conception of the unity of the spiritual and the physical in redemption – a conception typical of all the anti-Gnostic Fathers, even

---

79. *Against Heresies* III. 17.2; III.17.3; V. 1.1. See also: III. 24.1; IV. 38.1; V. 2.1; V. 2.3.
80. *Against Heresies* V. 34. 2.

if it is only exceptionally combined with a view of the work of Christ as Processive. The two events are the philosophy of Hegel, with its attempt to incorporate the whole of nature into the history of spirit, and the Darwinian theory of evolution, with its understanding of man as integral to natural processes. Because Hegel's philosophy is perhaps the single most important intellectual influence on the development of nineteenth and twentieth-century theology, it requires detailed consideration in its own right. But it may be appropriate to illustrate briefly the influence of evolutionary categories on the emergence of a contemporary Realist-Processive approach to the work of Christ.

The most dramatic example of the contemporary convergence of theological-Christological concerns with evolutionary theory is the thought of Pierre Teilhard de Chardin. Teilhard's views are thoroughly Processive and also teleological. He sees the cosmos as evolving toward what he terms increased 'radial energy' – toward a growing consciousness or increased spiritual energy. To designate this expanding quantum of consciousness, Teilhard coins the word 'Noosphere'. Man is the 'leading shoot' of the cosmic evolution resulting in a constantly expanding 'Noosphere'. As such he is the crown of the cosmos.[81]

Man is, however, also integral to nature as a whole. The expansion of radial energy follows natural laws just as physiological evolution does; radial attractions – love, for instance – may even be compared to gravitational forces.[82] To quote Teilhard's own epigrammatic summary: 'The only universe capable of containing the human person is an irreversibly "personalizing" universe'.[83] This Realist perspective is, moreover, reenforced by Teilhard's position that evolution has unavoidably become a unitary global process:

We are faced with a harmonized collectivity of consciousness equivalent to a sort of superconsciousness. The idea is that of the earth not only becoming covered by myriads of grains of thought, but becoming enclosed in a single thinking envelope so as to form, functionally, no more than a single vast grain of thought

81. *The Phenomenon of Man*, B. Wall, trans. (New York: Harper & Row – Torchbooks, 1965), esp. pp. 31–36, 62–66, 141–160, 163–164, 180–184 [*Le Phénomène Human* (Paris: Éditions du Seuil, 1955), pp. 25–30, 59–64, 153–175, 179–180, 199–203].
82. *The Phenomenon of Man*, pp. 64–66, 264–268 [62–64, 293–298].
83. *The Phenomenon of Man*, p. 290 [323].

on the sidereal scale, the plurality of individual reflections grouping themselves together, in the act of a single unanimous reflection.[84]

The result is a collective cultural and social evolution of the whole species which makes all forms of individualism obsolete: 'Beyond all nations and races, the inevitable taking-as-a-whole of mankind has already begun'.[85]
   Teilhard sees the process of cosmic evolution as redemptively significant. Consequently he may be said to outline not only a Realist-Processive metaphysics but also a Realist-Processive soteriology. In the Epilogue to the *Phenomenon of Man*, Teilhard leaves no doubt about his position on this point:

For reasons of practical convenience and perhaps also of intellectual timidity, the City of God is too often described in pious works in conventional and purely moral terms. God and the world he governs are seen as a vast association... conceived in terms of a family or government. The fundamental root from which the sap of Christianity has risen from the beginning and is nourished, is quite otherwise. Led astray by a false evangelism, people often think they are honoring Christianity when they reduce it to a sort of gentle philanthropism. Those who fail to see in it the most realistic and at the same time the most cosmic of beliefs and hopes, completely fail to understand its 'mysteries'. Is the kingdom of God a big family? Yes, in a sense it is. But in another sense it is a prodigious biological operation – that of the Redeeming Incarnation.[86]

Not only is the Point Omega – the supremely attractive goal toward which evolution moves – a conception continuous with the utterly inconceivable 'supernatural' God of Christian faith.[87] But the work of the Incarnate

84. *The Phenomenon of Man*, pp. 251–252 [279]; for the full argument, see pp. 239–253 [265–281].
   85. *The Phenomenon of Man*, p. 278 [309]. See also pp. 304–310 [338–344]. See also: Teilhard's How may we Conceive and Hope that Human Unanimisation will be Realized on Earth' in which he discusses an emerging 'Sense of Species'; and his critical comments on individualism in 'Some Reflections on Progress'. Both essays appear in the collection of Teilhard's writings entitled *The Future of Man*, N. Denny, trans. (London: Collins, 1964), pp. 61–81, 281–288 [*L'Avenir de l'Homme* (Paris: Editions du Seuil, 1959), pp. 83–106, 365–374].
   86. *The Phenomenon of Man*, p. 293 [326–327]. See also the essay 'Some Reflections on Progress' in *The Future of Man*, esp. pp. 74–81 [98–106].
   87. See especially the note on p. 298 [332] of *The Phenomenon of Man*.

Christ is precisely 'to subdue under himself, to purify, to direct and super-animate the general ascent of consciousness into which he inserted himself'.[88]

THE CONVERGENCE OF REALISM AND NOMINALISM IN PROCESSIVE INTERPRETATIONS

The thought of both Irenaeus and Teilhard indicates that a fully Processive Realist approach to understanding the work of Christ moves toward the very concerns central in Nominalist interpretations. In so far as the Atonement is understood as effected through the whole course of the historical process, the change which it entails is fundamentally related to the evolutionary transformation of man and his communities – although it need not be simply reduced to that transformation. Conversely, Nominalist interpretations which are fully Processive move toward Realist commitments. A Nominalist view of the influence of Christ can in principle focus exclusively on the transformation of the individual believer and still be Processive in the sense of attending to particular change in space and time. As the temporal mediation of change becomes a self-conscious affirmation, however, attention exclusively to the transformation of discrete individuals becomes a progressively less viable approach; for change mediated over an extended period of time unavoidably requires a social context. As a result, Nominalist-Processive interpretations also come to view the change effected in the individual as in some sense grounded outside of him – at least in the community in which he participates.

This convergence between the Realist and Nominalist types is one indication that the usefulness of specifying systematic alternatives should not be allowed to foster the illusion of static and unchanging typological structures. To outline and to illustrate the types which result from correlating the Realist-Nominalist and the Transactional-Processive distinctions

---

88. *The Phenomenon of Man*, p. 294 [327]. See also the entire Epilogue, pp. 291–299 [324–332]. Also relevant are the devotional reflections collected in *Hymn of the Universe*, G. Vann, trans. (Harper & Row – Colophon Books, 1965), pp. 133–155, esp. number 60 on p. 134 [*Hymne de l'univers: La messe sur le monde* (Paris: Éditions du Seuil, 1961), pp. 144–168, esp. number 60 on p. 145].

does, to be sure, illumine parallels not otherwise immediately apparent. But that exercise in systematic analysis is counterproductive if it is permitted to obscure the extent to which the multiple types are themselves the products of historical development. As the foregoing illustrations of each of the four types attempts to evidence at least suggestively, it is possible to discern each of the systematic alternatives in every historical age. That is especially the case in more recent centuries, since the reflection of earlier ages is available to moderns and hence reappears in a variety of forms. But even for the patristic and the early medieval periods, the full range of alternatives is represented. Though Nominalist and Processive motifs are not articulated self-consciously as alternatives to Realist and Transactional themes, they are nonetheless present, as, for example, the historical and psychological interests of an Augustine and the process metaphysics of an Origen testify. In spite of this representation of the various positions in each age, it is, however, also possible to correlate the relative dominance of individual types with definite historical developments.

My procedure in the chapter before this one of specifying the two sets of alternatives with reference to the social and cultural developments in relation to which they are recognized as systematic alternatives is, of course, consistent with this view of the typology as itself historically grounded. But the more detailed illustrations advanced in this chapter also confirm the relatedness of the types to the course of historical movement. It is possible to schematize this relatedness to Western history into a single line of development. The first position in this overall pattern is that of the Realist-Transactional type: redemption or salvation is derivative from a transformation in mankind as a whole, in the powers controlling the world, or in God himself – a transformation in principle effective quite apart from change in particular individuals in their concrete historical contexts. The second position in this developmental scheme is the Nominalist one: the focus of attention is precisely on the question of change in particular individuals which the various Realist-Transactional views tend to relegate to the status of a secondary concern. The contrast between these first two positions is what underlies the objective-subjective dichotomy of theories of the Atonement. That explains why this dichotomy may serve to illumine a considerable range of historical data. The difficulty with the objective-subjective distinction is, however, that it fails to attend in detail to the second variable which in effect allows the possibility of combining certain strenghts of the first two positions in a third one. That second variable is of course the temporal one. Attention to the question of time results in the recognition of a number of further systematic alternatives, since it is on examination evident not only that some Nominalist views are Transactional while others are Processive but also that Realist interpretations on occasion exemplify Processive motifs in addition to more characteristic Transactional emphases. No single coherent perspective can, to be sure, integrate all these disparate tendencies. But in so far as an interpretation of the Atonement as fully Processive moves toward combining Realist and Nominalist commitments, it may claim to be a third position in the overall pattern of development in Western approaches to the significance of Christ – and, indeed, in the pattern of development of Western thought and institutions.

This overall pattern of development from a relatively a-temporal monistic or wholistic view through radical particularity and pluralization to a reintegration of individuals into a temporalized whole is of critical importance for the philosophical perspective of Hegel. Consequently both his own system and the mutually antagonistic positions which stand under its influence may be construed as illustrating the problems and the promise of an attempt to conceptualize a consistently Processive interpretation of experience. The following study of the structure of Hegel's thought and its relation to nineteenth and twentieth-century theology is, then, a continued exploration of the possibility of combining Realist and Nominalist commitments in a thoroughly Processive approach not only to the significance of Christ but also to the whole of human experience.

PART TWO

Hegel and his Heritage

5

Beyond Orthodoxy and Enlightenment

A central thrust in the philosophical program of G. W. F. Hegel is the attempt to integrate Realist and Nominalist commitments in a coherent system. That attempt is evident throughout the Hegel corpus. Particularly in the *History of Philosophy* and in the *Logic*, the question of the status of universals is repeatedly addressed directly. But because Hegel is also a historian of culture in its multiple ramifications, the broader issues implicit in the Realist-Nominalist distinction receive extended treatment as well. In this chapter I attempt to provide a survey of those tendencies in Hegel's thinking which may be construed as exemplifying the attempt to integrate Realist and Nominalist perspectives into a self-consciously Processive approach. This initial examination of Hegel's systematic position offers a summary interpretation of his thought with reference to the categories I use in elaborating Christological types. In the following chapter I then turn more specifically to Hegel's understanding of the significance of Christ. That further undertaking entails a consideration of Hegel's interest from his earliest essays to his latest writings in the connections between Christ and his influence on the one hand and the course of the historical process on the other. Finally, in the seventh chapter I explore the central issues which emerge from the opposition between leading exponents and critics of Hegel's system in the nineteenth century. For those issues both the Realist-Nominalist and the Transactional-Processive distinctions continue to be instructive, as I seek to demonstrate through a consideration of the Christological and theological debates between right and left-wing Hegelians.

Even a cursory survey of the issues separating the heirs of Hegel is useful not only for understanding the continuing influence of his thought but also for underscoring the systematic implications of his own position. The nineteenth-century polarization between those who ground Christian faith on the historical Jesus and those who affirm a trans-historical Christ is perhaps the most transparent example of the renewed isolation of the Realist and

Nominalist perspectives which I argue Hegel seeks to combine. But even more central to the overall line of argument in this study is the Marxist critique of all those tendencies in Hegel's thought which at least may be construed as obviating the need for continuing transformation of man's historical life – a critique which, in short, rejects all Transactional formulations of Hegel's position and insists instead on a consistently Processive approach. In my exposition of Hegel's own thought, I argue that it may be interpreted as systematically Processive. It is, however, in any case important to recognize the extent to which there are Transactional tendencies in some of Hegel's formulations – tendencies which have exerted considerable influence. A consideration of Marx's critique serves to epitomize this fact and hence to underscore the need for a consistently Processive interpretation of Hegel's system like the one which this study advances.

NOMINALISM AND HEGEL'S DIALECTIC

The movement of Hegel's thought follows a recurrent pattern. That pattern governs the structure of his writings at every level from the most comprehensive organization of the system as a whole to specific analysis of particular logical or temporal developments. The structure is typically threefold: from a relatively less differentiated unity there is movement first to increased particularization or differentiation and then to a reestablished unity which in some sense preserves the greater individuation achieved in the process of differentiation. Because it informs Hegel's thought at every level, the pattern itself receives varied expression in accordance with the subject matter which is being analyzed and described. But the underlying structure nonetheless remains the same.

Hegel's *Logic* offers the paradigmatic instance of this pattern. For only in the *Logic* does Hegel attempt to begin with a totally undifferentiated unity. As he argues in detail in the first pages of Book One of the *Logic* (in the subsection entitled 'With What Must the Science Begin?'), his investigation can commence only with the concept 'being' conceived as the utterly abstract designation of everything that is, with no differentiation whatsoever within that whole. From this point of beginning the *Logic* then moves to increasing differentiation, as the untenability of a position which prescinds from all discrimination is demonstrated. Finally, in the third major division of the *Logic*, The Doctrine of the Concept (*Begriff* – usually translation 'Notion'), Hegel argues for an internally differentiated unity which preserves the values of particular judgment or discrimination while still affirming an ultimate unity of all conceptions in an organic system structuring all reality.

This pattern of the *Logic* in its entirety is also evident throughout Hegel's specific treatment of the relations between individual concepts and groups of concepts. In each case, the movement of Hegel's thought is, to use his terms, from the (relatively more) abstract to the (relatively more) concrete. Hegel employs the same vocabulary when he speaks not of relations internal to the *Logic* but rather of the relation between the *Logic* and the rest of his system. The meaning of the abstract-concrete distinction remains the same, although the reference changes. In each case, 'abstract' indicates an artificial extraction from the context to which 'concrete' refers. Thus in the *Logic* a concept is abstract in so far as its generality encompasses possible distinctions – in so far, that is, as it apprehends reality as undifferentiated; conversely, a conception is concrete in so far as it grasps reality as an internally differentiated system. In contrast, on the question of the structure of the entire system, the abstract-concrete distinction refers to the issue of whether or not phenomenal existence in space and time is included in the analysis. On this level, the *Logic* in its entirety is abstract, while the *Philosophy of Nature* and the *Philosophy of Spirit* are concrete. Yet if the shift in reference is recognized, the underlying pattern nonetheless remains the same: the movement is from a unity which prescinds from a specific mode of differentation through a radical form of that differentiation to a more comprehensive whole which includes differentiation or individuation within it.

This pattern is, of course, scarcely a novelty in the history of thought. But because of its pervasive influence on Hegel's procedure, it provides a useful vehicle for a summary characterization of his evaluation of Nominalism in all its varied cultural forms. That the dialectical movement exemplified in the *Logic* and in the structure of the system as a whole also informs Hegel's studies of more particular historical material is evident both in his detailed analysis of specific developments within the various series of lectures and in the overall structure of each series as a whole. The claim of Hegel's approach to be expositing the dialectical movement inherent in the material itself is undoubtedly least problematical in reference to the *History of Philosophy*. For the history of philosophy does exemplify more transparently than any other subject matter that principle of negativity or criticism which Hegel sees as providing the impetus for development from one position to another. To explore Hegel's appreciation of Nominalism, it is, however, more useful to consider his most comprehensive analyses of cultural development. That criterion dictates a focus on the *Phenomenology of Spirit* and the *Philosophy of History*. Especially the latter illustrates the systematic parallel between the second movement of Hegel's dialectic – that is, the movement to particularization or externalization or discrete individualization – and the emergence in Western cultural history of a self-conscious Nominalism.

HEGEL'S APPRECIATION OF NOMINALISM

The *Lectures on the Philosophy of History* follow the pattern characteristic of Hegel's thought. They begin with an undifferentiated unity, move to the extreme of differentiation or particularization, and finally return to a self-differentiated whole preserving individuation within it. In the political categories which dominate Hegel's interpretation of history, this development constitutes a movement from oriental despotism through Greek and Roman democratic and aristocratic experiments to the radical individualism of the Enlightenment and finally the constitutional monarchy of Western Europe. It is, to quote Hegel's most succinct formulation, a movement in the development of freedom:

The Orientals do not know that spirit or man as such is in principle free. Because they do not know this, they also are not free. They know only that one is free... This one is as a result a despot – not a free man, not a person at all. With the Greeks consciousness of freedom first arose; and therefore they were free. But they along with the Romans knew only that *some* are free – not man as such... As a result the Greeks not only had slaves... but their freedom was itself in part only an accidental, undeveloped and transient flower and at the same time in part a hard oppression of man's common nature, of the human. The teutonic nations, under the influence of Christianity, were the first to attain the consciousness that man as man is free, that it is the freedom of spirit which constitutes its peculiar nature.[1]

Hegel sees this development as one from political structures which completely submerge the individual to the development of equally universal or comprehensive political institutions which nonetheless allow full expression to individuality. Though it is preserved only in student notes, Hegel's introductory survey of the major divisions in the entire course of lectures offers a convenient summary of this development. The Greek contribution is the emergence of an individualism which Hegel typically describes in aesthetic categories: it is a beautiful or harmonious relationship in which the individual 'naturally' conforms to mores or conventions and thus is one with his society.[2] Rome makes a similarly provisional though nonetheless valuable and even necessary contribution. In forging a powerful state to which the individual is unambiguously subordinated, Roman political life at the same time creates a self-conscious awareness on the part of individuals of the definite rights which accrue to them simply because of their abstract existence as legal persons.[3] Because its awareness of the individual person is only that of an abstract entity with specified rights, the

1. *The Philosophy of History*, J. Sibree, trans. (New York: Dover Publications, 1956), p. 18 [Philosophie der Weltgeschichte, G. Lasson, ed. (Leipzig: Verlag von Felix Meiner, 1917–1920), p. 39]. This first edition of the Lasson text appears in four volumes plus a fifth volume of Lasson's study of Hegel as a philosopher of history. Since the four volumes of the lectures themselves are continuously paginated, I indicate page numbers only. For the long introduction – comprising the first volume – Hegel's own manuscript has been preserved; consequently Lasson can indicate which passages are from Hegel's manuscript and which from student notes. (The one I quote here is from Hegel's manuscript.) For the convenience of the English speaking reader I continue to give references to an English translation. In quoting from the *Philosophy of History*, I have, however, decided to supply my own translations for three reasons. First, there are numerous usually minor textual differences between the earlier edition which Sibree translates and Lasson's more critical edition. Second, there are occasional serious mistranslations in Sibree's work. In this passage, for example, *germanisch* is rendered as 'German' even though Hegel self-consciously avoids using *deutsch* and explicitly identifies *die germanische Welt* with all of Europe from Scandinavia to the Mediterranean and east as far as parts of Russia. Finally, Sibree's translation has the dubious distinction of being stylistically even more disastrous than Hegel's original while at the same time taking considerable liberty with the actual text.
2. *Philosophy of History*, pp. 106–107 [239–240].
3. *Philosophy of History*, pp. 107–108 [240–241].

Roman world can offer only individual despotism or anarchy as an alternative to the universal despotism of the state. But despite its political failure the Roman world provides the context for the emergence of that final spiritual individuality which is integral to the reestablished social whole of the European world.

In Hegel's survey the so-called teutonic world includes not only the reestablishment of a final social coherence but also the first development of full spiritual individuality. That spiritual individuality emerges with the Christian conviction of reconciliation: man himself is spirit and hence a moment in that process which constitutes ultimate reality. This individuality is, however, at first a matter of the inner life and stands over against all that is worldly – a radical subjectivity which only in time has an impact on social and political life.[4] The history of the West from the time of Christ on is for Hegel the continuing development of this self-conscious individuality and the gradual creation of institutional forms to integrate autonomous men into an organic social whole. As both the *Philosophy of History* and the *Phenomenology* amply illustrate, that double development is not a direct progress but rather, as always, a dialectical movement. Still, both the direction and the goal are set – with the result that even those tendencies which Hegel subjects to severe criticism are presented as making a useful and even necessary contribution.

One result of Hegel's analysis is that those developments which I have included under the characterization 'Nominalist' receive a thoroughly positive valuation – at the same time as they are granted only a provisional or penultimate validity. Although Hegel maintains that the awareness of the individual as possessing infinite value emerged 'in germ' with the appearance of Jesus and the faith of the early church, he focuses his own analysis of what he terms 'the principle of subjectivity' in the modern era. He notes the development of towns and guilds and private ownership in the late medieval period as institutionalizing greater possibilities for individual freedom. The church's blatant struggle for temporal dominion also is cited as contributing toward a rediscovery of the inner life – as in the monastic reform movements. Even the crusades are interpreted as providing the negative lesson that true spirituality is not to be found in the external trap-

4. *Philosophy of History*, pp. 108–110 [243–247].

pings of the historical Jesus. But despite such preparation, Hegel sees the decisive breakthrough of spiritual individuality in the Reformation. Indeed, in both the *Philosophy of History* and the *History of Philosophy* he repeatedly uses the designation 'the Protestant principle' to refer to what in his view is this peculiarly modern appreciation of the individual as a free and intrinsically valuable being.

That Hegel sees Luther as instrumental in explicitly asserting what is at least implicit in Christianity from the beginning does not, however, mean that further development is unnecessary. Instead the entire course of Western history since the Reformation is for Hegel the process through which the Protestant principle is realized in every sphere of life. Luther began this process. To use the summary formulation to which Hegel repeatedly returns, Protestantism substituted marriage, vocation in the world, and autonomy for the medieval trinity of chastity, poverty, and obedience. But there still remains a fundamental ambiguity in the Reformation position:

In the Protestant religion the principle of subjectivity was introduced through religious liberation and inner peace; [but] in the same movement there was also the belief in subjectivity as evil and as a wordly power.[5]

In contrast to the ambiguous status of temporal existence which results from Luther's intensely personal interpretation of justification and his understanding of the goal of man's life as beyond this world (*ein Jenseits*), post-Reformation cultural developments in the West focus decisively on the here and now. The result is the programmatic exaltation of man and the demand that his infinite value and his moral autonomy find expression throughout the secular order. This process Hegel analyzes and affirms both as necessary and as good in his consideration of the Enlightenment.

Hegel's relationship to the Enlightenment is complex. There is, moreover, no doubt that his judgment on his eighteenth-century predecessors is as much a negative as a positive one. Nonetheless, Hegel affirms the critical thrust of the Enlightenment in its assertion of individual self-confidence over against authority and in its questioning of the dualistic worldview and the dualistic criteria of knowledge typical of 'belief'. Hegel makes this point in each of his series of lectures – notably in the *Philosophy of Religion*, the

5. *Philosophy of History*, p. 438 [913] – my translation.

History of Philosophy and the *Philosophy of History*. But he formulates his position most sharply in the section in the *Phenomenology* on the Enlightenment, with its extended comparison between 'belief' and 'pure insight'.

In detailing the conflict between belief and pure insight – between an orthodoxy which had absorbed pietism into itself on the one hand and its Enlightenment opponents on the other – Hegel graphically portrays the systematic criticism to which uncompromising empiricism and self-confident moral individualism subject religious life and thought in the eighteenth century. Hegel does, to be sure, criticize the Enlightenment position on a number of fundamental points. But his line of argument nonetheless indicates his conviction that an advance beyond the Enlightenment position is possible only after the truth of that position is affirmed. Central to that truth is the conclusion that the attempt of belief to exempt itself from rational scrutiny is untenable:

> Enlightenment... brings to pass the abolition of that state of unthinking, or rather unreflective (*begrifflos*) cleavage, which finds a place in the nature of belief. The believing mood weighs and measures by a twofold standard, it has two sorts of eyes and ears, uses two voices to express its meaning, it duplicates all ideas, without comparing and relating the sense and meaning in the two forms used... Enlightenment illuminates that world of heaven with ideas drawn from the world of sense, pointing out there this element of finitude which belief cannot deny or repudiate.[6]

The result of this criticism is that the conflict between belief and pure insight becomes a conflict within Enlightenment itself. Belief is, to be sure, unsatisfied with a reduction of religious truth to the platitudes of Enlightenment rationalism; indeed, it finds this position, to quote Hegel, 'utterly and simply revolting' and 'sheer insipidity'.[7] But because belief cannot repudiate the focus on the finite which Enlightenment finds even in orthodoxy, a Deism emerges which is precisely parallel to the most consistent materialism of the day in restricting itself utterly to the finite while affirming an unknowable beyond analogous to the abstraction of pure matter which the materialists

6. *The Phenomenology of Mind*, J. B. Baillie, trans. (New York: Harper & Row–Torchbooks, 1967), pp. 587–588 [*Phänomenologie des Geistes*, J. Hoffmeister, ed. (Hamburg: Verlag von Felix Meiner, 1952), pp. 405–406].
7. *Phenomenology*..., pp. 580, 588–589 [400, 406–407].

posit.[8] For Hegel the absorption of belief into Enlightenment can only mean that further advance requires the demonstration of inadequacies in Enlightenment itself – but a demonstration which accepts an insistence on full attention to the morally responsible individual in the here and now. As Hegel summarizes the issue at the very end of the section on the Enlightenment in the *Phenomenology* (in a subsection entitled 'The Truth of Enlightenment'), it is precisely this 'principle of concrete actuality, or of certainty of self in the sense of this individual self' which belief lacks. In contrast to orthodoxy, movement beyond the Enlightenment position can only build on 'the truth of Enlightenment' that 'both worlds are reconciled and heaven is transplanted to earth below'.[9]

HEGEL'S THREEFOLD CRITIQUE OF NOMINALISM

His critique of the Enlightenment constitutes a central instance of Hegel's interpretation of historical data as manifesting the dialectical movement which structures his thought. Indeed, in view of Hegel's own struggle with overcoming while still appropriating the position of the Enlightenment, it is at least highly probable that the process of systematically understanding the history of eighteenth-century thought and culture itself functioned as a paradigmatic case in the development of the method which he employs in all of his mature work. In any case, Hegel's evaluation of the Enlightenment does exemplify the pattern in which his method characteristically results. That evaluation may be summarized in a single proposition: although the exclusive focus of the Enlightenment on the finite individual constitutes a necessary and at least provisionally good development of human subjectivity and moral responsibility, it must nonetheless be criticized and transcended so that the particular can be integrated into a universal whole.

Perhaps the most emphatic formulation of Hegel's critique of the Enlightenment position appears in his early essay *Faith and Knowledge*. In that work he takes the philosophies of Kant, Jacobi, and Fichte as epitomizing the mature expression of the problematic underlying the dominant movement of eighteenth-century thought. Although Hegel recognizes (and analyzes

8. *Phenomenology*..., pp. 591–594 [408–411].
9. *Phenomenology*..., pp. 597–598 [413].

in detail) differences among the three thinkers, he contends that they agree in affirming 'the absoluteness of the finite and of empirical reality and the absolute opposition between the infinite and the finite'.[10] Hegel takes this 'realism of finitude' as characteristic of the whole of modern culture in its unreflective or nonphilosophical manifestations; but he focuses on the thought of Kant, Jacobi, and Fichte because he sees their efforts to transcend empiricism and eudaimonism as having the unintended result of stating the Enlightenment position in its most consistent form. Hegel uses the example of eudaimonism to sharpen his polemic. In an uncritical and sensual ethic which declares happiness to be its highest value, there is no doubt a central emphasis on empirical satisfaction and sensual enjoyment. But there is in addition frequently the positing of some form of ultimate happiness or blessedness which stands over against the finite and is taken to have a reality or content at least analogous to that of the finite. In contrast, argues Hegel, the philosophies of Kant, Jacobi, and Fichte illustrate the reduction of the infinite to the status of a mere thought or a totally unknown something. The result is an exclusive and unqualified focus on the finite.[11]

Hegel's writings abound with his criticism of both the epistemological and the ontological implications of this Enlightenment position. He is particularly caustic in noting the paradox that this self-exaltation of the finite occurs in the context of the claim to take seriously the limitations of man's knowledge. A succinct passage from the *Philosophy of Spirit* may serve to epitomize his judgment on this claim: 'Such a *modesty* of thought, as treats the finite as something altogether fixed and *absolute*, is the worst of virtues'.[12] This systematic connection which Hegel sees between epistemological modesty or humility and ontological pride indicates the multiple dimensions of his critique of the Enlightenment – and illumines his program for transcending that position. The object of his critique is three-fold. He assails the absolutizing of the finite individual to which the Enlightenment

10. *Glauben und Wissen oder die Reflexionsphilosophie der Subjektivität* in *Erste Durckschriften*, G. Lasson, ed. (Leipzig: Verlag von Felix Meiner, 1928), pp. 229–230.

11. *Glauben und Wissen...*, pp. 225–235, esp. 227–230.

12. *Encyclopedia*, paragraph 386 in the numbering of the 1830 edition, which is the basis for all subsequent editions including that of which W. Wallace translates the first and third parts as *The Logic of Hegel* (Oxford: Clarendon Press, 1892) and *Hegel's Philosophy of Mind* (Oxford: Clarendon Press, 1894). In quoting from the first and third parts of the *Encyclopedia*, I use Wallace's translations.

is committed by default if not in intention. He also ridicules and castigates the conception of God as a mere abstract other over against the finite. Finally, he rejects every philosophical position which programmatically restricts human knowledge to the sensible and consequently relegates religious conviction to the sphere of the completely subjective. Hegel recognizes, moreover, that these three criticisms are inextricably interrelated – that a consistent absolutizing of man presupposes the view that God is unknowable, which in turn assumes either the critical philosophy of Kant or its empiricist predecessors. The conclusion is, therefore, unavoidable that the transcending of Enlightenment conceptions of God and man can only be achieved through a reappraisal of the epistemological analysis which is presupposed in the formulation of those conceptions.

HEGEL'S CRITIQUE OF NOMINALISM: THE EPISTEMOLOGICAL ISSUE

Hegel's reappraisal of the epistemological presuppositions of what he takes to be the typical Enlightenment position is adumbrated in the early essay *Faith and Knowledge*, particularly in the introductory and concluding remarks. But his argument appears in fully developed form only in the *Phenomenology of Spirit*. The *Phenomenology* does, to be sure, subject numerous successive stages or levels of consciousness to critical scrutiny, in each case advancing the contention that the attempt to explain man's experience in terms less comprehensive than what Hegel calls 'absolute knowledge' is internally inconsistent and therefore literally untenable. But the aim of this virtuoso review of the history of Western thought and culture is precisely to provide the appropriate context for the transcendence of the Enlightenment in general and Kant's critical philosophy in particular.

Although no summary can do justice to Hegel's vivid portrayal of the accumulated experience of mankind, his central line of argument is susceptible of concise formulation. Indeed, Hegel himself offers occasional summaries of the program which he attempts to carry out in the *Phenomenology* – summaries which indicate the centrality of Hegel's criticism of Kant in particular. In the *Phenomenology* itself, the most concise formulation of his argument occurs at the end of the introduction. Stated in its simplest form, Hegel's contention is that the common sense view of the object of knowing as an independent and external entity is untenable. As Hegel points out, the movement of the *Phenomenology* depends on the failure of the conception of objectivity as externality and independence 'to hold its ground' or 'to hold out':

The object... appears only to be in such wise for consciousness as consciousness knows it. Consciousness does not seem able to get, so to say, behind it as it is, not for consciousness, but in itself, and consequently seems also unable to test knowledge by it. But just because consciousness has, in general, knowledge of an object, there is already present the distinction that the inherent nature, what the object is in itself, is one thing to consciousness, while knowledge, or the being of the object *for* consciousness, is another moment. Upon this distinction, which is present as a fact, the examination turns. Should both, when thus compared, not correspond, consciousness seems bound to alter its knowledge, in order to make it fit the object. But in the alteration of the knowledge, the object itself also, in point of fact, is altered; for the knowledge which existed was essentially a knowledge of the object; with change in the knowledge, the object also becomes different, since it belonged essentially to this knowledge. Hence consciousness comes to find that what formally to it was the essence is not what is *per se*, or what was *per se* was only *per se for consciousness*. Since, then, in the case of its object consciousness finds its knowledge not corresponding with this object, the object likewise fails to hold out.[13]

In this characterization of the dissolution of a static subject-object dualism, Hegel claims simply to be describing man's normal experience: 'This dialectic process which consciousness executes on itself – on its knowledge as well as on its object – in the sense that out of it the new and true object arises, is precisely what is termed experience'.[14] The task of the *Phenomenology* – as the very name indicates – is, then, 'simply and solely to look on' as human consciousness 'tests and examines itself' in the process of moving to an increasingly adequate or comprehensive understanding both of itself as knower and of the object of its knowledge.[15]

This summary account of the program of the *Phenomenology* appears

13. *Phenomenology*..., pp. 141–142 [72].

14. *Phenomenology*..., p. 142 [73]. I have changed Baillie's arbitrary capitalization of 'experience', since that suggests a special or esoteric affair whereas Hegel refers simply to the apprehending and understanding or talking about empirical objects.

15. *Phenomenology*..., p. 141 [72].

as paradoxical or as highly speculative only if Hegel's central contention that there is no object outside of consciousness is misunderstood as denying the reality of a world external to the knower. But – as the ensuing exposition maintains in detail – that is emphatically not his position. Instead he is arguing only that any reference whatsoever to objects or objective reality is irreducibly conceptual. A distinction is, to be sure, made between what the object is in itself and what it is for consciousness – that is, in the knowledge which the subject has of it. But this distinction is itself a conceptual distinction, a distinction within the domain of man's knowing. The object in itself and the object for consciousness are, moreover, correlative. The movement of the *Phenomenology* from one level of consciousness to the next is the result of repeated testing of the adequacy of any given claim to knowledge. That testing assumes the form of the constantly (if sometimes implicitly) reiterated question of whether any given knowledge claim in fact corresponds to the real object. In so far as the answer is negative, the conception of the object is modified; but in that very process the object itself is changed, since the object is available to the knower only in so far as he can conceive or talk about it. Hegel insists that all knowing conforms to the pattern he describes. Even the 'common sense' which claims to apprehend independent external objects in practice modifies and revises its description of that objective order as its knowledge becomes progressively more adequate or sophisticated. Even 'common sense', in short, can refer to the objects it purports to know only in so far as it grasps them in its conceptions.

The immediate historical reference of Hegel's line of argument is its rejection of Kant's bifurcation between man's knowledge and the so-called thing-in-itself. That his analysis constitutes a criticism of Kant is very frequently stated explicitly and is at least implicit in virtually every formulation of Hegel's position. But the preface to the second edition of the *Logic* provides what is perhaps his most succinct and lucid summary of the contradiction which he sees not only in Kant's thought but in any view which maintains a simple subject-object dichotomy – a view which he terms 'natural logic':

For us the object can be nothing else but our notions of it. The way in which the critical philosophy understands the relationship of these three terms is that we place our thoughts as a medium between ourselves and the objects, and that this medium instead of connecting us with the objects rather cuts us off from them. But this view can be countered by the simple observation that these very things which are supposed to be beyond us and, at the other extreme, beyond the thought referring to them, are themselves figments of subjective thought, and as wholly indeterminate they are only a single thought-thing – the so-called thing-in-itself of empty abstraction.[16]

Even the thing-in-itself is, then, a conception which exists within man's knowledge and hence cannot claim the status of external or independent existence. That it abstracts from all particular determinations or specifications is not denied. The appropriate conclusion following from this fact is, however, that the concept of the thing-in-itself is a limiting concept – not that it is sheer objectivity independent of all man's concepts.

Kant's epistemological program unavoidably entails a final agnosticism as to whether man's conceptions in the last analysis correspond to the things-in-themselves. This agnosticism is particularly pronounced in the case of the 'ideas' of God, the world, and the self, since they organize other conceptions instead of unifying and referring to sense data. But even in the case of empirical concepts which do refer to sensible objects and hence qualify as knowledge in Kant's usage, there is a programmatic denial that the knowledge in question can legitimately claim to be knowledge of things as they really are, of things apart from any knower, of the things-in-themselves. In contrast, Hegel insists on an ideal of 'absolute knowledge' or 'pure science' in which the system of man's conceptions is completely adequate to reality itself. As Hegel remarks in summarizing the result of the *Phenomenology* in his introduction to the *Logic*, this ideal of absolute knowledge or pure science 'presupposes liberation from the opposition of consciousness'.[17] Because the object itself can be thought only if it is integral to the whole system of man's conceptions, it is not possible even to talk about an objective order without already undercutting any claim that it is in principle inaccessible to man's knowledge. Once this fundamental contention is granted, the process of immanent criticism of the adequacy of any given

16. *Hegel's Science of Logic*, A. V. Miller, trans. (London: George Allen & Unwin, 1969), p. 36 [*Wissenschaft der Logik*, G. Lasson, ed. (Leipzig: Verlag von Felix Meiner, 1923), part 1, p. 15].

17. ...*Logic*, p. 49 [part 1, p. 30].

knowledge claim to its object is unavoidable; and the ideal which any such criticism presupposes is that perfectly coherent and comprehensive system of concepts which is completely adequate to the whole of reality.

HEGEL'S CRITIQUE OF NOMINALISM: THE ONTOLOGICAL IMPLICATIONS

The contrast between Hegel's approach and the Enlightenment position which he criticizes is epitomized in the question of how God is conceived. One of the most illuminating extended discussions of the issues which Hegel sees in this question is his consideration of the conceptions of finitude and infinity in the *Logic*. In that discussion Hegel develops in detail his distinction between the true and the spurious infinite.

Hegel frequently identifies the spurious infinite simply as the infinite of the understanding. Its identification with the understanding in contrast to reason already indicates a correlation with Hegel's eighteenth-century predecessors – an indication which is confirmed throughout the discussion. Hegel maintains that the typical Enlightenment position cannot escape the fundamental contradiction of affirming an infinite which is, in the last analysis, only another finite entity:

This contradiction occurs as a direct result of the circumstance that the finite remains as a determinate being opposed to the infinite, so that there are *two* determinatenesses; *there are* two worlds, one infinite and one finite, and in their relationship the infinite is only the *limit* of the finite and is thus only a determinate infinite, an *infinite which is itself finite*.[18]

Any position which defines God in unqualified contrast to the phenomenal world is included in Hegel's criticism. The God of Deism who is utterly beyond the autonomous world which he has established is, of course, a paradigmatic case of what Hegel is rejecting. Because that 'beyond' is an abstraction defined as external to the finite, it is itself limited. It is, in short, 'the finitized infinite'.[19] Hegel sees the same model as applicable to the 'perennial ought' of Kant and Fichte. In this case, too, the infinite is con-

18. ...*Logic*, pp. 139–140 [part 1, p. 128].
19. ...*Logic*, p. 137 [part 1, p. 125].

ceived as a fixed beyond which can never be reached – a beyond defined in opposition to the finite and hence itself not unlimited.

The true conception which Hegel contrasts to this spurious infinite is the mutual overcoming of the abstract or independent existence of the finite and the infinite:

Infinity *is* only as a transcending of the finite; it therefore essentially contains its other and is, consequently, in its own self the other of itself. The finite is not sublated by a power existing outside it; on the contrary, its infinity consists in sublating its own self.[20]

Hegel's argument is that the very conceptions of the finite and the infinite mutually imply each other and hence cannot be consistently defined simply as opposed to each other. That the finite cannot exist over against the true infinite follows from the very definition of infinity as not limited. As Hegel observes, 'One only needs to *be aware of what one is saying* in order to find the determination of the finite in the infinite'.[21]

Hegel is not, however, satisfied with a formulation which simply affirms the unity of the finite and infinite. The appearance of this discussion of the finite and the infinite in the first of the three major divisions of the *Logic* already indicates that it does not yet offer a detailed exposition of his own position. But Hegel also registers his reservations explicitly. Criticizing the word 'unity' as implying an 'abstract, inert self-sameness', he insists instead that the true infinite must be conceived as a becoming, as a process, through which the opposition of the finite and the (spurious) infinite is continuously transcended.[22] Hegel does not, then, simply deny the fact of opposition between the finite and what it takes to be the infinite. Such a denial would constitute an undialectical repudiation of the Enlightenment. The result would be a return to a consciousness of unity with the one or the all which belies the emergence of radical individuation and self-consciousness as cul-

---

20. ...*Logic*, pp. 145–146 [part 1, p. 135]. The 'transcending', 'sublated', and 'sublating' in the translation are renderings of the German noun *Aufhebung* and the corresponding past participle *aufgehoben*. Because there is no adequate English equivalent for this crucial Hegelian conception, it is important to keep in mind its dual meanings of 'overcoming' and 'preservation'. Despite its awkwardness, 'sublating' at least has the merit of not emphasizing overcoming to the exclusion of preservation – as 'transcendence' tends to do.

21. ...*Logic*, p. 143 [part 1, p. 132].

22. ...*Logic*, pp. 147–148 [part 1, pp. 137–138].

tural facts. In contrast to glorification of any such undifferentiated unity, Hegel insists on an infinity which preserves the finite as a moment in the process of the whole. He affirms, to quote the formulation at the conclusion of the *Logic's* discussion of finitude and infinity, 'the finite as it is in the true infinite – as a determination, a content, which is distinct but is not an *independent, self-subsistent* being, but only a *moment*'.[23]

THE RESULT OF HEGEL'S CRITIQUE: A NEW REALISM

The recognition that Hegel's relationship to the Enlightenment is not one of undialectical rejection is crucial for an adequate comprehension of his own position. The issue is whether Hegel asserts a new Realism which emerges from an immanent criticism of Nominalism or whether he simply reasserts the old Realism which had succumbed to its Nominalist opponents. That Hegel himself emphatically claimed to be doing the former is beyond dispute. But it remains to specify further the difference which he sees between his position and its antecedents.

The form of Realism which Nominalism has rendered forever obsolete is, to use Hegel's vocabulary, the affirmation of universals which are and remain only abstract. The exemplars of this position which he cites most frequently are the Hindus, the Eleatics, Spinoza, and Schelling. The criticism is in each case in principle the same. It may be epitomized in Hegel's well-known epigrammatic characterization of Schelling's absolute as "the night in which all cows are black."[24] Stated in terms of the pattern which structures Hegel's thought, this form of Realism exemplifies the first moment of the dialectic: it affirms an undifferentiated unity encompassing all of being. Because this view denies significance to the individual, it survives the emergence of a self-conscious Nominalism only as an anachronism.

One index of Hegel's concern to distinguish his position from this affirmation of an undifferentiated unity is the frequency with which reference to Spinoza occurs throughout his works. The issue which Hegel elaborates

23. . . .*Logic*, pp. 149–150 [part 1, pp. 139–140].
24. *Phenomenology. . .*, p. 79 [19]. Hegel uses the same metaphor in his 1801 essay *The Difference between the Fichtean and the Schellingian System of Philosophy;* see the reference to 'the night of totality' in *Erste Druckschriften*, p. 21.

again and again may be summarized in his programmatic contrast between conceiving the absolute as substance and as subject:

In my view – a view which the developed exposition of the system itself can alone justify – everything depends on grasping and expressing the ultimate truth not as Substance but as Subject as well.[25]

As the preface to the *Phenomenology* indicates, both the epistemological and the ontological dimensions of Hegel's critique of his predecessors are reflected in this programmatic formulation. The central epistemological issue is with Kant and the empiricists. In rejecting the thing-in-itself as an empty conceptual abstraction, Hegel argues that the object of knowledge cannot consistently be thought of as a static entity but rather only as what is grasped in that developing and increasingly sophisticated web of conceptions through which alone man can know or speak of anything at all. That even the simplest empirical object proves to be conceivable only as integral to a whole complex of conceptions is Hegel's response to any form of subject-object dualism. But equally important is Hegel's insistence against Spinoza that this whole complex of conceptions is itself constantly undergoing revision and development as man seeks to make his knowledge more adequate to the reality he experiences.

This epistemological observation has, moreover, ontological implications. Whatever man claims to know at all, he knows through his concepts. Consequently any object about which he thinks or talks is integrally related to a complex system of other objects which are also known through human conceptions. No more than any other object of man's awareness or knowledge can the absolute or the true infinite be thought of apart from the entire complex of conceptions through which man organizes his experience. Indeed, only the whole of man's developing knowledge can correspond to the absolute in Hegel's sense of the true infinite. Hence man's conception of the absolute is adequate only when it is that of a self-differentiated process. Hegel offers his own summary statement of this point:

The truth is the whole. The whole, however, is merely the essential nature reaching its completeness through the process of its own development. Of the Absolute

25. *Phenomenology . . .*, p. 80 [29].

it must be said that it is essentially a result, that only at the end is it what it is in very truth; and just in that consists its nature, which is to be actual, subject, or self-becoming, self-development.[26]

The absolute is, then, not a static entity which may be grasped through Spinoza's deductive method on the model of geometry. Instead the absolute is for Hegel a process which includes finite self-consciousness and which can be known only through the whole evolving system of man's conceptions. Spinoza's conception of substance or Parmenides' conception of being is undifferentiated, contains no distinctions within it, does not serve to discriminate one quality from another – is, to use Hegel's word, abstract. In contrast the absolute of the *Logic* undergoes progressive redefinition until it becomes an internally mediated or differentiated system which preserves distinctions within itself. The conceptions comprising this system constitute a single whole – a whole which Hegel terms 'the conception' (*der Begriff*, usually translated 'the Notion'). But because this system in preserving distinctions within itself does not annihilate the finite, it is, in Hegel's terminology, concrete. The result is that Hegel grants the profound significance of the development of self-conscious individuality in the modern period. But he does so without affirming the finite individual as the absolute. Instead he integrates the commitments of Nominalism into a Realism which unabashedly maintains the reality of the universal as the structure of the whole and the end toward which it is developing.

In the first chapter of the *Logic* Hegel himself interprets the difference between his position and that of Spinoza or Parmenides in theological categories. The contrast is between a pantheistic denial of becoming and an acceptance of creation *ex nihilo*:

The proposition: out of nothing comes nothing, nothing is just nothing, owes its peculiar importance to its opposition to *becoming* generally, and consequently also to its opposition to the creation of the world from nothing. Those who maintain the proposition: nothing is just nothing, and even grow heated in its defence, are unaware that in so doing they are subscribing to the abstract pantheism of the *Eleatics*, and also in principle to that of Spinoza. The philosophical view for which 'being is only being, nothing is only nothing', is a valid principle, merits the name of 'system of identity'; this abstract identity is the essence of pantheism.[27]

26. *Phenomenology...*, pp. 81–82 [21].
27. *...Logic*, p. 84 [part 1, pp. 68–69].

The rejection of every such 'system of identity' in favor of affirming process or becoming is the most salient feature of Hegel's Realism. The positive evaluation of change and development which results informs every dimension of his thought. The reference to the doctrine of creation is, moreover, particularly illuminating; for it is possible to interpret Hegel's system as a philosophical formulation of that apprehension of reality as inherently and significantly historical which is expressed in the Christian symbols of creation and redemption. To pursue that line of interpretation is the purpose of the following chapter.

6

Hegel on the Significance of Christ and the Historical Process

In attempting to summarize Hegel's position as concisely and as systematically as possible, the foregoing discussion focuses for the most part on specifically philosophical issues. That procedure should not, however, be taken to suggest that Hegel's coming to terms with his eighteenth-century predecessors may legitimately be construed as an exclusive preoccupation with epistemological and ontological questions. Such a restriction is in any case untenable, since the positions which a thinker takes on underlying ontological and epistemological issues have definite practical implications. But in the case of Hegel, a separation of philosophical issues in the strict sense from the full spectrum of other cultural questions also misrepresents his own procedure. Not only does he in time offer multiple series of lectures detailing the connections between his philosophical analysis and the various forms of cultural history; but specifically religious concerns and political events are also instrumental in the development of his position on philosophical issues. This significance of religious and political questions in the formation of Hegel's mature position is strikingly illustrated in his early manuscripts.

THE 'EARLY THEOLOGICAL WRITINGS'

There has been considerable controversy surrounding the question of whether or not it is appropriate to characterize Hegel's early manuscripts as theological in character. The genesis of the debate is a reaction against the dominant portrayal of the young Hegel in German scholarship of the late nineteenth and early twentieth century. That dominant tradition of interpretation attains its most influential expression in Wilhelm Dilthey's *Life of the Young Hegel* (1905). Dilthey emphasizes the pantheistic and mystical tendencies in Hegel's early essays. Although the studies on the political situation in Germany at the turn of the century and on political and economic theory are occasionally mentioned, they are thoroughly subordinated to religious themes in Dilthey's treatment. This pattern in turn becomes an organizing principle for editing the early manuscripts. Describing his 1907 edition of the early manuscripts as a continuation of Dilthey's work, Herman Nohl includes in his collection of essays and fragments everything that Hegel wrote between 1790 and 1800 – except for four brief notes, several sermons, and the political writings.

This focus of attention on religious themes to the exclusion of Hegel's social and political writings has not, of course, been without effect. On the one hand, scholars like Theodor Haering have tended systematically to divorce Hegel's thought from social-political interests. In his two-volume *Hegel: His Intention and His Achievement* (1929, 1938), Haering draws extensively on Dilthey and devotes more space to discussing the essays collected in Nohl's edition of the early writings than to all the published works and public lectures. On the other hand, there has been a very strong reaction – particularly among Marxist scholars – against the portrayal of the young Hegel either as a mystical pantheist or as a pro-Christian theologian. The most influential example of this reaction is George Lukács's *Der junge Hegel*. The traditional designation of Hegel's student years as a 'theological period' is, in Lukács's view, simply a 'reactionary legend'.[1] Lukács has exerted considerable influence because he does not rest his case simply with references to Hegel's letters and his political writings but instead addresses himself centrally to the very fragments and essays which Nohl presents as theological in character. Thus Lukács acknowledges the importance of religious questions for the young Hegel while at the same time rejecting the quietistic social and political perspective implied in the mystical-pantheistic line of interpretation.

Because Dilthey and Nohl and those writing under their influence tend to abstract Hegel's theological reflection from his manifest concern with broader social and cultural developments, Lukács provides a necessary corrective. He is, to be sure, not sympathetic to Hegel's interest in religious questions as such. But he does not attempt to deny the role which that interest plays in Hegel's thinking. Instead he analyzes Hegel's treatment of specifically religious and theological concerns in relation to economic

1. Georg Lukács, *Der junge Hegel* (Zürich: Europa Verlag, 1948), p. 27 and the entire section pp. 27–45.

and political issues. One result is a significant contribution to the understanding of the genesis of Hegel's appreciation of the role of development in all of social and cultural life.

THE CONCEPT OF POSITIVITY IN HEGEL'S EARLIEST WRITINGS

Lukács argues persuasively that the conception of positivity provides a revealing index of changes in Hegel's interpretation of social and cultural development.[2] In the earliest fragments from his student years in Tübingen and in the further fragments and the long essay *The Positivity of the Christian Religion* written during his time in Bern as a tutor, positivity has unambiguously negative connotations. In the earliest fragments, which Nohl collects under the heading '*Volksreligion* and Christianity', the word 'positivity' does not itself appear. The conception as Hegel later uses it is, however, implicit in the contrast which he develops between objective and subjective religion. Objective religion is formulated as a theoretical system, is taught on authority, is oppressive; in contrast, subjective religion expresses itself in personal experience and in moral action. Hegel's preference between the two is as unambiguous as his formulation of the alternatives would lead one to expect: 'Everything depends on subjective religion – this has a genuinely true value'.[3] In the long essay *The Positivity of the Christian Religion*, Hegel

2. See *Der junge Hegel*, especially pp. 46–61, 110–130, 295–309. Lukács's focus on the social implications of Hegel's early writings has its parallels in a number of theological studies. Very explicit in acknowledging his debt to Lukács is Günther Rohrmoser, *Subjektivität und Verdinglichung: Theologie und Gesellschaft im Denken des jungen Hegels* (Gütersloh: Verlaghaus Gerd Mohn, 1961), esp. pp. 21–60, 101–114. Another recent instance of theological interest in the early essays with particular reference to their social and ethical implications is Hans Schmidt. *Verheissung und Schrecken der Freiheit* (Stuttgart: Kreuz-Verlag, 1964). Schmidt laments what he sees as Hegel's eventual 'logicizing' of history' and attributes this to the final domination in his thought of his early attraction to the Greeks. See esp. pp. 267–334. Wolf-Dieter Marsh is another contemporary theologian-ethicist who criticizes the tendency toward a de-historicized system in the position of the late Hegel. But he finds in Hegel's early concerns the possibility of uniting the perspectives of Marx and Kierkegaard. See *Gegenwart Christi in der Gesellschaft: Eine Studie zu Hegels Dialektik* (München: Chr. Kaiser Verlag, 1965), esp. pp. 236–305.

3. *Hegels theologische Jugendschriften*, H. Nohl, ed. (Tübingen: J. C. B. Mohr – Paul Siebeck, 1907), p. 8. The distinction is developed in pp. 6–12. See also pp. 48–50. Unfortunately the English translation *On Christianity: Early Theological Writings*, T. M. Knox,

continues his polemic against 'objective religion' in his critique of positivity. In the draft of this essay written in Bern in 1795 or 1796, positivity is identified with teachings and institutional patterns imposed on believers through appeals to authority other than rational insight. To underscore his negative judgment on positivity in this sense, Hegel repeatedly compares Christianity unfavorably with philosophical sects which maintain the autonomy of the individual's reason.[4]

In the *Positivity* essay, Hegel formulates the content of Jesus' teaching as embodying the ethical program of Kant:

The teaching of Jesus requires an unconditional and disinterested obedience to the will of God and the moral law and makes this obedience a condition of God's favor and the hope of salvation.[5]

The similarity in content between the teachings of Jesus and Kant's ethics is, however, less central than the difference between Christians and the philosopher on the authority which establishes the knowledge of God's will. For Kant it is, of course, human reason; in contrast, the Christians whom Hegel criticizes 'base the knowledge of God's will and the obligation to obey it solely on the authority of Jesus, and then set up the recognition of this authority as part of the divine will and so a duty'.[6] The at least implicit preference for Kantian autonomy over Christian positivity which recurs throughout *The Positivity of the Christian Religion* receives still more pointed expression when Socrates and his followers are explicitly singled out as the model for a non-authoritarian philosophical sect.[7] This parallel between

---

trans. (New York: Harper & Brothers – Torchbooks, 1961) does not include the earliest fragments.

4. *Early Theological Writings*, pp. 74–75, 81–83, 100–101, 104 [157–158, 162–164, 177, 180]. See also the fragment (not included in the English translation) in which Hegel vehemently protests the loss of human autonomy entailed in authoritarian religion (*Theologische Jugendschriften*, pp. 233–239). These and the other passages to which I call attention in the following pages are the basis on which Walter Kaufmann concludes about the young Hegel: 'Emphatically, he was not a believer'. See *Hegel: Reinterpretation, Texts, and Commentary* (London: Weidenfeld & Nicolson, 1966), p. 41. As the argument of this chapter as a whole indicates, I consider this judgment in any case to be superficial and for all but the most narrow definition of 'believer' to be inaccurate as well.

5. *Early Theological Writings*, p. 85 [165]. See pp. 71, 75 [155, 158] for similar summary formulations.

6. *Early Theological Writings*, p. 85 [165].

7. *Early Theological Writings* pp. 81–83 [162–164]. See also the second of the fragments

the Greek and the modern German philosopher is, moreover, an admittedly polemical but not misleading illustration of the conclusion which Hegel draws from his earliest analysis of positivity.

The alternative which Hegel poses (and endorses) to the present state of Christendom is consistent with his negative evaluation of positivity in the earliest fragments and in *The Positivity of the Christian Religion*. It is a return to the pattern exemplified in classical Greece. The contrast which Hegel draws has reference not only to the religious dimension but to all of cultural and social life. His ideal is a *Volksreligion* – that is, a public, civic, popularly-based complex of social, ethical, and cultural commitments which are willingly affirmed and hence provide a genuine coherence and unity of purpose to their adherents. Hegel specifies three characteristics of a *Volksreligion*: it gives assent only to truths in principle available to unaided reason (even if they are taught as a divine revelation); it appeals to the senses and the imagination, the heart, and not exclusively the mind; and it is through its festivals and ceremonies integral to the social and cultural life of the people.[8] Over against this ideal of a *Volksreligion*, Christianity is for Hegel deficient because it is in its origin an exclusively 'private religion' which loses its 'meaning and spirit' when it assumes a public institutional form.[9]

In his idealization of the Greek city-state Hegel is, of course, reflecting a widespread tendency among the intellectuals of his time. That this interest in Greek social and cultural life continued in the 1790s with the French republican experiment serving to accentuate awareness of the feudalistic pattern of German political life indicates the practical issues at stake. His insistence on the tremendous significance of the French Revolution may serve to epitomize Hegel's own commitment to the political implications

---

which Nohl collects in the first untranslated section of his edition, *Theologische Jugendschriften*, pp. 30–35.

8. *Theologische Jugendschriften*, pp. 19–29; see also pp. 32–35 for Hegel's description of Socrates as a free man in a republican state which encouraged individual autonomy. In introducing his summary characterization of a *Volksreligion*, Hegel observes parenthetically that he is considering it as objective (p. 20). That objectivity in this instance is not intended as a contrast to what he terms 'subjective religion' in the first fragment is evident from the immediately ensuing description which carefully excludes 'objective' (in the sense of 'positive') tendencies. Hegel's *Volksreligion* is public and institutional – and in that sense 'objective'; but it also exemplifies the characteristics of his 'subjective religion' in being based on experience and eliciting voluntary assent from its adherents.

9. *Theologische Jugendschriften*, pp. 19–20, 41–42, 49–50.

of emulating the Greek city-state.[10] Despite his life-long affirmation of agreement with the principles of the French Revolution, Hegel's overall analysis does not, however, remain without fundamental change for even a few years. The model which informs the earliest fragments is one of return or re-establishment of an ideal which classical Greece represents. No value is seen in the intervening history. In contrast, Hegel's writings by 1800 reveal a definite appreciation of that intervening development.

THE CONCEPT OF POSITIVITY AND HEGEL'S VIEW OF DEVELOPMENT

The change in Hegel's use of the conception of positivity is one indication of this modification in his position. At least a considerable difference in emphasis is evident in *The Spirit of Christianity and its Fate:* positivity is identified with Jewish piety, while Jesus is presented as repudiating the objectivity, positivity, and heteronomy characteristic of his people's faith in favor of subjectivity and an ethic of love.[11] In *The Positivity of the Christian Religion*, Jewish religious life is also criticized sharply and the teachings of Jesus himself are presented in a much more sympathetic vein than is the disciples' codification of Christianity. But the relationship between Jesus and his disciples and hence the earliest form of Christian church is explicitly criticized as positive and is unfavorably compared both to Kantian ethics and Socratic philosophy. In contrast, *The Spirit of Christianity and its Fate* does not refer to Jesus' message as positive and presents his teaching of love as transcending Kantian morality with its opposition between duty and

10. For a concise but still comprehensive summary of Hegel's attitudes toward the French Revolution, see Joachim Ritter, 'Hegel und die französische Revolution' in *Metaphysik und Politik: Studien zu Aristoteles und Hegel* (Frankfurt/Main: Surkamp Verlag, 1969), pp. 183–255.
11. For summary passages explicitly identifying positivity with Jewish piety and presenting Jesus as criticizing it, see *Early Theological Writings*, pp. 210–213 and 224 [265–267 and 276]. In addition there are very numerous passages which do not use the conception of positivity but nonetheless make the same point in referring to Jesus' criticism of Jewish subservience to an alien authority and its formalistic commmands. Particularly in view of Kierkegaard's well-known reflections on Abraham as the paradigm of the faithful man, it is interesting in this connection that Hegel interprets the Jewish patriarch as a central illustration of the alienated man suffering the oppression of an alien God (*Early Theological Writings*, pp. 182–188 [243–248]).

inclination – an opposition which is itself declared to be positive in as much as it requires subjection to an alien (even if internal) lord.[12]

The important substantive difference between the two writings is, of course, a considerable change in the interpretation and evaluation of Jesus' teaching. But this difference in turn seems to have prompted a re-examination of the conception of positivity itself. Hegel addresses this issue directly in a revision of the first sections of the *Positivity* essay – a revision written shortly after completion of *The Spirit of Christianity*. In this new introduction Hegel expresses concisely and with precision an understanding of positivity as a function of historical development. In the earlier version of the *Positivity* essay this view on occasion appears at least by implication. Perhaps the clearest example is his contention that the authoritarian cast of Christianity made the emergence of Christian sects inevitable once individuals sensed 'that they had the right to legislate for themselves.'[13] But in his revision of the opening sections of the essay, Hegel's analysis becomes explicit and programmatic:

Any doctrine, any precept, is capable of becoming positive, since anything can be proclaimed in a forcible way with a suppression of freedom... For this reason the following essay does not profess to inquire whether there are positive commands and doctrines in the Christian religion. An answer to this question in accordance with universal concepts of human nature and God's attributes is too empty; the frightful chatter, endlessly prolonged in this key and inwardly vacuous, has become so wearisome that it is now utterly devoid of interest. Hence what our time needs instead perhaps is to hear someone proving the very opposite of what results from this 'enlightening' application of universal concepts... An attempt to do this presupposes that the convictions of many centuries, regarded as sacrosanct, true, and obligatory by the millions who lived and died by them in those centuries, were not, at least on their subjective side, downright folly or plain immorality.[14]

Hegel's argument against the Enlightenment's absolute contrast between natural and positive religion is, then, that development through what is in retrospect perceived as positivity is unavoidable. Hence religions are

12. *Early Theological Writings*, pp. 210–213, 216–217, 223, 225 [265–267, 270, 275, 277].
13. *Early Theological Writings*, pp. 142–145 [210–213].
14. *Early Theological Writings*, pp. 171–172 [143].

not inherently positive but rather become positive as a function of an evolution in the self-consciousness of their adherents. Hegel insists that this view does not in any way sanction or legitimate established religious systems as they are. It does, however, maintain that the process of social and cultural development through which the positivity of institutions and systems of belief is recognized cannot be circumvented or ignored – as it is, for instance, in appeals to abstract rational propositions or to an earlier ideal state.[15]

Even such a cursory examination of his early unpublished writings demonstrates that the emphasis on process or development evident throughout Hegel's mature writings is not simply the result of epistemological disagreements with Kant or criticisms of Spinoza's static ontology. Instead, Hegel's distinctive metaphysical position itself emerges from his reflection on specific instances of social and cultural developments. The example of his interpretation of primitive Christianity has its parallel in writings on political and economic questions. There, too, the conception of positivity is used – and in a precisely analogous way.

The parallel is most striking in Hegel's long essay of 1802 entitled *Concerning Scientific Analyses of Natural Law*. As he does in rejecting any undialectical distinction between natural and positive religion, Hegel maintains that positivity is not a characteristic of institutions themselves but is rather a function of the level of awareness of the individuals making judgments about the institutions. He offers his own succinct summary:

When accepted practice and law were one and the same, there was nothing positive about particularity (in customary behavior); but when the whole does not progress in tandem with the growth of the individual, then law and accepted practice diverge. The living unity which binds the members together becomes weak... Here the individual cannot be apprehended simply in himself, for his particularity is without that life which explains it or makes it comprehensible. And in as much as the new custom or practice also begins to interpret itself in laws, an inner contradiction of laws among themselves simply becomes unavoidable.[16]

15. *Early Theological Writings*, pp. 169–171 [141–143].
16. *Schriften zur Politik und Rechtsphilosophie*, G. Lasson, ed. (Leipzig: Verlag von Felix Meiner, 1923), pp. 407–408. For a specific example, see pp. 405–406 where Hegel argues that feudalism is 'positive' only once it is perceived as such and therefore criticized and resisted. Once the perception of the positivity of an institution or a belief becomes widespread, it is, however, doomed. In his 'Concerning the Latest Domestic Affairs of Württemberg', Hegel makes this point with dramatic flair: 'How blind are those who

In political as in religious history, positivity is, then, the necessary concomitant of any development whatsoever. Only as some measure of critical consciousness stands over against the accepted order can there be that tension or contradiction which results in movement. The perception of positivity is, in short, the functional equivalent in Hegel's early essays of the principle of negativity which in the later writings is said to generate the dialectical movement of both thought and reality.

Immediate Influences on Hegel's Conception of Development

In Hegel's turning away from the ideal of a reestablished Greece and in his attention to the process through which social and cultural development occurs, at least some measure of influence may without undue speculation be attributed to Friedrich Schiller. That the epigram 'World history is [itself] the Last Judgment' ('*Die Weltgeschichte ist das Weltgericht*') is a quote from Schiller's poem 'Resignation' and that another of his poems is entitled 'The Four Ages of World History' are intimations of this influence. But almost certainly more important in shaping Hegel's own position is the series of letters (which appeared in the journal *Die Horen* in 1795) entitled *On the Aesthetic Education of Man*. Schiller, along with such other cultural leaders of his and the preceding generation as Lessing, Winckelmann, and Goethe, had participated in the enthusiasm for Greek civilization which gripped Germany in the last third of the eighteenth century. While Winckelmann appealed to Germans to imitate Greek art and Lessing used the *Poetics* of Aristotle to ridicule the formalisms of French classical drama, Goethe and Schiller moved from the powerful but relatively unstructured style of their *Sturm und Drang* writings to classical models of dramatic form and poetic meter. This mood in turn provided the context for the enthusiasm which the next generation (including Hegel and his friends Schelling and Hölderlin) displayed for classical Greece. In this context,

---

want to believe that arrangements, constitutions, laws which no longer agree with the practices, the needs, the opinions of men, which have lost their inner life [aus denen der Geist entflohen ist], can continue to exist – that forms in which understanding and feeling no longer have any interest can continue to provide cohesion for a people!' (*Schriften zur Politik...*, p. 151).

then, Schiller's letters *On the Aesthetic Education of Man* forthrightly declare the necessity and irreversibility of the course of development which Western civilization has followed since antiquity. While insisting that he too laments the dearth of simplicity and harmony in modern life, Schiller rejects as impossible any attempt to return to the less differentiated (occupationally) and less complex (politically) existence of either some state of nature or an idealized Greece. He summarizes his own ambivalence:

I admit that however little delight individuals may derive from this disintegration of their being, the species could not have progressed in any other way... There was no other way of developing the various faculties of man, than by opposing them to each other. This antagonism of forces is the greatest instrument of culture.[17]

On the Aesthetic Education of Man is especially noteworthy, since Hegel himself refers to having read it and considering it a 'masterpiece' in a letter to Schelling in April of 1795.[18] But the expression of this viewpoint is not of course confined to one instance. Even if attention is restricted to those recent German books with which Hegel was almost certainly familiar, Lessing's 'Education of the Human Race' (1777), Herder's *Ideas for a Philosophy of the History of Mankind* (1784–1791), and Kant's 'Idea for a Universal History from a Cosmopolitan Point of View' (1784) as well as other of his short essays indicate the range of important works in which the idea of historical development figures prominently. Schiller's views may have been more influential than those of some others because he affirms the necessity of further development and rejects as illusory visions of a return to classical or natural harmony and simplicity in spite of his profound attraction to the Greeks. The substance of Schiller's position is, however,

---

17. *On the Aesthetic Education of Man, in a Series of Letters* in *Schiller's Complete Works*, C. J. Hempel, trans. (Philadelphia: I. Kohler, 1861), vol. 2, p. 511 [*Über die aesthetische Erziehung des Menschen, in einer Reihe von Briefen* in *Schillers Sämtliche Werke*, vol. 12, O. Malzel, ed. (Stuttgart: J. G. Cotta'sche Buchhandlung Nachfolger, 1905), p. 22]. See also Schiller's repeated insistence that the state of culture which man is ultimately to attain is infinitely superior to the state of nature in his *On Naive and Sentimental Poetry* in *Complete Works*, vol. 2, pp. 549, 557–558 [*Über naive und sentimentalische Dichtung* in *Sämtliche Werke*, vol. 12, pp. 163, 189–190]. This essay also appeared in the journal *Die Horen*, which Schiller edited, in the years 1795–1796.

18. *Briefe von und an Hegel*, J. Hoffmeister and R. Flechsig, eds. (Hamburg: Verlag von Felix Meiner, 1952–1960), vol. 1, p. 25.

least novel precisely in those emphases which are most strikingly similar to Hegel's view as expressed most vigorously in the *Phenomenology*. For those commitments which Schiller and Hegel share are anticipated to a remarkable degree in one of Kant's brief excursions into speculative history.

In his essay 'Conjectural Beginning of Human History' Kant uses chapters 2 through 6 of Genesis as a background for sketching an outline of man's initial stages of moral and then social development. He interprets the fall as man's coming to awareness of his rational capacities and his power of free choice – a reading very similar to the one Hegel expounds again and again.[19] He also adumbrates a very interesting theory of cultural sublimation in the course of explaining man's development through the first stages of purposive activity to his view of himself as a social being capable of dominating nature.[20] Finally, he traces man's social development through agricultural and nomadic stages and concludes with an affirmation of divine providence.[21] Throughout the short essay, a commitment to the necessity and the irreversibility of this development is at least implicit; and on occasion his very wording anticipates Schiller and then Hegel, as, for example, when he speaks of the goal of cultural development as a time in which 'art will be strong and perfect enough to become a second nature' or when he roundly declares that the 'wish for a return to an age of simplicity and innocence is futile'.[22]

There were, then, numerous influential proponents of the idea of a progressive cultural evolution in the closing third of the eighteenth century. That Hegel was not without significant predecessors should not, however, obscure the extent to which his works shaped the powerful impact which the idea of development has had in the nineteenth and twentieth centuries. For despite the writings of men like Lessing and Kant and Schiller, all of whom were profoundly committed to the optimism of the Enlightenment, many of Hegel's contemporaries could see no alternative to idealizing some

19. 'Conjectural Beginning of Human History', E. L. Fackenheim, trans., in *Kant on History*, L. W. Beck, ed. (Indianapolis: Bobbs-Merril Library of Liberal Arts, 1957), pp. 54–57 ['Muthmasslicher Anfang der Menschengeschichte' in *Kant's gesammelte Schriften*, edition of the Königliche Preussische Akademie der Wissenschaften (Berlin: Walter de Gruyter, 1902–1938), vol. 8, pp. 110–113].
20. 'Conjectural Beginning. . .', pp. 57–63 [113–118].
21. 'Conjectural Beginning. . .', pp. 63–68 [118–123].
22. 'Conjectural Beginning. . .', pp. 62–63, 68 [117–118, 122].

past culture. Hölderlin and Novalis are in this connection more representative of their generation than is Hegel. Thoroughly disillusioned with the outcome of the French revolutionary experiment – in *Hyperion* (1797–1799) the freedom fighters whom the protagonist joins finally prove to be only a band of thieves – Hölderlin was confined to a tower in Tübingen for the last forty years of his life at least in part because he could see no genuine alternative in the present to his beloved Greeks. And Novalis' *Christianity or Europe* (1799) anticipates the growing number of intellectuals who in the early nineteenth century idealized the medieval period and, in that spirit, joined the Roman Catholic Church. In contrast to all such tendencies, Hegel forged a unified and comprehensive system of thought which incorporates the conception of process at its very core and consequently expresses philosophically the fundamental commitment to cultural development which he shares with his late eighteenth-century mentors.

HEGEL ON THE IMAGE OF CHRIST'S DEATH AND RESURRECTION

Both Hegel's early writings and the essays of Schiller in particular serve to focus the question of development on Western history between antiquity and the present. As long as classical Greece is thought of as providing a possible alternative model to that of modernity, one's evaluation of the intervening history is, of course, of central importance. But Hegel's later interpretation of the conception of positivity also focuses on that period. Indeed, that later form of Hegel's understanding of positivity provides in germ the whole of the final stage in his *Philosophy of History*. In as much as Jesus himself denounces the positivity of Jewish piety, the Christian tradition has immanent in it that critical self-consciousness which in principle repudiates all alien authority. Hence the apprehension of man as inherently possessing the dignity of self-conscious spiritual existence rather than standing over against an authoritarian God who is totally other – an apprehension which is in Hegel's view fundamental to the understanding of both the Reformation and the Enlightenment – serves only to articulate fully a crucial dimension of the Christian perspective itself.

Hegel states this position in dramatic form through his employment of the image of the dying and rising Christ. His interpretation of the crucifixion and resurrection assumes a thoroughly dialectical relationship between the historical appearance of Christ and his continuing significance in the self-consciousness of believers. He repeatedly alludes to the Biblical portrayal of Jesus' life and death in summarizing what he sees as the critical transition to the modern European world. In the survey of the course of world history with which the *Philosophy of Right* concludes, for example, reference to 'the absolute turning point' toward the modernity of Western Europe is correlated with the 'infinite grief' into which 'spirit and its world are ... both alike lost and plunged'.[23] Though the crucifixion is not explicitly mentioned, the context makes the connection unmistakable. Similarly, in his preliminary survey of the religion of art in the *Phenomenology*, Hegel describes the transition from this form of religion to revealed religion as 'the night in which the substance was betrayed, and made itself subject'.[24] Though there are no allusions to Christ's death in particular, summary reference to the centrality of Christ as a historical turning point also appears in the lectures on the *Philosophy of History*.[25] As is evident in the fuller discussion in *Phenomenology* and the *Philosophy of Religion*, none of these numerous historical references can, however, be understood apart from an analysis of the impact which the image of the dying and rising Christ has on believers.

Hegel's view of the crucifixion and resurrection as it informs the believer's consciousness is one of a double movement. On the one hand, the finite self recognizes that it is not an independent particular entity but rather a moment or a constituent of a universal spiritual process – a double recognition which constitutes the self's crucifixion and resurrection:

When the death of the mediator is grasped by the self, this means the sublation

---

23. *Philosophy of Right*, paragraph 358.
24. *The Phenomenology of Mind*, J. B. Baillie, trans. (New York: Harper & Row–Torchbooks, 1967), p. 712 [*Phänomenologie des Geistes*, J. Hoffmeister, ed. (Hamburg: Verlag von Felix Meiner, 1952), p. 492]. In this passage the focus is, as is usual in Hegel's thought, on the death of Christ. The motif of resurrection is, however, implicitly present as the new reality – namely subject – which results from the repudiation of substance or abstract universality.
25. *The Philosophy of History*, J. Sibree, trans. (New York: Dover Publications, 1956), pp. 108–109 [*Philosophie der Weltgeschichte*, G. Lasson, ed. (Leipzig: Verlag von Felix Meiner, 1917–1920), pp. 243–245].

of his factuality, of his particular independent existence: this particular self-existence has become universal self-consciousness.[26]

On the other hand, the conception of deity as totally other is seen to be an abstraction which must die in order that the true God may be affirmed and realized – raised again from the dead – as subject. Hegel himself indicates the inter-relatedness of the two movements:

On the other side, the universal, just because of this, is self-consciousness, and the pure or non-actual Spirit of bare thought has become actual. The death of the mediator is death not merely of his *natural* aspect, of his particular self-existence: what dies is... also the abstraction of the Divine Being.... That death is the bitterness of feeling of the 'unhappy consciousness', when it feels that God Himself is dead.... This feeling ... means, in point of fact, the loss of the Substance and of its objective existence over against consciousness. But at the same time it is the pure subjectivity of Substance, the pure certainty of itself, which it lacked when it was object or immediacy, or pure essential Being. This knowledge is thus spiritualization, whereby Substance becomes Subject, by which its abstraction and lifelessness have expired, and Substance therefore has become real, simple, and universal self-consciousness.[27]

This interpretation of the image of the dying and rising Christ and of the dramatic announcement 'God is dead' recurs again and again in Hegel's writings. Even more cryptic formulations appear earlier in the section on revealed religion in the *Phenomenology* and also in the preface to the *Phenomenology* as a whole.[28] But the theme and even many of the central phrases are also repeated from his earliest sketches to the latest writings. The 1802 essay *Faith and Knowledge*, for example, concludes with a highly rhetorical passage which sets 'the speculative Good Friday' over against the Enlightenment absolutizing of the finite to dramatize Hegel's insistence that the experience captured in the outcry 'God is dead' is a crucial moment, 'but also not more than a moment', in the life of spirit.[29] The unpublished manu-

26. *Phenomenology*..., p. 781 [545–546].
27. *Phenomenology*..., pp. 781–782 [546].
28. *Phenomenology*..., pp. 93–94, 752–753 [29–30, 523].
29. *Erste Druckschriften*, G. Lasson, ed. (Leipzig: Verlag von Felix Meiner, 1928), pp. 345–346. Here again, the resurrection motif remains implicit but is nonetheless adumbrated in the contention that God's death is 'no more than a moment' in the life of spirit.

scripts from this period also include an elaboration of this theme.[30] Finally, the *Philosophy of Religion* offers a more detailed treatment of the death and resurrection of Christ, including a brief consideration of the meaning of the statement 'God is dead'.[31]

Hegel's analysis of the crucifixion-resurrection into two converse though complementary movements is at least implicit in each of his treatments of this theme. The delineation of this pattern enables Hegel to oppose two central tendencies of his Enlightenment predecessors and contemporaries while nonetheless appropriating what he considers the genuine insights of distinctively modern thought. On the one hand, he rejects the correlative conceptions of an alien and abstractly transcendent God and an absolutized finite self. On the other hand, he affirms the ultimate dignity of self-conscious man in understanding him as ingredient in the divine life itself; and through this affirmation he reconceives God as intimately related to man's experience in this world rather than as an alien power utterly beyond human experience. To specify Hegel's position further, it is, then, necessary to

30. *Dokumente zu Hegels Entwicklung*, J. Hoffmeister, ed. (Stuttgart: Fr. Frommanns Verlag, 1936), pp. 319–321.

31. *Lectures on the Philosophy of Religion*, E. B. Spiers and J. B. Sanderson, trans. (London: Routledge and Kegan Paul, 1895), vol. 3, pp. 84–100, esp. 91, 98 [*Vorlesungen über die Philosophie der Religion*, G. Lasson, ed. (Leipzig: Verlag von Felix Meiner, 1925–1929), part 3/1, pp. 155–174, esp. 157–158, 167]. Unfortunately, the English translation of the *Philosophy of Religion* follows the German editions prior to that of Lasson in failing to discriminate between Hegel's own manuscript and reconstructions based on student notes of his lectures. In this case, only pp. 155–164 of Lasson's text is from the manuscript. Because text and reconstructions are throughly interwoven in the 1840 edition of P. Marheineke (which the English translates), precise equivalents for Hegel's own manuscript can be given only on a sentence by sentence basis. Indeed, in some cases even passages originating from the manuscript cannot be correlated in detail with the text which Lasson provides because of editorial amplifications of Hegel's sometimes cryptic lecture notes.

There is no doubt that the lectures on the *Philosophy of Religion* have exerted an enormous influence on subsequent theology and philosophy of religion. But in them Hegel tends to interweave what he elsewhere distinguishes as religious images or representations on the one hand and philosophical concepts on the other. The result is that Hegel's consideration of popular or mythological images which in his view require interpretation may easily be misunderstood as a literal formulation of his own position. Textual problems (which have the effect of incorporating student notes into the lectures themselves) of course exacerbate the danger of misinterpreting Hegel's own position. Consequently I do not rely on the *Philosophy of Religion* lectures in this study. Instead I use them only as illustrative material to support my interpretation of Hegel's position as it is developed in the major books which he published himself.

investigate the changes both in man and in God which his interpretation of the dying and rising Christ implies. That investigation requires a consideration of Hegel's understanding of the believer's appropriation of reconciliation and an examination of the connection between God, the crucifixion-resurrection, and the course of the historical process.

THE CONTINUING INFLUENCE OF CHRIST

From Hegel's earliest fragments to his lectures in the last years of his life there is a persistent rejection of any form of objectivity which fails to relate integrally to the subject. This emphasis is perhaps expressed in its most unqualified form in his early exaltation of 'subjective religion' over 'objective religion'. But even in the late *Lectures on the Philosophy of Religion*, Hegel continues in his insistence that allegedly objective facts or truths apart from subjective appropriation are powerless.

Hegel's distinction between an external or outward apprehension of history and inner or spiritual comprehension is one indication of his unwillingness to accept a disinterested objectivity as finally normative.[32] This distinction is most frequently elaborated in his consideration of miracles or of the resurrection; but it reflects Hegel's focus on the significance of doctrine for contemporary piety rather than as a record of isolated historical facts. The same tendency is evident in his rejection of any fundamentalism of the historical Jesus:

What this self-revealing spirit is in and for itself, is therefore not brought out by the rich content of its life being, so to say, untwined and reduced to its original and primitive strands, to the ideas, for instance, presented before the minds of the first imperfect religious communion, or even to what the actual human being has spoken. This reversion to the primitive is based on the instinct to get at the notion, the ultimate principle; but it confuses the origin, in the sense of the immediate existence of the first historical appearance, with the simplicity of the notion. By thus impoverishing the life of spirit, by clearing away the idea of the communion and its action with regard to its idea, there arises, therefore, not the notion but

32. See, for example, ...*Philosophy of Religion*, vol. 3, pp. 77, 86, 91–92, 98, 115–120 [part 3/1, pp. 154, 169–170, 173–174, 186–189, 199–200]. Only pp. 186–189, 199–200 of the German and most of 115–120 of the English appear in Hegel's own manuscript.

bare externality and particularity, merely the historical manner in which spirit once upon a time appeared, the soulless recollection of a presumably (*gemeinten*) individual historical figure and its past.[33]

One reason for Hegel's consistent refusal to equate origin and validity is his conviction that the truth captured in the image of the dying and rising Christ presupposes its continuing effectiveness and, indeed, its ever greater realization. For the reconciliation of God and man in a unified spiritual process to which Christian faith testifies is an as yet not fully actualized potentiality. Hegel maintains this position in reference both to the individual life and to world history as a whole.

The least ambiguous statements of his view in regard to men as individuals appear in the introduction to his section on medieval philosophy in the *History of Philosophy* and in his treatment of man as fallen in the *Philosophy of Religion*. In both discussions he insists emphatically that man is not yet what he ought to be, that what is in Christ represented as implicitly or potentially accomplished must still be actualized in the lives of believers, that in contrast to pantheism, 'which leaves the immediate just as it is', the Christian doctrine of reconciliation portrays man as accepted 'only in his truth' in as much as he is capable of the divine and not in his natural state.[34] Hegel's interpretation of the story of Adam's fall may serve to

---

33. *Phenomenology...*, pp. 764–765 [532–533]. I include the extended quotation to indicate the remarkable degree to which Hegel anticipates the issues underlying the historical Jesus debates of the nineteenth century. Hegel returns to this question repeatedly. For similar discussions, see: *Philosophy of History*, pp. 325, 326, 328, 331, 393 [737, 738, 741, 742–743, 847, 849–850]; ...*Philosophy of Religion*, esp. vol. 3, pp. 115, 123–127 [part 3/1, pp. 200–201, 202–205]; *Hegel's Lectures on the History of Philosophy*, E. S. Haldane and F. H. Simson, trans. (London: Routledge and Kegan Paul, 1968), vol. 1, pp. 73–74, vol. 3, pp. 12–15 [*Einleitung in die Geschichte der Philosophie*, J. Hoffmeister, ed. (Hamburg: Verlag von Felix Meiner, 1959), pp. 179–181 and *Vorlesungen über die Geschichte der Philosophie* in *Sämtliche Werke*, H. Glockner, ed. (Stuttgart: Fr. Frommanns Verlag, 1928), vol. 19, pp. 109–112]. The double reference to the German text of the *History of Philosophy* is necessary because the Meiner Verlag has unfortunately issued only the first volume of its critical edition. In subsequent references to the *History of Philosophy*, the page numbers between brackets indicate the Hoffmeister edition equivalents of passages from the first volume of the English translation and the Glockner edition equivalents for passages from volumes two and three.

34. ...*History of Philosophy*, vol. 3, pp. 2–5, 8–10 [101–103, 105–106]; ...*Philosophy of Religion*, vol. 3, pp. 45–66 [part 3/1, pp. 95–129]. Throughout the *Philosophy of Religion* there are, of course, frequent references to the natural man's imperfection or to the only

epitomize the dual emphasis in his position: first, man is not in his natural state reconciled to God; but, second, this state of alienation is the necessary result of man's attaining self-conscious individuality and moral autonomy and hence is in fact itself integral to the process of establishing a genuine spiritual community.[35]

The establishment of that genuine spiritual community is, then, the aim of reconciliation. The obstacle to the individual's achieving participation in this community is his unwillingness to relinquish his sense of personal independence – a self-preoccupation, a focus on one's own particular interests, which for Hegel constitutes evil. In interpreting the crucifixion and resurrection so as to reject the correlative conceptions of an absolutized finite self and an abstract other-worldly God, Hegel indicates the pattern which reconciliation must appropriate. In addition, his repeated analysis of religious cultic activity specifies a central form which that appropriation assumes – or at least has assumed in the past.

In his *Lectures on the Philosophy of Religion*, the conception of cult or cultus is a central analytical category. In the introductory comments, in the detailed development of 'the conception of religion', and finally in each of the descriptions of the various 'definite religions', the conception of cult is used again and again both analytically and descriptively. As Lasson's critical edition of the text indicates, Hegel's own manuscript is considerably less expansive in its treatment of cultic materials than are student records of his oral presentation. The contrast is particularly marked in the general characterization of the cultus at the outset of the lectures. Consequently the details of Hegel's analysis cannot in all cases be established with complete certainty. The outlines of his interpretation are, however, evident both from the remarks which do appear in his own manuscript and from the over-all tendency of the further illustrative material.

---

implicit or potential status of reconciliation; but the passage I have indicated is the single most sustained systematic discussion both in Hegel's own manuscript and in the student notes.

35. Hegel seems to have been inordinately attached to his interpretation of this story in Genesis 3. In addition to the passages in the *History of Philosophy* and the *Philosophy of Religion* to which I refer in the preceding note, he summarizes his views on the fall in: ...*Philosophy of Religion*, vol. 1, pp. 275–279, vol. 2, pp. 202–204 [part 2/1, pp. 29–32, part 2/2, pp. 86–88]. – both passages are from student notes; *Phenomenology*..., pp. 770–772 [537–539]; *Philosophy of History*, pp. 321–322 [727–730]; and the addition (reconstructed from student notes) to paragraph 246 of the *Encyclopedia*.

Hegel interprets cult as epitomizing the character of the religious system of which it is a part. In what Hegel terms 'natural religion', for example, cultic activity includes no sense of overcoming alienation, of repentance leading to reunion with the religious object, because this stage of religious development is characterized as possessing an underlying confidence of an immediate unity with the infinite.[36] In contrast, the Jewish cult exemplifies alienation in extreme form: fear, abasement, servitude are typical of the attitudes which it expresses.[37] Hegel's analysis of Greek and Roman cultic activity similarly provides a microcosm of his description of their religious systems – as well as of their social and cultural patterns. The public festivals of Greece illustrate its institutionalization of full individual participation in a cohesive social whole;[38] and the cults of Rome reveal the same shallow utilitarianism which Hegel sees in that culture in its entirety.[39]

Hegel's view of the Christian cult conforms to this pattern. Like its Jewish antecedents, it expresses the worshipper's alienation from his God. But it also becomes a means through which believers apprehend their ultimate unity with that God. Hegel acknowledges the role which faith in the community's teaching plays as the presupposition of the worshipper's experience and therefore as integral to the cult. His paradigm for the Christian cult is, however, the mass:

The sustenance of the congregation . . . [is] the eternal repetition of the life, death, and resurrection of Christ in the members of the church . . . . In [the] mass. . . Christ is brought into the present daily. . . [This is] the realization of this movement in the spirit. . . In the cult, then, and more particularly in the sacrament – the main sacrament: whether there are more [we will] not go into – there is given for immediate enjoyment, for immediate certainty, the unity of the subject with the absolute object, the kingdom of God.[40]

36. . . .*Philosophy of Religion*, vol. 1, pp. 230–239 [part 2/1, pp. 68–76]. This is Hegel's general description of the various cultic forms in the different 'natural religions'. In the English translation, most of this material appears (in the pages to which I refer) in the introduction to the entire series of lectures. Further detailed illustrations occur in the discussion of the individual religions classified as 'natural'.

37. . . .*Philosophy of Religion*, vol. 2, pp. 205–220 [part 2/2, pp. 89–110].

38. . . .*Philosophy of Religion*, vol. 2, pp. 256–288, esp. pp. 267–278 [part 2/2, pp. 149–191, esp. 163–173].

39. . . . *Philosophy of Religion*, vol. 2, pp. 309–323 [part 2/2, pp. 219–234].

40. . . .*Philosophy of Religion*, vol. 3, p. 132 [part 3/1, p. 208]. I have translated directly from Lasson's edition of Hegel's manuscript instead of quoting the Speirs-Sanderson

In the eucharist, then, the believer participates in the sacrifice of isolated individual autonomy to be integrated into that unified spiritual process inclusive of both God and man.

RELIGION, POLITICS, AND PHILOSOPHY

That Hegel focuses his analysis of the appropriation of reconciliation on the life of the church does not mean he views the work of reconciliation as confined to that one institution. Although the emphasis on this point is much more pronounced in the student records of his lectures than in his own manuscript, even the *Philosophy of Religion* repeatedly notes the need for giving concrete expression in the secular order to the fact of reconciliation which believers experience in the church.[41] And in the *Philosophy of History* and the *Philosophy of Right* the question of the relationship between the religious experience of believers in the church and secular culture and institutions receives considerable attention. The critical significance of this question is evident from the fact that Hegel views the whole of the history of 'the teutonic world' as actualizing the reconciliation expressed in the Christian gospel. That the Reformation and the Enlightenment – to take the two periods on which he most frequently focuses – are construed as moving toward establishing the Christian perception of spiritual individuality in all of life indicates the direction in which Hegel sees the historical process moving: the end or *telos* is the integration of fully self-conscious individuality into a social and cultural whole which excludes

---

rendering. Hegel's cryptic notes require some supplementation, as the brackets indicate; however, the P. Marheineke edition of 1840 (from which the Speirs-Sanderson translation works) not only intersperses student notes but also amplifies Hegel's manuscript so freely that even in a case like this one, where the passage originates from the manuscript, what appears in previous editions cannot be correlated in detail with the text as Lasson provides it. One of the few recent studies which stresses the importance of cultic activity in Hegel's interpretation of religious life in general and of the Christian community in particular is Emil L. Fackenheim, *The Religious Dimension in Hegel's Thought* (Bloomington, Ind.: Indiana University Press, 1967); see esp. pp. 122–124, 143–149.

41. The two most sustained passages illustrating this concern are preserved only in student notes. See ...*Philosophy of Religion*, vol. 1, pp. 246–258, vol. 3, pp. 134–139 [vol. 1, pp. 302–311, part 3/1, pp. 215–219]. The distinction between 'volume' and 'part' in the reference to the German equivalent corresponds to the Meiner Verlag's designation of its separately paginated volumes and part-volumes.

no dimension of man's experience. The church is, to be sure, the initial locus of this spiritual community. But the full realization of its own commitments in Hegel's view entails the transformation of secular existence as well.

The *Philosophy of History* returns to this contention again and again. In his introductory comments characterizing the historical process as a development toward freedom, he formulates his position in reference to this definition of the end of history when he elaborates his contention that European nations were the first to attain a full consciousness that man as such is free:

This consciousness arose first in religion, the inmost region of spirit; but to integrate this principle into the secular order is a further task – a task or problem which can be carried out or solved only through a severe and long process of culture.[42]

Hegel's analysis of this process of culture – that is, of European history – portrays a dialectical interaction between church and state. His own summary repeatedly describes the outcome of that interaction as the 'harmonizing of the antitheses'.[43] More specifically, he insists that it is an error to construe the distinction between 'church' and 'world' as an ultimate opposition:

On the one hand, the inner sphere has the assignment of training the citizen of the religious life so that he becomes conformed to God's spirit. On the other hand, this sphere is the point of origin for the correlative secular order and the task of Christian history. Pious conversion must not remain exclusively a matter of interior disposition; it must rather become an actual present world conforming to the determination of that absolute spirit.[44]

42. *Philosophy of History*, p. 18 [39] – my translation. The text is from Hegel's own manuscript.
43. *Philosophy of History*, pp. 343, 345 [759, 765–766]. See also: pp. 335–336 [747–748] where he makes the same point in characterizing the transition from the Roman to the teutonic word; and pp. 109–110 (244–247) for a parallel summary at the end of the general introduction.
44. *Philosophy of History*, p. 335 [474] – my translation. See also the addition to paragraph 270 of the *Philosophy of Right* for a concise statement of the contrast between the state as the public actualization of what remains 'inward' and 'subjective' in religion. Because the additions included in the T. M. Knox translation, Hegel's *Philosophy of Right* (Oxford: Oxford University Press, 1967), are those which E. Gans somewhat

For Hegel religion is, then, a matter of 'the inmost region of spirit' or 'the inner shrine of man' or 'the recesses of the heart'; but that private and subjective dimension of human experience is not to be severed from the public arena in which the spiritual insights of religious experience receive institutional form. The activity of men is, moreover, the means through which the actualization of reconciliation is to be achieved:

What is only in principle or in itself is a possibility, a potentiality; but it has not yet emerged from its inner being into existence. A second moment must be added to produce actuality. This is activity, actualization, the principle of which is the will – the activity of men in the world. It is only through this activity that those concepts, those implicit determinations, are realized or actualized. Laws and principles do not live or have force immediately in themselves. The activity which puts them into operation and gives them definite existence is the need, the drive, the inclination, the passion of man.[45]

Because Hegel identifies the 'idea' which he sees being actualized in the historical process whith the divine plan or purpose, he understands the activity of finite spirit as constitutive of the activity of absolute spirit. In maintaining that the process of reconciliation finally passes beyond the confines of the church, Hegel is, therefore, radically committed to what he interprets in a variety of contexts as the typically Protestant legitimation of secular activity on the grounds that it is inherently of spiritual value. One summary passage may serve to epitomize his position:

The spirit of God lives in the church: it is the inner driving spirit. But it is in the world, in a material which is not yet conformed to it, that spirit is to be actualized... In the religious dimension we often see the change that a man who all his life ... has struggled in and enjoyed secular pursuits gives up everything in order

---

arbitrarily selected from student notes for inclusion in his edition of the *Philosophie des Rechts* (Berlin: Verlag von Duncker und Humblot, 1833), they must be used with some care; but they do frequently provide graphic formulations of points which Hegel makes less dramatically in the version he published. For a discussion of Gans' procedure in editing the additions, see J. Hoffmeister's foreword in his critical edition, *Grundlinien der Philosophie des Rechts* (Berlin: Akademie Verlag, 1956). In those few instances when I refer to Hegel's preface and consequently to pages instead of to paragraphs, the German edition which I indicate parenthetically is that of Hoffmeister and the English translation is that of Knox.

45. *Philosophy of History*, p. 22 [59] – my translation. This passage is from Hegel's manuscript.

to devote himself to religious solitude. But in the world this kind of work cannot be rejected but rather must be carried through to completion. And at last it turns out that spirit finds the end of its struggle and its satisfaction precisely in what it had opposed. It turns out that precisely secular pursuits are a spiritual occupation.[46]

Hegel's most dramatic formulation of his position that all of secular existence is in the process of becoming a spiritual whole takes the form of eulogizing the state as a determination or expression of the divine idea or, most memorably, as 'the march of God in the world'.[47] The state is in this view the comprehensive public institutionalization of the reconciliation which remains only private and subjective in the individual believer and public but still provincial in the life of the church. The pattern is the same as that in Hegel's interpretation of the cross. In recognizing finite spirit as a moment in the universal spiritual process, self-conscious individuality is affirmed without being absolutized. Hegel insists that this understanding of the state as incorporating the citizen into a greater whole is not a denial of self-conscious individuality. Especially in the *Philosophy of Right* he returns to this issue repeatedly in attempting to distinguish between the unself-conscious unity of the ancient *polis* and the highly differentiated integration of the modern state.[48] His intention is, then, to move beyond the fragmentation which the Enlightenment's absolutizing of the individual

46. *Philosophy of History*, pp. 354–355 [789] – my translation.

47. *Philosophy of History*, pp. 39, 51 [92–93, 108]; *Philosophy of Right*, the addition to paragraph 258. Hegel's precise wording here is not well attested. His published works and his own manuscript of the *Philosophy of History* confine themselves to such descriptions as 'the spirit on earth' or 'the realization of the Idea'. Lasson's edition does not even include the phrases which Sibree translates as 'the Divine Idea as it exists on Earth' or 'the phenomenal existence of the Divine Essence' in its redaction of the student notes – though these phrases occur in earlier editions. (The references I give are to these specific passages in the English translation and to the corresponding though somewhat less colorful contexts in Lasson's edition of the German.) Despite uncertainties about his exact words, the repeated appearance in student notes of phrases correlating the divine idea or spirit with the state does provide considerable (though not conclusive) evidence that Hegel did on occasion formulate his view of the spiritual reality of the state by identifying it explicitly with God or the divine.

48. *Philosophy of Right*, paragraphs 150, 206, 260–261, 270 (a long and important discussion of the relation between the state and religion), 299, 253–260 (a compressed formulation of Hegel's philosophy of history) and the additions to paragraphs 155, 156, 270, 299, 316, 317.

produces while nonetheless preserving the ascription of value to self-conscious individuality characteristic of modern Western culture.

Hegel's attempt to see the process of reconciliation between finite and infinite spirit as operative in the state as well as in the church is at least in part the expression of his conviction that the infinite cannot in the last analysis be less than completely comprehensive or universal. The state is thus for him not simply a complex political institution but rather that totality which includes in itself all dimensions of life and culture. Hegel's concern with maintaining the universal scope of reconciliation and his consequent refusal to ascribe finality to the cultic experience of the church is, moreover, reinforced by his judgment that the critical historical role of the church is a matter of the past. Perhaps the most dramatic expression of this judgment is the concluding section of the *Philosophy of Religion*. In his own manuscript this brief division bears the superscription, 'Passing Away of the Church' (the German is '*Gemeinde*', which has the specific meaning of congregation or parish).[49] In characteristic fashion, Hegel laments what he sees as the rampant subjectivity of his time and compares the contemporary situation to that period of decline in the Roman Empire when private rights and private well-being became so dominant that the unity or coherence dependent on political and religious institutions disappeared. He acknowledges that to speak of the church's passing away is to conclude on a discordant note; but he does so nonetheless.

Hegel qualifies the severity of his concluding discord with a reference to philosophy's role as preserving the truth of religious insight. He alludes to Matthew 16: 18 with the significant substitution of 'teaching' for 'church': 'Christ [says], "The gates of hell shall not prevail against my teaching"'. He then proceeds to a declaration that religion must flee to philosophy now that its external institutional form is passing away.[50] That the content expressed in religious representations (*Vorstellungen*) finds its definitive

---

49. . . .*Philosophy of Religion*, vol. 3, pp. 149–151 [part 3/1, pp. 229–232]. Interestingly, this caption is omitted in the English translation; and even Lasson's edition has the added words 'and Renewal' – along with the indication that these words are not in Hegel's own text.

50. . . .*Philosophy of Religion*, vol. 3, pp. 149–150 [part 3/1, p. 231]. Unfortunately, this transition is obscured in the English translation both because the order of Hegel's sentences is changed and because his quotation is 'corrected' so that it reads 'church' instead of 'teaching'.

articulation in philosophical conceptions (*Begriffe*) is, of course, a recurrent contention in Hegel's thought. It finds its most sustained expression in the *History of Philosophy* and in the sections on revealed religion and absolute knowledge in the *Phenomenology*, on the absolute idea in the *Logic*, and on religion and philosophy in the *Philosophy of Spirit*. To appreciate the issues involved in Hegel's distinction between religious images and symbolic representations on the one hand and philosophical concepts on the other, it is, however, necessary to examine the broader question of the relationship in his thought between reconciliation and temporal process.

TELEOLOGY AND HISTORY: THE STATUS OF TEMPORAL DEVELOPMENT

Hegel's concern with concrete social and cultural patterns in their historical development pervades his writings from the earliest fragments and essays on the themes of *Volksreligion*, political change, and positivity as a function of evolution to the *Philosophy of History*, the *History of Philosophy* and the *Philosophy of Religion*, all of which are products of the last decade of his life. In his thought there is, moreover, a self-conscious attempt to understand Christian symbols as interpreting the course of history. In spite of this relating of Christian commitments to definite social and cultural developments, Hegel's position on whether or not those temporal changes are ultimately significant is not, however, completely unambiguous.

What is probably the passage most frequently cited in this connection appears in the edition of the *Encyclopedia* published for the first time in 1840 under the auspices of an association of Hegel's friends and former students:

The object is the notion implicity: and thus when the notion, in the shape of End, is realized in the object, we have but the manifestation of the inner nature of the object itself. Objectivity is thus, as it were, only a covering under which the notion lies concealed. Within the range of the finite we can never see or experience that the End has been really secured. The consummation of the infinite End, therefore, consists merely in removing the illusion which makes it seem yet unaccomplished. The Good, the absolutely Good, is eternally accomplishing itself in the world: and the result is that it needs not wait upon us, but is already by implication, as well as in full actuality [*an und für sich*], accomplished. This is the illusion under which we live. It alone supplies at the same time the actualizing force on which the interest in the world reposes. In the course of its process the idea creates that illusion, by setting an antithesis to confront it; and its action consists in getting rid of the illusion which it has created.[51]

This passage appears neither in the original edition of the *Encyclopedia* nor in the 1827 and 1830 editions, in which Hegel included numerous notes and additions. It is instead among those additions which Leopold von Henning, the editor of the 1840 edition, reconstructed from Hegel's post-humously available papers and from student notes. The passage itself is, therefore, of sufficiently dubious authority that it cannot legitimately be employed as a key to Hegel's thought. Nonetheless, the position that the apparent incompleteness of the realization of ultimate cosmic purpose is illusory and the contention that the absolute good is already accomplished may serve to indicate a tendency also evident in the writings which Hegel himself published – a tendency continued in such works as F. H. Bradley's *Appearance and Reality* (1893), J. E. McTaggart's *Studies in Hegelian Cosmology* (1901), and P. T. Raju's *Thought and Reality: Hegelianism and Advaita* (1937).

Nowhere in Hegel's published works is the complex of issues involved in this tendency to minimize or even dismiss apparent historical deficiencies raised more sharply than in the well-known statement in the preface to the *Philosophy of Right* that '*What is rational is actual and what is actual is rational*'.[52] His equation of the rational with the actual here and then again in an explicit defense of this passage in an addition to paragraph six of the *Encyclopedia* unavoidably becomes a focus for the perennial controversy over whether Hegel was (particularly toward the end of his life) a political reactionary. Fortunately, a decisive adjudication of that dispute is not the necessary prerequisite for an attempt to understand Hegel's philosophy. It is, however, important in the context of this study to counter at least the most extreme caricatures of his political views, since to portray Hegel's position as obviating all need for further transformation in the historical order is to construe his thought as Transactional rather than Processive.

---

51. *Encyclopedia*, the editorial addition to paragraph 212 (in the numbering of Hegel's 1830 edition). The translation is that of W. Wallace, *The Logic of Hegel* (Oxford: Clarendon Press ,1892), same paragraph numbering.

52. ...*Philosophy of Right*, p. 10 [14].

There can be no denying that especially the *Philosophy of Right* propounds
views which indicate a conservative strain in Hegel's political thought. To
take a central example with multiple ramifications, Hegel rejects the individualistic egalitarianism of contemporary liberals and instead insists on
the legitimacy of functional inequalities and class divisions.[53] At the other
end of the spectrum of social institutions, he also rejects any attempt to
integrate the state into a super-national unity and even allows that war
between states may be edifying.[54] In his first public lecture after arriving
at the University of Berlin in 1818 he expresses his personal satisfaction
at being able to withdraw from the turmoil of political events to the stability
of Prussia and the uninterrupted study of philosophy.[55] In spite of his
consistent rejection of all that he viewed as even mildly utopian and not-
withstanding his personal desire for stability, Hegel's political commitments
cannot, however, persuasively be called reactionary. Indeed, even apparently
very conservative positions frequently prove to be aimed at avoiding a
return to the rule of arbitrary privilege which preceded the French Revolution and the Napoleonic Reforms. In his analysis of the political situation
in Württemberg in 1818, for example, Hegel supports the king against the
constitutional demands of the Diet; but his position is developed in opposition to the attempt of the deputies to reassert their pre-Napoleonic powers
and on the basis of the experience in the years following 1805 when Duke
Frederick allied himself with Napoleon and forced through a widespread
reform of feudalistic privileges.[56] Similarly, Hegel's support of Prussia
during the last decade of his life reflects his appreciation of the very significant advances which Hardenberg's administration effected in institutionalizing the Napoleonic reforms.[57] It does seem that Hegel misjudged the

53. *Philosophy of Right*, paragraphs 199–208, 298–320.
54. *Philosophy of Right*, paragraphs 321–329.
55. *Berliner Schriften*, J. Hoffmeister, ed. (Hamburg: Verlag von Felix Meiner, 1956),
pp. 3–9. See also the concluding paragraph of Hegel's 1831 essay on the English Reform
Bill in *Schriften zur Politik* ..., p. 323.
56. For an excellent summary of this complex of issues along with detailed references
to revelant historical studies, see John Robert Rodman, *The Rational State: Hegel's
Political Philosophy in the Context of its Time*, Harvard University Ph.D. dissertation,
1958, pp. 232–304, 603–634. See also: Hegel's *Schriften zur Politik* ..., pp. 157, 159–161,
166–167, 186, 200 for summary formulations of Hegel's central line of argument.
57. For details, see Rodman's thesis, pp. 692–740. The attempts of the Stein-Harden-
berg administrations to effect at least limited and carefully controlled reform are docu-

growing power of the forces of reaction during his tenure in Berlin and consequently supported the *status quo* against liberals who were in any case increasingly powerless. But Hegel himself was not among the reactionaries – as is evident in his scathing criticism of Karl Ludwig von Haller's *Restoration of Political Science*, first published in 1816.[58] Nor was his support of Prussia completely uncritical: even the *Philosophy of Right* prescribes that a constitutional body should have unrestricted national representation, publicity of debate, and legislative power, all of which the Prussian parliament lacked.[59]

Even if it is granted that Hegel's personal political position was not that of simply legitimating the existing state of affairs, the question of the systematic implications of identifying the rational and the actual remains as a focus for understanding the status which Hegel ascribes to historical change. Like Hegel's personal politics, those implications resist every undialectical schematization. For the identification of the rational as the truly actual is just as revolutionary as the identification of the actual with rationality is conservative. Especially in the *Philosophy of Right* Hegel does, to be sure, use the criterion of actuality to criticize what he sees as abstract ideals having no grounding whatever in the empirical world. His negative verdicts on an unqualified egalitarianism and on the goal of a cosmopolitan political structure are cases in point. But Hegel also employs the criterion of rationality to criticize – indeed, to characterize as finally unreal – those facts of empirical existence at variance with the ends which reason is attaining in the historical process.

This double functioning of the equation between the rational and the actual follows from Hegel's definition of actuality. As he explicitly points out in the addition to paragraph six of the *Encyclopedia* in which he defends his remarks in the preface to the *Philosophy of Right*, the conception of actuality as he develops it in the *Logic* does not refer simply to all of empirical existence. Instead actuality is defined as 'the *unity of essence and Existence*'.[60]

mented in Walter M. Simon, *The Failure of the Prussian Reform Movement*, 1807–1819 (Ithaca: Cornell University Press, 1955), esp. pp. 6–37 and 51–56.

58. ...*Philosophy of Right*, paragraph 258.

59. Compare ...*Philosophy of Right*, paragraphs 298–320 and Simon's discussion of the fate of constitutionalism in *The Failure of the Prussian Reform...*, pp. 105–142.

60. For Hegel's summary formulation, see *Hegel's Science of Logic*, A. V. Miller, trans. (London: George Allen & Unwin, 1969), p. 529 [*Wissenschaft der Logik*, G.

This definition expresses Hegel's contention that the actual is not simply synonymous with all of existence. Only in so far as what exists conforms to its ideal rational structure is it actual; the rest of existence is mere appearance or contingency. Hegel summarizes this point in presenting his conception of the idea as the teleological structure of reality:

We must recognize that everything actual *is* only in so far as it possesses the Idea and expresses it. It is not merely that the object, the objective and subjective world in general, *ought to be* congruous with the Idea, but they are themselves the congruence of Notion and reality; the reality that does not correspond to the Notion is mere *Appearance*, the subjective, contingent, capricious element that is not the truth.[61]

In view of this definition of actuality as that which expresses the rational ideal or concept, Hegel's equation of the actual and the rational is, then, tautologous. In so far as Hegel distinguishes between actuality (*Wirklichkeit*) and the whole of empirical reality (*Realität*) or existence by including in the latter not only the actual but also the fortuitous or mere appearance, his position cannot, moreover, be accurately charged with simply legitimating everything as it is. But any criticism of an existing state of affairs assumes that a greater actualization of ideals than the one realized in the present is in principle possible. In his analysis of teleology Hegel adopts this premise: 'The teleological process is the *translation* of the Notion that has a distinct

---

Lasson, ed. (Leipzig: Verlag von Felix Meiner, 1923), part 2, pp. 156–157]. The whole section entitled 'Actuality' develops his position in detail. The parallel passage in the *Encyclopedia* is paragraph 142; the addition – reconstructed from student notes and Hegel's posthumous papers – is particularly interesting because it records a play on words whereby the actual (*das Wirkliche*) is characterized as what is also active, productive, effective (*das Wirkende*).

61. ...*Logic*, p. 756 [part 2, pp. 408–409]; pp. 755–760 [part 2, pp. 407–413] summarizes the argument of this whole concluding section of the *Logic*. See also pp. 734–735 [part 2, pp. 383–385] for a formulation of the same point in the beginning of the discussion of teleology. Perhaps the most influential recent discussion of the critical power of Hegel's thought is that of Herbert Marcuse in *Reason and Revolution: Hegel and the Rise of Social Thought* (Boston: Beacon Press, 1966), esp. pp. 1–29. That the equation of the actual and the rational is a potentially revolutionary doctrine is not, however, a new discovery among students of Hegel. See, for example, Kuno Fischer, *Hegel's Leben, Werke und Lehre* (Heidelberg: Carl Winter's Universitätsbuchhandlung, 1901), pp. 1153–1155.

concrete existence as Notion into objectivity'.[62] At the same time, however, he argues that in this process the notion or concept in fact only actualizes itself. He states the conclusion of this argument succinctly:

It can therefore be said of the teleological activity that in it the end is the beginning, the consequent the ground, that it is a becoming of what has become, that in it only what already exists comes into existence.[63]

The totality which is in the process of being actualized and is therefore already at least potentially present is, in Hegel's vocabulary, the idea. That this idea constitutes the very structure of reality is the central contention of Hegel's system. Though his definition of the terms renders the identification of the rational and the actual tautologous, that equation nonetheless expresses in epigrammatic form his position that ideals are not other-worldly abstractions but rather effective potentialities realizing themselves in history. This position may, of course, also be stated theologically – though Hegel's most explicitly theological formulations are preserved only in student notes. One particularly striking example appears in the introduction to the *Philosophy of History:*

The truly good, the universal divine reason, is also the power to realize itself. This good, this reason in its most concrete representation, is God. The good, not just as the idea alone, but rather as effective power [*Wirksamkeit*] is what we call God. The insight of philosophy is that no power prevails over the power of the good, of God, so as to frustrate his effectiveness... God governs the world; the content of his rule, the actual carrying out of his plan, is the history of the world.[64]

As Hegel puts the matter in the closing paragraph of the *Philosophy of History*, world history is itself the true theodicy. And Hegel's thought – both in its philosophical and in its more directly theological expression – is the attempt to articulate the process through which the spiritual purpose at work in the world is realized.

62. ...*Logic*, p. 747 [part 2, p. 399].
63. ...*Logic*, p. 748 [part 2, p. 399]. For the same point in reference to organic nature, see *Phenomenology*, pp. 293–301 [193–199].
64. *Philosophy of History*, p. 36 [54–55] – my translation.

RECONCILIATION AND THE PHILOSOPHICAL TRANSCENDENCE OF TIME

As his comments in the addition to paragraph six of the *Encyclopedia* emphasize, Hegel opposes his identification of the real and the actual to the 'perennial ought' of the understanding which seeks to impose its 'dreams' on the world. The issue is in effect a variation on the contrast between the false or spurious and the true infinite – the contrast between the unending struggle to attain an other over against the finite and the recognition that the infinite includes the finite within itself. Hegel does not deny that much in the empirical world is deficient:

The intelligent observer may meet much that fails to satisfy the general requirements of right; for who is not acute enough to see a great deal in his surroundings which is really far from being as it ought to be. [65]

But he nonetheless insists that the business of philosophy is to delineate the at least potential rationality which is actualizing itself rather than to articulate the in the last analysis unreal distortions of that teleological reality. The result is a definite subordination of the practical activity of effecting empirical change to the cognitive enterprise of philosophy. As is the case with every Hegelian *Aufhebung*, the subordinated member is not simply eliminated. Hence the contribution of human action is not denied. But the absolutizing of any finite activity is seen to be untenable.

Hegel returns to this issue again and again. The section of the *Phenomenology* entitled 'Dissemblance' (*Verstellung*) offers a detailed critique of the distortions and inconsistencies which in his view result from the Kantian conception of the highest good as a mere postulate or as only a 'beyond'. In both versions of the *Logic* the relating of theoretical and practical activity is the final transition to the absolute idea. And in the *Philosophy of Spirit* the reconciliation of the theoretical and the practical again appears, this time as the culmination of Hegel's treatment of subjective spirit and hence as the transition both to objective spirit and to absolute spirit.

Hegel sees the integration of the idea of cognition and the idea of the good, the theoretical and the practical, as a microcosm of his thought as a whole. He summarizes the movement himself:

65. *Encyclopedia*, paragraph 6. This passage is an addition, but one included in Hegel's 1827 and 1830 editions rather than one of those editorially reconstructed for the 1840 edition.

In this result *cognition* is restored and united with the practical Idea; the actuality found as given is at the same time determined as the realized absolute end; but whereas in questing cognition this actuality appeared merely as an objective world without the subjectivity of the Notion, here it appears as an objective world whose inner ground and actual subsistence is the Notion. This is the absolute Idea.[66]

Hegel praises the idea of the good as 'superior to the idea of cognition' because 'it possesses not only the worth of the universal but also of the out-and-out actual'.[67] In contrast to the practical idea, the idea of cognition seeks to know the objective order simply as a static given. Hegel maintains that Kant's philosophy has forever destroyed the possibility of this undialectical metaphysics. But the perspective epitomized in the brief discussion of the idea of the good is also inadequate because it is in Hegel's view internally inconsistent. On the one hand, it rightly stresses the role of activity in realizing or mediating the goal of that good which the idea of cognition wrongly takes to be simply a given. On the other hand, it denies the efficacy of the very activity it extolls when it supposes that this end is in fact never attained – that it is an ideal which is only a beyond and not a present reality. Hegel's resolution of this contradiction is, then, that the 'objective world' is a teleological process in which the end is being realized and which may, therefore, be known philosophically as ultimately rational in its inner reality.[68]

In this transition to the absolute idea Hegel's understanding of the goal of philosophy is clearly articulated. Many commentators have assumed that Hegel presents his own system as attaining this goal. None of the passages typically cited in support of this interpretation is, however, so unambiguous as to allow no other reading. The concluding pages of the *Philosophy of History* and the *History of Philosophy*, which are frequently

66. ...*Logic*, p. 823 [part 2, p. 483]. See also the parallel passage in the *Encyclopedia*, paragraphs 234 and 235. The editorially reconstructed addition to paragraph 234 is, particularly lucid in its emphasis on the processive character of this resolution: 'The good, the ultimate purpose of the world, is only in that it is ever bringing itself into being'. This addition also explicitly distinguishes between the life of nature and that of spirit on the grounds that nature always only returns to itself while genuine advance or progress (*Fortschreiten*) is possible for spirit.
67. ...*Logic*, pp. 818–819 [part 2, p. 478].
68. See especially ...*Logic*, pp. 821–823 [part 2, pp. 481–483]; for a more detailed discussion of the contradictions into which the practical idea falls, see pp. 629–641 [434–444] of the *Phenomenology*.

quoted (and not infrequently misquoted) to support an understanding of Hegel as claiming finality for his thought, in fact only announce that his historical treatment necessarily concludes in as much as the present has been reached -- a present which is more adequate in its knowledge than any past, but which does not preclude further development. The structure of Hegel's *Philosophy of History* does, to be sure, move from boyhood through youth and manhood to the maturity or old age which is identified with the teutonic world. The structural organization of his various histories in analogous ways also make it difficult to conceive of a move beyond Hegel's standpoint. But as the famous epigram at the conclusion to the preface of the *Philosophy of Right* epitomizes, Hegel acknowledges the impossibility that any philosophy can anticipate the future: 'The owl of Minerva spreads its wings only with the falling of the dusk'.[69] Although it is beyond dispute that Hegel appears to have an almost limitless estimate of the significance of his philosophy which results in considerable rhetorical excess, he nonetheless also recognizes the cultural dependence of his thought. Even the *Logic* is presented as meeting a definite need because 'spirit, after its labours over two thousand years [since Aristotle], must have attained to a higher consciousness about its thinking and about its own pure, essential nature'.[70]

Whether or not Hegel is understood as claiming that he himself has carried out the program with complete success, he does, however, in any case indicate what the ideal of absolute knowledge entails. That ideal is a completely adequate grasp or conception of the rational structure of reality as a whole: it is Aristotle's thought thinking thought. The *Logic* in particular is Hegel's attempt to attain this ideal. In systematizing the concepts through which man knows whatever reality he can talk about at all, the philosopher does not simply order his categories but rather thinks the very structure of reality. Because this ideal of absolute knowledge comprehends the teleological structure of the real, it is, moreover, the

69. *Philosophy of Right*, p. 13 [17].
70. ...*Logic*, p. 51 [part 1, p. 33]. See also the comments in the preface to the second edition on the exhibition of logical concepts in the medium of language, pp. 30–33 [part 1, pp. 9–11] and the remark in the preface to the first edition, p. 26 [part 1, pp. 4–5] that logic must reflect 'the new spirit which has arisen in the sciences no less than in the world of actuality' in as much as 'once the substantial form of spirit has reconstituted itself, all attempts to preserve the forms of an earlier culture are utterly in vain'.

overcoming of dependence on any particular point in the temporal process. Hegel advances this contention in his discussion of absolute knowledge in the *Phenomenology*:

Time is the notion definitely existent, and presented to consciousness in the form of empty intuition. Hence spirit necessarily appears in time, and it appears in time so long as it does not grasp its pure notion, i. e. so long as it does not annul time... When this notion grasps itself, it supersedes its time character, (conceptually) comprehends intuition, and is intuition comprehending. Time therefore appears as spirit's destiny and necessity, where spirit is not yet complete within itself.[71]

Absolute knowledge is, then, a transcending of particular temporal reference. To construe this position as a relegation of temporal process to the status of illusion or unreality is, however, seriously to distort Hegel's thought. Because the content of absolute knowledge, the absolute idea, is the systematic conception of the end toward which the whole of reality is in process, it presupposes and therefore includes within itself the entire course of its historical development. The philosophical formulation of the ultimate truth of that process may be expressed in what is in effect an eternal present – a present which encompasses the whole of the temporal movement. But that eternal knowing necessarily presupposes the historical process through which it emerges.

A failure to appreciate Hegel's conception of the nature of absolute knowledge unavoidably results in a correlative misunderstanding of his philosophical interpretation of the Christian doctrine of reconciliation. As the process through which the infinite spiritual community embracing self-conscious individuality within itself is realized, the Atonement is an inher-

71. *Phenomenology*, p. 800 [558]. Hegel's exposition at this point is extremely important for the interpretation which Alexandre Kojève proposes in his *Introduction to the Reading of Hegel*, J. H. Nichols, Jr., trans. (New York: Basic Books, 1969) [*Introduction à la lecture Hegel* (Paris: Raymond Queneau, 1947)]. This particular passage underlies Kojève's discussion in pp. 100–149 [336–380]. I find Kojève's emphasis on the empirical and descriptive character of Hegel's thought both provocative and sound. See esp. pp. 170–259 [445–526]. But I do not think his argument for the conclusion that Hegel must then be a 'Wise Man' at the end of history is persuasive. See esp. pp. 75–99, 150–169 [271–291, 427–441]. That Hegel is a 'realist' (in the nineteenth-century meaning) does not preclude 'idealism' in the sense of his conceiving ends or *teloi* which are not yet fully actualized in history. For what I think is a needed corrective of Kojève here, see Jan van der Meulen, *Hegel: die gebrochene Mitte* (Hamburg: Verlag von Felix Meiner, 1958), esp. pp. 332–345.

ently temporal affair. The religious imagination in the first instance apprehends the unity of the infinite and the finite or the divine and the human
in a single historical individual. Through their appropriation of the symbolic
representation of the life, death, and resurrection of the Christ, believers
themselves then move through the recognition of their spiritual individuality
to a denial of absolute discreteness or autonomy in favor of self-conscious
integration into the life of infinite spirit. Hegel repeatedly acknowledges
the necessary role which this symbolic representation plays both in the
development of the spiritual community and in continuing pre-reflective or
unreflective piety. But he nonetheless insists that a full comprehension of
the process of reconciliation requires the translation of images and symbols
into concepts. At the end of his discussion of revealed religion in the *Phenomenology* Hegel summarizes the deficiencies he sees in the portrayal of reconciliation in the symbolic representation of the religious consciousness:

Reconciliation ... enters its consciousness as something remote, something far
away in the future, just as the reconciliation, therefore, is in its heart, but still
with its conscious life sundered in twain and its actual reality shattered... What
appears as actually present, as the aspect of immediacy and existence, is the world
which has yet to await transfiguration. The world is no doubt implicitly reconciled
with the essential Being; and that Being no doubt knows that it no longer regards
the object as alienated from itself, but as one with itself in its Love. But for self-
consciousness this immediate presence has not yet the form and shape of spiritual
reality.[72]

In contrast to this inherently temporal portrayal of reconciliation, philosophy
knows that the unity of the finite and the infinite is an eternally present
spiritual reality – a reality coming into being in time which is nonetheless
also fully actual in the teleological perspective of absolute knowledge. Man
need not, then, look to an Atonement in the distant past; nor is reconciliation to be found in an anticipated future. Instead he can know in the present
his unity with that infinite spiritual process in which he is a moment, a process which is truly infinite precisely because it ultimately encompasses even
that finitude which attempts to stand over against it.

72. *Phenomenology*, pp. 784–785 [548]. The *Philosophy of Religion* makes the same
point in a variety of contexts. But because its intention is to grasp religious insights philosophically, conceptual comprehension and representational portrayal are constantly in
interaction. See the discussion of reconciliation in volume 3, especially pp. 66–100 [part
3/1, pp. 130–174].

7

Hegel's Continuing Relevance for Theology

That Hegel sees philosophical concepts as transcending or even annulling time is a recurrent source of controversy among the heirs of his thought. The most general formulation of the issue dividing the various lines of interpretation is in reference to the question of the status attributed to the concepts which Hegel systematizes in the *Logic*. This question may, of course, also be stated theologically: it is then the question of the existence of a God in principle antecedent to or not dependent on man and his world. But despite the persistence of this form of the question, in the writings of Hegel's students the earliest focus for the same complex of issues is a Christological one. The question then is that of the relationship between the determinate historical individual Jesus of Nazareth and the absolute truth claims made in reference to the Christ of faith. Because both questions are typically articulated throughout the nineteenth and into the twentieth century in the context of conversation with Hegel, they may serve to epitomize his past influence on and his continuing relevance for theological reflection.

STRAUSS AND THE CHRISTOLOGICAL ISSUE

The most incisive formulation of the Christological issue in the years following Hegel's death is that of David Friedrich Strauss in his 1835 book *The Life of Jesus, Critically Examined*. As Strauss indicates in his preface to the first edition, the aim of his study is that 'the whole history of Jesus ... is to be subjected to a critical examination, to ascertain whether it have not some admixture of the mythical'.[1] Strauss undertakes this task because

1. *The Life of Jesus, Critically Examined*, M. Evans, trans.(New York: Calvin Blanchard, 1860), vol. 1, p. 3 [*Das Leben Jesu, kritisch bearbeitet* (Tübingen: Verlag von C. F. Osiander, 1835–1836), vol. 1, p. v]. The Marian Evans (George Eliot) translation is of the fourth German edition; but because the first edition is decisive as far as historical influence is concerned, I give the parallel references to that edition. (I refer only to passages

of his conviction that the approaches to the Gospel records of both super-naturalism and rationalistic naturalism are inadequate or, to use his word, 'antiquated'. He recognizes that he has antecedents in his scrutiny of Biblical materials for mythical motifs; and in his introduction he surveys the tradition of critical study first of the Old Testament and then of the Gospels. In contrast to previous efforts, however, Strauss sees his own investigation as encompassing the entire history of Jesus in a systematic fashion and therefore as establishing 'whether in fact, and to what extent, the ground on which we stand in the gospels is historical'.[2]

Strauss presents his philosophical perspective as fulfilling 'the main requirement' for the comprehensive task of criticism which he undertakes:

The majority of the most learned and acute theologians of the present day fail in the main requirement for such a work, a requirement without which no amount of learning will suffice to achieve anything in the domain of criticism, namely, the internal liberation of feelings and intellect from certain religious and dogmatical presuppositions; and this the author early attained by means of philosophical studies. If theologians regard this absence of presupposition from his work, as un-christian: he regards the believing presuppositions of theirs as unscientific.[3]

As he indicates in the immediately following paragraph, Strauss grounds this 'internal liberation' for his study on the conviction 'that the essence of Christian faith is perfectly independent of his [the author's] criticism'.

The 'Concluding Dissertation', which comprises the last major division of *The Life of Jesus*, elaborates this cryptic statement. In that discussion Strauss sketches the Christology of 'the most recent philosophy', namely that of Hegel and his followers. He notes that for the Hegelian theologians the truth of Christianity follows from the very conceptions of God and man:

Thus by a higher mode of argumentation, from the idea of God and man in their reciprocal relation, the truth of the conception which the Church forms of Christ appears to be confirmed, and we seem to be reconducted to the orthodox point of view, though by an inverted path: for while there, the truth of the conceptions

---

that appear in virtually the same form in the first and fourth editions.) After a consider-ably revised third edition, Strauss returned in his fourth edition to his original position and, for the most part, to his first edition text – a fact which makes the English trans-lation much more useful than it would otherwise be.

2. *Life of Jesus...*, vol. 1, p. 4 [vol. 1, p. v].
3. *Life of Jesus   .*, vol. 1, p. 4 [vol. 1, p. vi].

of the Church concerning Christ is deduced from the correctness of the evangelical history; here, the veracity [*Richtigkeit*] of the history is deduced from the truth of those conceptions.[4]

Strauss himself assents to the argument that certainty about the truth of Christianity is not dependent on knowledge of any particular historical facts – and acts on the total freedom of historical criticism which that position implies. But as his qualified wording suggests, he rejects the somewhat uncritical supposition that the independent speculative truth of Christianity can in turn support the historical claims of the Gospels.

The issue which Strauss sees between his own position and that of such speculative theologians as Philipp Marheineke, Karl Rosenkranz, and Kasimir Conradi is discussed in his final paragraph (divided in two in the fourth edition) entitled 'Last Dilemma'. In contrast to every attempt of his fellow Hegelians to retain the focus of orthodoxy on a single historical individual, Strauss insists that 'the general propositions on the unity of the divine and human natures, do not in the least serve to explain the appearance of a person, in whom this unity existed individually, in an exclusive manner'.[5] Commenting that the idea is 'not wont to lavish all its fullness on one exemplar, and be niggardly towards all others'' Strauss offers his alternative in a series of rhetorical questions:

And is this no true realization of the idea? is not the idea of a unity of the divine and human natures a real one in a far higher sense, when I regard the whole race of mankind as its realization, than when I single out one man as such a realization? is not an incarnation of God from eternity, a truer one than an incarnation limited to a particular point of time?[6]

He insists that only this position resolves the contradiction present in every Christology focusing on the historical individual Jesus of Nazareth:

This is the key to the whole of Christology, that, as subject of the predicate which the church assigns to Christ, we place, instead of an individual, an idea; but an idea which has an existence in reality, not in the mind only, like that of Kant. In an

4. *Life of Jesus*..., vol. 2, p. 894 [vol. 2, p. 732].
5. *Life of Jesus*..., vol. 2, p. 894 [vol. 2, p. 733].
6. *Life of Jesus*..., vol. 2, p. 895 [vol. 2, p. 734].

individual, a God-man, the properties and functions which the Church ascribes to Christ contradict themselves; in the idea of the race, they perfectly agree.[7]

It is interesting at least historically that the argument which Strauss presses here provides the origin for the division of Hegelians into the right, the left, and the center. Strauss develops this set of distinctions in his third series of polemical writings (*Streitschriften*) in defense of his *Life of Jesus*. He uses the classification to differentiate answers to the question of 'whether and to what degree the Gospel history as history is given with the idea of the unity of divine and human nature'.[8] As is evident from his discussion of specific thinkers (including himself), this somewhat oblique phrasing refers to the extent to which the definite historical content of the Gospels is taken to be defended or guaranteed by speculative theology. The right – Strauss singles out Carl Friedrich Göschel, Georg Andreas Gabler, and (somewhat ironically in view of his later writings) Bruno Bauer – is said to maintain that speculative theology preserves the whole of the Biblical history: faith and knowledge, religious representation and philosophical concept, may be fully harmonized. The center, illustrated in the thought of Karl Rosenkranz, concedes that much the Gospel history cannot be salvaged but nonetheless contends that the central commitment of Christianity to an individual historical incarnation finds support from speculative philosophy. Finally, the left, which Strauss himself represents, insists that although philosophy may verify the conceivability of a single individual who attains the goal of uniting the divine and the human, the adjudication as to whether or not this possibility has occurred can be executed only through historical investigation.

Strauss vacillated considerably in his own thinking. In the 1864 edition of the *Life of Jesus* – a radically revised and popularized version which combines its Biblical study with a legitimation of middle class conventions – he returns to the kind of compromise that marks the third edition of 1838 but is repudiated in the fourth edition of 1840. Then in his 1872 *The Old*

7. *Life of Jesus*..., vol. 2, p. 895 [vol. 2, pp. 743–735].
8. *Streitschriften zur Verteidigung Meiner Schrift über das Leben Jesu und zur Charakteristik der gegenwärtigen Theologie* (Tübingen: Verlag von C. F. Osiander, 1841), collection 3, p. 95. The whole discussion is pp. 94–126. This volume combines a number of previously published collections of essays. This particular essay, 'Verschiedene Richtungen innerhalb der Hegel'schen Schule in Betreff der Christologie', was first published in 1837.

and the New Faith he once again builds on the more negative critical position of his first and fourth editions. But despite changes in his own approach to and conclusions about the reliability of the Gospel records, the incisiveness of his formulation of the issue is evident in the fact that the position wihch he characterizes as the left articulates the alternatives which the academic tradition of theological reflection at least in Germany has more or less self-consciously pursued from his time on.

THE HISTORICAL JESUS AND THE TRANSHISTORICAL CHRIST

Strauss' critical studies of the Gospels did not, of course, in themselves create a fundamentally new theological situation. Along with his polemical writings they did, however, serve to focus the difficulties inherent in a number of previously significant approaches. That is most patently the case in reference to the two polar positions against which Strauss self-consciously advocates his mythical interpretation. Rationalistic defenses of the facticity of even the details of the Gospel accounts through elaborate explanations appealing only to laws of nature as the means of God's activity were no longer viable once even Strauss' line of questioning was accepted. A thinker like H. E. G. Paulus could write his *Life of Jesus* (1828) only before 1835. The problematical character of a consistent supernaturalism had no doubt become generally evident before the time of Strauss. But his work nonetheless served to underscore the difficulties. The most unrelenting of the orthodox – the Biblical literalists J. T. Beck and E. W. Hengstenberg, for example – simply refused even to entertain Strauss' program and instead welcomed *The Life of Jesus* as evidence of the unavoidable result of allowing any Biblical criticism whatsoever. But those conservatives who attempted to respond substantively to Strauss' claims in effect only demonstrated the untenability of their own supernaturalism. The accounts of Jesus' life by August Tholuck and August Neander, both written in 1837 as replies to Strauss, illustrate this tendency.

More important than his systematization of the evidence against the tenability of rationalism and supernaturalism is Strauss' repudiation of the most influential mediating positions. As he states in his criticism of what he characterizes as the right and the center, he rejects every attempt implicitly or explicitly to validate historical data through philosophical argument. This criticism is in effect directed at the position of Schleiermacher as well as at that of Hegel and his followers. It may be possible to interpret Schleiermacher's argument for the historicity of Christ as simply the sociological contention that the piety of the Christian community is historically inexplicable without a founder. But Strauss focuses instead on precisely those tendencies in which more specific historical conclusions are presented as following from non-historical premises. In the last section of *The Life of Jesus* he criticizes in particular Schleiermacher's defense of Jesus' sinlessness on grounds that sinful man could not conceive of a sinless ideal unless he existed historically. He then concludes:

We may now estimate the truth of the reproach, which made Schleiermacher so indignant, namely, that his was not an historical, but an ideal Christ. It is unjust in relation to the opinion of Schleiermacher, for he firmly believed that the Christ, as construed by him, really lived; but it is just in relation to the historical state of the facts, because such a Christ never existed but in Idea.[9]

In critizing both the Hegelians and Schleiermacher, Strauss is not denying the validity of either the speculative-dogmatic or the historical task. He insists only that they are in principle discrete enterprises neither of which can support the other. The result is that only two alternatives remain for approaching the question of Christology. One is to accept a system of beliefs or propositions on some authority other than verification of historical facts about Jesus' life or teaching. The other is to decline allegiance to both orthodox and speculative doctrines and instead to pursue historical investigation to see what may plausibly be affirmed about the founder of Christianity. This specification of alternatives is, to be sure, scarcely a new one. Strauss was himself fully aware of two of his recent antecedents: Lessing, with his 'ugly broad ditch' between necessary truths of reason and contingent facts of history; and Kant, with his systematic differentiation in *Religion within the Limits of Reason Alone* (1793) in particular between the moral-rational and the historical. Hegel, Schleiermacher, and their respective followers were also not unaware of the importance of this distinction, even if their attempts to justify Christianity not infrequently combine historical and phil-

9. *Life of Jesus*, vol. 2, p. 887 [vol. 2, p. 720]. The comments on Schleiermacher are on pp. 881–887 [710–720].

osophical argumentation. But Strauss' formulation of the issue nonetheless has an unprecedented urgency because of his simultaneous demonstration through detailed critical analysis that the historical reliability of the Gospels is at virtually every point highly questionable.

As the response which it provoked amply illustrates, the publication of Strauss' *Life of Jesus* did not have the effect of forever clarifying the relationship between historical and philosophical questions in the theological enterprise. Despite the continued combination of historical claims and philosophical arguments in an uncritical fashion, the two alternatives indicated by Strauss' formulation of the issue did, however, become increasingly important as methodologically distinct approaches. The single most striking development is the consolidation of a movement which Strauss certainly did not initiate but in which he participated and to which he gave further impetus: the movement toward a systematic and cumulative program of Biblical criticism not as an attack on Christianity but rather as a sympathetic effort to understand it in its historical origins. There are, to be sure, significant contributions to this undertaking throughout the Enlightenment. Many had their roots in attempts to discredit Christianity; but much serious scholarship also occurred from within the church. Both traditions very much influenced Strauss. For him in particular they may be epitomized in the figures of H. S. Reimarus, about whom he wrote a biography in his later life, and J. S. Semler, the prolific eighteenth-century scholar who battled tirelessly against Biblical literalism. Despite the undeniable existence of antecedents, the Hegelian presuppositions which Strauss and scholars like his teacher F. C. Bauer and his contemporary Bruno Bauer accept do, however, provide a highly conducive context for systematic critical inquiry. On the one hand, the sharp distinction between the question of the truth of Christianity and the findings of historical research encourages the total freedom of criticism which Strauss' *Life of Jesus* exemplifies. On the other hand, the emphasis on development which F. C. Bauer in particular appropriated from Hegel imbues the subject matter of history with a fundamental interest and importance.

That systematic and disciplined historical-critical study not only of Biblical materials but also of the church's tradition emerges as an accepted academic enterprise in the course of the nineteenth century is in itself a development of enormous significance. The role of Hegelians in the consolidation of this movement is, moreover, amply illustrated in the history of the so-called Tübingen school from F. C. Bauer on. But also significant for an understanding of nineteenth-century theology is an appreciation of the role which the demise of allegiance to Hegel's metaphysics plays in the emergence of an exclusively historical approach to theological scholarship. Rejecting both orthodox dogmas and the speculative claims of Hegel's system, theologians in practice increasingly follow the alternative of accepting the findings of historical scholarship as the basis for belief. This program is a return to the Enlightenment rationalist attempt to establish what may plausibly be affirmed – but with the difference that the more radical and systematic critical study in the intervening period makes the historical remnants much more dubious. The result is a confrontation with Strauss' critical conclusions in the absence of his confidence that the truth of Christianity is in any case secure.

Certainly not all of the writers who turned to the Jesus of history admitted the seriousness of the findings of Biblical criticism. As Albert Schweitzer argues persuasively in his epoch-ending *The Quest of the Historical Jesus* (1906), most of the biographies of Jesus owe far more to the imagination and the cultural presuppositions of their authors than to reliable New Testament data. But despite a lack of sophistication about what can and cannot be surmised on the basis of available sources, this preoccupation with the Jesus of history illustrates a methodological preference for even sparse and uncertain historical facts over philosophical or dogmatic assertions. This preference finds expression not only on popular and devotional writings but also in the academic tradition of nineteenth-century liberalism. Perhaps the single figure who best illustrates both tendencies in their fully developed form is the formidable church historian Adolf Harnack.

Harnack's massive scholarly studies in the history of Christian thought testify to his academic preference for the historical over the dogmatic or the philosophical mode of enquiry or assertion. But his very popular *Essence of Christianity* indicates that he also grounded his constructive interpretation of Christian faith on the findings of historical research. Harnack summarizes his preference concisely at the end of his discussion of Christology in the eighth of his lectures:

Let us rid ourselves of all dogmatic sophistry, and leave others to pass verdicts of exclusion. The Gospel nowhere says that God's mercy is limited to Jesus' mission. But history shows us that he is the one who brings the weary and heavy laden to God...[10]

In speaking confidently of what 'history shows', Harnack presupposes a greater degree of reliability of the Biblical records than does Strauss. Harnack is explicit on this point:

Sixty years ago David Friedrich Strauss thought he had almost entirely destroyed the historical credibility not only of the fourth but also of the first three Gospels as well. The historical criticism of two generations has succeeded in restoring that credibility in its main outlines.[11]

Harnack acknowledges that even the Synoptic Gospels are not 'historical works' but rather 'books composed for the work of evangelization'. He also recognizes that 'the historian's task of distinguishing between what is traditional and what is peculiar, between kernel and husk, in Jesus' message of the kingdom of God is a difficult and responsible one'.[12] But in spite of the difficulties, Harnack proceeds on the assumption that the available historical data is the only possible basis for formulating the essence of Christianity. Even his meager distillate of Jesus' teaching as propounding the coming of the kingdom, the Fatherhood of God and the infinite value of the human soul, and the command of love may, to be sure, be disputed as indefensibly expansive of what historical scholarship can plausibly assert. That dispute is, however, a disagreement with Harnack's execution of his program; though it may in the last analysis call into question the viability of his approach, it nonetheless agrees that his method is to restrict the claims of Christian faith to what is historically either demonstrable or at least probable.

Preoccupation with establishing Christian faith on a reliable historical foundation is not, of course, the only response to the theological situation as Strauss articulates it. The speculative alternative also continues to be represented. The Hegelian theologian A. E. Biedermann provides an exam-

10. *What is Christianity*, T. B. Saunders, trans. (New York: Harper & Row–Torchbooks, 1957), p. 145 [*Das Wesen des Christentums* (Leipzig: J. C. Hinrichs'sche Buchhandlung, 1900), p. 92].
11. *What is Christianity*, p. 20 [14].
12. *What is Christianity*, p. 55 [36].

ple of a sophisticated execution of this approach. Himself influenced by Strauss, Biedermann accepts his central criticism of orthodoxy:

The fundamental contradiction in the ecclesiastical Christology ... is rooted in the immediate identification of the Christian principle with the human person whose religious life is its revelation in history, so that a spiritual principle is described as a person, and from this the mythologizing of the dogma was the necessary consequence.[13]

Against what he sees as Strauss' unnecessary abstraction of the 'Christian principle' from Jesus, Biedermann maintains that the conviction of the ultimate unity of God and man 'entered history with the religious person of Jesus' and is, therefore, 'a definite concrete historical religious principle'.[14] But he also insists – most frequently against Schleiermacher – that every attempt to identify the final truth or significance of Christianity with the historical influence originating in the person Jesus unavoidably compromises the universalism of the Christian principle.[15] The result is that despite his affirmation of an intimate relationship between the Jesus of history and the Christian principle, that 'principle of divine childhood' is construed as an ontological reality the universal truth of which is not dependent on any particular fact concerning its temporal manifestation or its historical influence.[16]

Biedermann's theological program draws heavily and explicitly on Hegel's thought. The same concern to develop a theological stance not vulnerable to the findings of historical scholarship is, however, evident in the writings of less overtly Hegelian thinkers as well. Perhaps the most frequent formulation of this concern is in fact in the anti-speculative tendency to ground the truth of Christianity not in some past but in the present of immediate experience. In a thinker like Søren Kierkegaard, this position is still very much dependent on Hegel's categories. The same tendency is, however, also illustrated in the less philosophical vocabulary of at least some pietists.

13. *Christian Dogmatics in God and Incarnation in Mid-Nineteenth Century German Theology*, C. Welch, trans. (New York: Oxford University Press, 1965), p. 332 [*Christliche Dogmatik* (Berlin: Verlag von Georg Reimer, 1884–1885), vol. 2, p. 425]. For a more detailed discussion of Strauss, see pp. 334–336 [vol. 2, pp. 434–436].

14. *Christian Dogmatics*, pp. 337, 367–368 [vol. 2, pp. 437, 583].

15. *Christian Dogmatics*, pp. 337–342 [vol. 2, pp. 438–442] gives a summary of his criticism of Schleiermacher in particular.

16. *Christian Dogmatics*, pp. 373–377 [vol. 2, pp. 590–595].

Appeals to the Jesus of history and testimonies about personal experience continue to be combined in the rhetoric of evangelical piety. But challenges to historical claims only serve to underscore the central commitment of pietism to present experience in confirming the truth of faith.

The first decades of the twentieth century witness a movement toward combining this existentialist approach with the speculative alternative which Biedermann may be taken to represent. In response to a generally negative consensus about the possibilities of constructive theological work in the historical mode of the nineteenth-century liberals, a new attempt is made to establish a defensible theological position in principle independent of the findings of historical and Biblical criticism. The diversity of the forms in which this attempt finds expression is illustrated in the fact that the theological systems of Karl Barth and Paul Tillich, however different on other specific issues, stand in complete agreement in undertaking the non-historical alternative which Strauss' formulation of the Christological problem indicates. Confronted with the highly problematical character of any statements about the Jesus of history, theology resolutely turns to the Christ of faith.

Anti-Theology and the Historical Process: Feuerbach and Marx

In articulating the Christological issue which confronts theology, Strauss also stands in direct continuity with those left-wing Hegelians who challenge the viability of the theological enterprise as such. Because of the difference in the specific questions which they discuss, the systematic similarities in the positions of Strauss on the one hand and Ludwig Feuerbach and Karl Marx on the other may not, however, be immediately apparent. Whereas Strauss argues against grounding the truth of Christianity on the historical individual Jesus of Nazareth, Feuerbach and Marx insist that historical existence is the sole locus of the real. But despite appearances, the atheism of Feuerbach and Marx and Strauss' affirmation of a transhistorical Christ in fact are systematically analogous. In both instances there is a repudiation of commitments which are construed as transcending the experienced order of natural and human phenomena. For Feuerbach and Marx, that repudiation takes the form of denying God. For Strauss it is the rejection of a

Christology which contradicts man's phenomenal experience in ascribing absolute predicates to a particular individual.

The connection between Strauss and Feuerbach is the more direct one. Indeed, Feuerbach's argument in *The Essence of Christianity* in particular may be construed as simply extending Strauss' analysis of Christology to the question of God. Whereas Strauss proffers the whole human race as the realization of the Christological affirmation that God and man are one, Feuerbach maintains that human nature or mankind as a species is in fact the subject of all the predicates traditionally ascribed to God.[17] In contrast to Strauss' terse summary formulation of his position, Feuerbach develops his argument in inordinate and repetitious detail. As he indicates in the preface to the second edition of *The Essence of Christianity*, Feuerbach attempts to use his contention that theological statements refer only to man in order to illumine the full range of primary religious data. Thus he considers not only theological doctrines but also religious practices. Throughout his discussion Christology is, however, the prism through which all Christian thought and practice is viewed; for the affirmation of Christ as the Godman is taken to be the critical movement toward the ultimate recognition of humanity as divine. The development of his position is evident in Feuerbach's repeated identification of humanity and in particular of love between men with God and with Christ as the image of that reality:

That God, who is himself nothing else than the nature of man, should also have a real existence as such, should be as man an object to the consciousness – this is the goal of religion; and this the Christian religion has attained in the incarnation of God, which is by no means a transitory act, for Christ remains man even after his ascension.[18]

The most unequivocal expression, the characteristic symbol of this immediate identity of the species and individuality in Christianity is Christ, the real God of the Christians.[19]

17. The most extended single presentation of Feuerbach's contention that only man or human nature can be the subject to which all the anthropomorphic attributes of God refer appears in *The Essence of Christianity*, M. Evans, trans. (New York: Harper & Row–Torchbooks, 1957), pp. 14–19 [*Das Wesen des Christenthums* (Leipzig: Otto Wigand, 1843), pp. 21–28].

18. *Essence of Christianity*, p. 145 [216]. For a similar summary statement, see p. 208 [311].

19. *Essence of Christianity*, p. 154 [229].

Christ is nothing but an image, under which the unity of the species has impressed itself on the popular consciousness.... Christ is the love of mankind embodied in an image... Thus Christ, as the consciousness of love, is the consciousness of the species. We are all one in Christ.[20]

Perhaps the most frequent criticism which Feuerbach advances against his philosophical antecedents in the tradition of German Idealism is that they indulged their speculation in theoretical abstractions divorced from man in the concreteness of his needs and impulses.[21] It is, therefore, paradoxical that Karl Marx and Friedrich Engels in turn charge Feuerbach with himself confining his program to a reordering of conceptions. They do, to be sure, recognize Feuerbach's commitment to a sensationalist epistemology and to a programmatic materialism. Both Marx and Engels also acknowledge their debt to Feuerbach's analysis of religious phenomena and view that analysis as the paradigm for all critical advance beyond Hegel. As Engels puts the matter late in his life in reviewing the intellectual ferment of the 1840's, with the publication of *The Essence of Christianity*, 'we all became at once Feuerbachians'.[22] Or as Marx maintains in 1844, Feuerbach's works are 'the only writings since Hegel's *Phänomenologie* and *Logik* to contain a real t heoretical revolution' and he is, therefore, 'the true conqueror of the old philosophy'.[23] But despite this recognition of their debt to Feuerbach, Marx

20. *Essence of Christianity*, pp. 268–269 [399–400]. For an epigrammatic identification of this human love with God, see the 1843 essay *Grundsätze der Philosophie der Zukunft* in *Ludwig Feuerbach: Kleine Schriften*, K. Löwith, ed. (Frankfurt/Main: Surkamp Verlag, 1966), p. 217: 'Man *with* man – the *unity of I and Thou is God*'.

21. For a summary formulation of this criticism, see the second edition preface to *The Essence of Christianity*, pp. xxxiii–xxxvi [viii–xii]. The single most sustained instance of this line of criticism appears in *Grundsätze...*, pp. 177–192. The same theme is anticipated and reiterated on pp. 146–151, 160, 199, 208. Feuerbach also adumbrates this critique in the 1842 programmatic essay 'Vorläufige Thesen zur Reform der Philosophie' in ...*Kleine Schriften*, pp. 126–128, 134–135, 141–142. The emphasis on his own thought as concrete and sensual over against the system of Hegel in particular as illegitimately abstract is much less pronounced in Feuerbach's earlier (1839) article 'Zur Kritik der Hegelschen Philosophie' in ...*Kleine Schriften*, pp. 78–123.

22. *Ludwig Feuerbach and the Outcome of Classical German Philosophy* (New York: International Publishers, 1935), p. 28 [*Ludwig Feuerbach und der Ausgang der klassischen deutschen Philosophie* (Stuttgart: Verlag von J. H. W. Dietz, Nachf., 1910), p. 11]. Unfortunately I cannot refer to the appropriate volume of the German critical edition of the works of Marx and Engels because that volume was not available to me.

23. *Economic and Philosophic Manuscripts of 1844*, M. Milligan, trans. and D. J. Struik,

and Engels nonetheless still criticize him for remaining content to focus on man's religious alienation instead of pursuing the implications of this ideational problematic to its economic and social sources.

As is particularly evident in *The German Ideology*, appraisal and critical appropriation of Feuerbach serves to focus the same process in reference to Hegel. The first of the three major divisions in *The German Ideology* underscores this point. That division, which is simply entitled 'Feuerbach', elaborates a parallel between Hegel's older more conservative (politically and religiously) students and the allegedly radical younger generation exemplified in Feuerbach in particular:

Since the Young Hegelians consider conceptions, thoughts, ideas, in fact all the products of consciousness, to which they attribute an independent existence, as the real chains of men (just as the old Hegelians declared them the true bonds of human society) it is evident that the Young Hegelians have to fight only against these illusions of consciousness.

Against so-called old and young Hegelians alike Marx and Engels insist that attempts 'to interpret reality in another way' are in practice demands 'to accept it by means of another interpretation'.[24] As a result, even Feuerbach with his emphasis on the physical needs of men nonetheless remains satisfied with things as they are once he has reinterpreted them.[25] Both *The German Ideology* and Marx's 1844 manuscripts leave no doubt that this criticism is intended to apply to Hegel as well as the young Hegelians. In the manuscripts in particular, Marx argues at length that the fatal flaw in Hegel's system is his focus on consciousness. From that focus there follows what Marx sees as the correlative position that reconciliation or the overcoming of alienation and estrangement is a function exclusively of self-consciousness. There follows, in short, Hegel's '*false* positivism' – his

---

ed. (New York: International Publishers, 1964), pp. 64, 172 [*Ökonomisch-philosophische Manuscripte aus dem Jahre 1844* in *Karl Marx–Friedrich Engels historisch-kritische Gesamtausgabe*, vol. I/3, V. Adoratskij, ed. (Berlin: Marx–Engels Verlag, 1932), pp. 34, 151].

24. *The German Ideology, Parts I and III*, R. Pascal, ed. (New York: International Publishers, 1947), pp. 5–6 [*Die deutsche Ideologie* in . . .*Gesamtausgabe*, vol. I/5, V. Adoratskij, ed. (Berlin: Marx–Engels Verlag, 1932), pp. 9–10]. For similar statements of parallels, see the paragraphs preceding and the sentences immediately following the quoted passages, pp. 1–6 [3, 7–10] and also pp. 33–37 [31–34].

25. *German Ideology*, p. 34 [31–32].

'merely apparent criticism' – which can affirm what is in spite of its deficiencies because the phenomenal order is transcended (*aufgehoben*) in thought.[26]

That Hegel is also implicated in Marx's critique of Feuerbach need not be belabored. The last of the 'Theses on Feuerbach' (which Marx wrote in 1845 and Engels discovered in a notebook after his death and then revised and published) may serve to epitomize the extent to which Hegel is seen standing behind Feuerbach: 'Philosophers have only *interpreted* the world differently; the point however is to *change* it'.[27] But despite his criticism of Hegel along with Feuerbach and despite his recognition of the role of *The Essence of Christianity* in the development of his own position, Marx nonetheless also attempts to correct Feuerbach with Hegel.

The first of the 'Theses of Feuerbach' indicates this tendency. There Marx registers his dissatisfaction with 'all hitherto existing materialism – that of Feuerbach included' because its sensationalist epistemology fails to do justice to 'the *active* side' or '*practice*'. In as much as Marx credits idealism with developing precisely this dimension of man's life at least on the abstract level of cognition, he insists that any post-idealistic materialism cannot simply reaffirm its pre-Kantian antecedents. In the manuscripts of 1844 the same contention appears in Marx's observation that his 'naturalism or humanism distinguishes itself from idealism and materialism, constituting at the same time the unifying truth of both'.[28] In this context Marx again correlates materialism with suffering or passivity and idealism with activity.

Consistent with this appreciation of the emphasis of idealism on human activity is Marx's appraisal of the *Phenomenology*. While agreeing with Feuerbach's repudiation of the abstract treatment of estrangement or alienation and reconciliation in the *Logic*, Marx sees in the *Phenomenology*'s analysis of social existence and in particular of man's estrangement '*all* the elements of criticism' which he in turn develops.[29] He does, to be sure,

26. ...*Manuscripts of 1844*, pp. 184–187 [163–166]. All of pp. 170–193 (150–172) develops this line of criticism of Hegel's thought. For a summary formulation of this argument see K[arl] Marx and F[riedrich] Engels, *The Holy Family* (Moscow: Foreign Languages Publishing House, 1956), pp. 253–256 [*Die heilige Familie* in ...*Gesamtausgabe*, vol. I/3, pp. 369–372].

27. These 'theses' are available in numerous editions – as appendices to the English translations of *The German Ideology* and of Engels' *Ludwig Feuerbach*..., for example. Consequently I refer to them only by number. This last one is number 11.

28. ...*Manuscripts of 1844*, p. 181 [160].

29. ...*Manuscripts of 1844*, p. 176 [156].

reject Hegel's focus on man's consciousness. But the recognition of the importance of man's activity and consequently of historical development remains as a central commitment in his writings. Indeed, that commitment provides the very structure of his thought; for each general exposition of his program – in *The German Ideology*, in *The Communist Manifesto*, in the preface to *The Critique of Political Economy*, and in the 1844 manuscripts – takes the form of a world history. The result is, then, that with Marx the historical dimension of Hegel's thought attains unambiguous predominance. That achievement stands in contrast to the right-wing Hegelians, as is evident in their continued discussion of human immortality and of the inner-Trinitarian life of God as independent of the world.[30] And it also stands in contrast to such left-wing Hegelians as Strauss and Feuerbach whose focus on logical or speculative issues and arguments obscures whatever connections there are between their contentions and interpreting the course of the historical process.

THE CONTINUING APPEAL OF AN HISTORICIZED HEGEL

The influence of Marx on theological reflection in the nineteenth century is typically a negative or at most an indirect one. Increasing disenchantment with Hegel's system as a system does, to be sure, have the parallel result of preserving his thought almost exclusively in its application to historical data. This tendency is evident both in theological and in secular historical

30. For examples of writings by Hegelian theologians which discuss in detail and then affirm human immortality, see: Carl Friedrich Göschel, *Von den Beweisen für die Unsterblichkeit der menschlichen Seele* (Berlin: Verlag von Duncker und Humblot, 1835); Göschel, *Der Mensch nach Leib, Seele und Geist diesseits und jenseits* (Leipzig: Dörffling und Franke, 1856); Carl Ludwig Michelet, *Vorlesungen über die Persöhnlichkeit Gottes und Unsterblichkeit der Seele oder die ewige Persöhnlichkeit des Geistes* (Berlin: Verlag von Ferdinand Dümmler, 1841), esp. pp. 289–314. Perhaps the most influential example of a Hegelian theologian who discusses knowledge of God in himself as well as knowledge of God in relation to the world is Philipp Marheineke. See his *Die Grundlinien der christlichen Dogmatik als Wissenschaft* (Berlin: Duncker und Humblot. 1827), pp. 123–134 for an explication of the inner Trinitarian divine life as distinguished from any relation to the world. For an explicit criticism of Strauss and 'the younger Hegelians' and an insistence that God is fully self-conscious independently of the world, see Georg Andreas Gabler, *Die Hegelsche Philosophie* (Berlin: Verlag von Alexander Duncker, 1843), pp. 89–215.

study: while F. C. Bauer and the Tübingen School illustrate the former, Leopold von Ranke and the so-called German Historical School are important representatives of the latter. This line of development is not, however, directly dependent on the thought of Marx. The influence which Feuerbach exercises on theological reflection in the nineteenth century is similarly peripheral. Preoccupied with the Christological issue as Strauss formulates it, few theologians at least in the German academic tradition focus on the question of God as the critical doctrine demanding exposition or defense.

Not until the publication of Barth's *Epistle to the Romans* (1919) does the question of God again move to the center of theological discussion. Sharing with thinkers like Biedermann and Kierkegaard the conviction that Christian faith cannot be dependent on the vagaries of historical research or the developments of human culture, Barth reasserts a position which in effect isolates both Christological and theological affirmations from secular history. The question of God is, in short, formulated precisely to exclude not only Feuerbach's challenge but also any such historicized version of Hegel as that of Marx. As a result, the influence of Hegel on theology during the period of dominance of Neo-orthodoxy is confined for the most part to those epistemological considerations so central to the Barthian conception of revelation. Not surprisingly it is, therefore, only with the demise of Barthianism as the controlling ethos of academic theology that the historical and cultural dimension of Hegel's thought is again appreciated as a constructive contribution to reflection on Christian faith.

Recognition of the need to relate theological reflection to developmental-evolutionary-historical categories is not, of course, confined to those self-consciously working under the influence of Hegel. With the growing appreciation of the difficulties attendant on Barth's attempt to isolate the theological enterprise from other academic disciplines, a number of tendencies chronologically parallel to Neo-orthodoxy have attained a new prominence. Perhaps most decisive is the academic study of the history of religions (including much Biblical scholarship, especially of the Old Testament) which has continued the commitment of nineteenth-century liberalism to seeing all religious traditions as integrally related to social and cultural developments. Also significant is the concern to relate Christian faith to the categories of process philosophy. Although Alfred North Whitehead himself (and consequently many of those writing under his influence) never stresses or even acknowledges the similarities between his thought and that of Hegel, their philosophies not only have a common concern with developing a metaphysics of process but also reveal numerous structural similarities – similarities frequently overlooked because of the striking stylistic and temperamental contrast between the absolutistic German philosopher and the tentative Anglo-Saxon theoretician of a scientific worldview. Whitehead's thought, frequently conjoined with that of Charles Hartshorne, has been particularly influential in American theology. Self-consciously post-Barthian examples of that influence include John B. Cobb's *A Christian Natural Theology* (1965) and *God and the World* (1969), Schubert M. Ogden's *The Reality of God* (1963), and Daniel Day Williams' *The Spirit and the Forms of Love* (1968).

Not only are there a number of more or less independent tendencies toward making historical development or process a central focus of theological reflection; there are also several distinguishable (though not necessarily separable) approaches leading to a revival of theological interest in this dimension of Hegel's thought. One is through the Barthian perspective itself. Jürgen Moltmann's *Theology of Hope* (1965) illustrates the tendency to move toward addressing questions of historical development from an immanent criticism of Barth's theological program. Similarly, the thinking of Gordon D. Kaufman exemplifies the process through which attention to the work of such Hegel-influenced philosophers and historians as R. G. Collingwood and Wilhelm Dilthey may combine with an appreciation of Barth to form a theological perspective which focuses increasingly on social and cultural history. Another approach to a revived theological interest in Hegel is that mediated at least to a considerable degree through the Marxist tradition. Here Ernst Bloch's books *Subject-Object: Some Comments on Hegel* (1951) and *The Principle of Hope* (1959) have exerted extensive influence. Because his Marxist perspective combines with an attempt to interpret Hegel sympathetically, Bloch consistently historicizes Hegel's thought. He thereby provides an interpretation of Hegel congenial to those theologians dissatisfied with Neo-orthodoxy, as is argued systematically in Wolf-Dieter Marsch's *The Presence of Christ in the Social Order: A Study in Hegel's Dialectic* (1965).

There is, then, a revival of theological attention to Hegel's thought and a community of interest between that revival and at least some tendencies in process philosophy and in the historical study of religious traditions. The question remains as to whether or not renewed consideration of Hegel's philosophy offers the possibility of a viable theological position after the demise of Neo-orthodoxy. The intention of the following chapters is to address that question first in outlining a constructive approach to the Christological issues elaborated in the foregoing historical and systematic study and then in appraising this approach in comparison with the ideal-typical alternatives on the specific question of interpreting the fact of religious pluralism.

PART THREE

Christology and Religious Pluralism

8

Christ, the Christian, and the Kingdom of God

In so far as Hegel's thought moves toward an integration of Nominalist soteriological commitments into a Realist metaphysics of history, it provides a significant point of reference for post-Barthian attempts at constructive theology. To avoid the limitations of numerous previous theological appropriations of his system, renewed interest in Hegel must, however, acknowledge Marx's contribution in focusing critical attention on what are at least potentially anti-historical tendencies in his mentor's thought. Like Marxist theory, Christian theology must repudiate any formulation of Hegel's position which allows the implication that conceptual knowledge obviates or qualifies the need for transformation in the concrete personal, social, and cultural lives of men and their communities. It must, in short, be unambiguously Processive in its understanding of the work of reconciliation.

The following discussion of the effect which the various images of Christ have on the religious consciousness may seem to ignore this injunction that Christian theology appropriate Marx's critique of Hegel. It may, to be more specific, appear to be 'idealist' in the pejorative sense of ascribing efficacy to abstract ideas apart from the historical institutions which are their necessary correlates. Consideration of the various images of Christ need not, however, deny that his significance is to be seen in his impact on concrete historical life. Nor need it deny Marx's demand for continuing change or transformation in man's world. Attention to the various images of Christ does, to be sure, imply a rejection of any undialectical contention that ideas simply reflect the economic organization of the societies in which they are expressed. But that dogma is in any case not entailed in an appreciation of Marx's criticism of Transactional tendencies in Hegel's thought. As the final sections of this chapter indicate, I certainly want to maintain that the significance of Christ is intimately related to the social, economic, and political as well as the religious development of those communities coming under his influence. The relation between the ideal and the real is, however, thoroughly dialectical. There is no denying that the teaching and

the actions of Jesus himself and the subsequent images of Christ elaborated
in the church are historically conditioned through innumerable forces. But
recognition of this historical relativity does not obviate the need to examine
the personal, social, and cultural dynamics through which the figure of
Christ shapes man's consciousness of himself and his role in the world.
Indeed, any reference to the comprehensive historical impact of Christ
presupposes this more directly or explicitly religious influence.

To maintain this dependence of the more comprehensive or the universal
on the particular is simply to restate the contention that a Realism which
is systematically Processive in effect incorporates the commitments of Nominalism. The question of universality is then a derivative one. It arises only
if and in so far as definite individuals and specific historical communities
advance more comprehensive claims for the change or renewal which they
experience. It is, therefore, consistent with the program of proposing a
Realist-Nominalist-Processive approach to the significance of Christ to begin
with the characteristically Nominalist concern about the effect of the figure
of Christ on particular individuals.

THE CENTRAL ROLE OF THE BIBLICAL PORTRAYAL OF CHRIST

Even the direct or self-conscious influence of Christ on particular individuals
is not, of course, confined to the effects on believers. It is, however, mediated
through the church, since even those whose interest in or apprehension
of Christ is extra-ecclesiastical are finally dependent on the Christian tradition in general and the Biblical writings in particular for at least the impetus
to whatever picture of Jesus they elaborate. The Biblical portrayal of Christ
is, therefore, fundamental to the enterprise of describing the influence which
that figure exerts on particular historical individuals and their communities.

That the influence of Jesus of Nazareth is inseparable from the Biblical
portrayal of Christ is a matter of historical fact. For most of the history
of Christian piety, the Biblical records were, moreover, accepted as reliable
reports of actual events. As a result, Christian faith in the modern period
and in particular after the work of Strauss is in a position different from
that of its pre-critical antecedents. With the recognition that virtually any

detail of the Biblical accounts is of questionable historical accuracy, Christian faith cannot be based on any particular historical claim. Indeed, any appeal whatever to the historical Jesus is problematical. Despite the undeniable difference in the situation before and after the advent of a generally acknowledged tradition of systematic Biblical criticism, there are, however, two considerations which mitigate the sharpness of the contrast. The first is that the Biblical portrayal of Christ continues to inform man's religious imagination whether or not it represents an accurate record of past occurrences. The second consideration also qualifies the contrast between the pre- and post-critical situation – though from the opposite direction. It is the fact that detailed analysis of the Biblical accounts as historical sources does allow relative judgments as to historical reliability.

The first consideration is, of course, in the tradition of Strauss and all those whose soteriology is grounded in a transhistorical Christ rather than in the particular individual Jesus of Nazareth. That religious power is possible without direct dependence on historical fact is amply illustrated in man's religious history; but this possibility is also demonstrated in the history of the New Testament itself, perhaps most transparently in the enormous influence which the Fourth Gospel has exercised. From the possibility of religious efficacy apart from reliable historical grounding, Strauss and others argue that religious insight may be formulated in timeless truths in principle not dependent on temporal origins. This position in turn elicits the criticism that there is then no need for a historical redeemer at all, since the mere idea alone is all that is required. The criticism in its sharpest form contrasts a once for all historical transaction in the first century effecting salvation in principle for all men with a conception of Christianity as offering a possibility of renewal always available to all men in all times. The former view is the Realist-Transactional position; it in effect precludes any genuine significance to historical development under the guise of 'taking history seriously'. The difficulty with the contrast is its inaccurate suggestion that the only alternative to the Realist-Transactional position is another non-temporal understanding of the significance of Christ. But for any interpretation which attends to the mediation of Christ's efficacy through a concrete tradition, the question of ideas independent of their historical particularity can arise only as a strictly hypothetical case. Hence attention to the concrete personal and social processes integral to the genesis and development of a historical tradition precludes acceptance of either position in this formulation of the issue: a possibility of renewal available to all men in all times is scarcely more compatible with the conditions of historical mediation than is commitment to a transhistorical transaction that in itself transforms the situation of all mankind.

Those approaches which emphasize the sociological and psychological fact that religious insights emerge within definite historical contexts are, then, at least implicitly resisting the attempt to insulate theological claims from the history which they presuppose and in turn interpret. A concise and forceful statement of this resistance is an essay by Ernst Troeltsch on the significance of Jesus for faith.[1] This essay is, however, only an especially lucid exposition of the position implicit in interpretations which stress the relatedness of theological affirmation and historical tradition. From this perspective there can be agreement with Strauss both that the truth of essential religious beliefs is not dependent on particular historical facts and that no historical knowledge can guarantee the truth of faith; but there is also the recognition that historical study unavoidably influences the very understanding of those beliefs and the interpretation of traditional commitments.

This interaction between faith and historical study is, of course, particularly evident in the case of Biblical scholarship. That the church ascribes canonical status to the Old and New Testaments is one indication of the special relationship between faith and scripture – and hence between faith and critical study of the Bible. This ascription of normative status to the Bible is not simply an act of ecclesiastical authoritarianism. Instead it is a recognition of the peculair situation of the first generation(s) of believers and therefore of the power which their testimony both to Christ and to their common life is able to exercise.[2] The self-reflection of the early church cannot, to be sure, simply be repeated uncritically in subsequent centuries;

---

1. *Die Bedeutung der Geschichtlichkeit Jesu für den Glauben* (Tübingen: J. C. B. Mohr – Paul Siebeck, 1911). Despite the considerable differences between their approaches to many issues, Josiah Royce's formulation of this question is strikingly parallel to that of Troeltsch. See *The Problem of Christianity* (Chicago: Henry Regnery – Gateway Edition, 1968), esp. vol. 1, pp. 412–419 and vol. 2, pp. 334–340, 366.

2. For a provocative discussion of this set of issues, see Karl Rahner's concise essay, *Inspiration in the Bible*, C. H. Henkey and M. Palmer, trans. (New York: Herder and Herder, 1964) [*Über die Schriftinspiration* (Freiburg: Herder, 1961)].

but it is nonetheless a significant reference point for the self-consciousness of succeeding generations of believers.

That the Bible in some sense retains its normative status may serve to epitomize the two considerations which qualify any contrast between theology before and after systematic Biblical criticism. On the one hand, inclusion in that canon of such writings as the Fourth Gospel which freely adapt and transform historical traditions underscores the observation that myths and images can be effective in shaping man's consciousness whether or not they report historical facts. On the other hand, the focus of the New Testament canon on the earliest available records indicates a fascination with origins characteristic especially of modern Western thought but also in at least an unsystematic fashion of all traditions declaring allegiance to a founder. In extreme form this fascination results in an equation of origin and validity: only those formulations echoing the earliest expression of the tradition can claim to be true. An awareness of the development which any tradition undergoes precludes any such absolutizing of the original. But the recognition that what is of value in a tradition cannot be reduced to what is stated or implied in its earliest expression does not preclude an interest in whatever can be determined as historically probable about that formative period. Indeed, such interest in the generation of a religious tradition is the natural correlate of an appreciation for the development which it undergoes throughout its history.

Even a cursory survey of the extensive literature on the question of differentiating strata in the New Testament corpus is, of course, beyond the scope of this essay. That there is a tendency to claim more as the result of historical reclamation projects than can plausibly be defended may, however, be epitomized in a general reference to both the nineteenth-century quest for the historical Jesus and the current 'new quest'.[3] Yet in spite of

---

3. For a critical survey of late Enlightenment and nineteenth-century fascination with Jesus' life, the best work is still the classic of Albert Schweitzer, *The Quest of the Historical Jesus*, W. Montgomery, trans. (New York: MacMillan, 1948) [*Von Reimarus zu Wrede: Eine Geschichte der Leben-Jesu-Forschung* (Tübingen: Verlag von J. B. C. Mohr – Paul Siebeck, 1906)]. James Robinson, *A New Quest for the Historical Jesus* (London: SCM Press, 1959) provides a general overview of the revival of interest particularly in the intentionality and self-understanding of Jesus. An early programmatic announcement of the concerns motivating this 'new quest' is Ernst Käsemann's 'Das Problem des historischen Jesus', *Zeitschrift für Theologie und Kirche*, LI (1954), 125–153. For a concise

the difficulties which the attempt entails, there is a virtual consensus among Biblical scholars that judgments can be made as to relative historical reliability of the various traditions incorporated into the Gospels in particular. Perhaps the most systematic recent statement of the issues involved in this undertaking is Van A. Harvey's *The Historian and the Believer*. Harvey's distinction between 'the Biblical Christ' and 'the perspectival image or memory-impression of Jesus' discriminates between theological transformations of historical traditions and a portrayal which while it is undeniably highly selective nonetheless is based on memories and historical reports. This distinction allows judgments as to which tendencies in the Biblical accounts are most readily compatible with 'the actual Jesus' or at least with 'the historical Jesus' in so far as he is available to critical study at all.[4]

To make such distinctions need not entail the position that only the historically most reliable data may be employed for theological reflection. Indeed, any such restriction would result in a tragic impoverishment of theological resources not only in Biblical themes but also in post-Biblical developments. It is, however, appropriate that theological construction in a post-critical age remain in conversation with the historically most plausible outlines of the figure portrayed in the Gospels. Further elaboration and adaptation is no doubt unavoidable. The tradition of elaboration and adaptation in theological reflection from Biblical times to the present is, moreover, a further resource. But an attempt to interpret the significance of Christ can hope to succeed only if its appropriation of the tradition conveys something of the power of the historical figure who so forcefully shaped the religious consciousness of the first disciples.

Because of the endless varieties of misuse to which Biblical texts are subject, it may be helpful to summarize the foregoing remarks with explicit

---

but still devastating critique of this whole undertaking, see Van A. Harvey and Schubert Ogden, 'How New is the "New Quest for the Historical Jesus"?' in C. E. Braaten and R. A. Harrisville, eds. *The Historical Jesus and the Kerygmatic Christ* (Nashville: Abingdon Press, 1964), pp. 197–242.

4. See *The Historian and the Believer* (New York: MacMillan, 1966), esp. pp. 246–291. Especially important in the process of evaluating the Biblical accounts as historical sources are those emphases which remain even though they are potentially embarrassing. Jesus' baptism by John, his repeated association with the disreputable, even the crucifixion with the disciples' attendant inadequacy are examples.

reference to the question of how the authority of the New Testament functions in the overall line of argument of this study. That the New Testament is authoritative I take to be an empirical fact about the Christian church. This fact has the consequence that any exploration of the effects of the various images of Christ on the Christian consciousness must include in its purvue an examination of Biblical motifs. If a Christology is to have power in Christian communities, it may, moreover, have to be able to sustain a claim for continuity with at least some Biblical traditions. This requirement is, however, only a necessary and not a sufficient condition for the adequacy of a particular interpretation of the significance of Christ. Hence while this study does advocate the Realist-Nominalist-Processive perspective, it does not do so on the grounds that this perspective reflects the historically most reliable data about Jesus with unsurpassable fidelity. Instead it argues only that the Realist-Nominalist-Processive position represents one possible systematization of the Biblical and ecclesiastical portrayals of Christ. The contention for the greater adequacy of this position in comparison with the alternatives then entails a further appeal to the criteria of coherence and adequacy to total experience which inform the line of argument developed throughout the study and which are articulated most explicitly in the tenth chapter.

THE SYNOPTIC PICTURE OF JESUS' LIFE AND TEACHING

Limitations of space and of competence preclude not only an analysis of the relative historical reliability of specific passages but also any comprehensive characterization of the Synoptic portrayal of Jesus. Instead I propose to outline a central complex of themes in the Synoptic accounts of Jesus' life and teaching: the good news of the imminent rule of God; and the correlative demand for human transformation and commitment. To focus on this complex of themes is not, of course, to argue that all the pericopes evidencing them are historically reliable. But even the most radical of Biblical scholars do not dispute the presence in the earliest traditions of teaching about the kingdom or the rule of God and of accounts in which Jesus calls for repentance or μετάνοιά or transformation in men. The Synoptic pericopes no doubt already include considerable elaboration of the earliest reports; it is, however, highly probable that they are elaborations and not inventions.

Both sets of motifs are prominent in what is generally regarded as a summary statement of Jesus' preaching at the outset of Mark's Gospel:

Jesus came into Galilee preaching the gospel and saying, 'The time is fulfilled, and the kingdom of God is at hand; repent, and believe in the gospel'.[5]

The call to repentance and the injunction to believe in the gospel epitomize the double tendency evident in the Synoptic accounts of his teaching about the kingdom and of the events of his ministry. In the Gospels themselves this double tendency is admittedly expressed in a somewhat stylized fashion in the contrast between the pharisees and scribes on the one hand and the tax collectors or publicans and sinners on the other. But it is among the least problematical of historical judgments about Jesus that he engendered hostility among recognized Jewish spiritual leaders and at the same time associated with the disreputable strata of his society. This dual focus of the events in his public ministry in turn serves to accentuate the dialectic in his religious perspective. He preaches both judgment and grace: he demands repentance, radical personal change, rejection of all complacence or self-righteousness; yet this demand is good news of forgiveness, healing, deliverance for those who trust it and commit themselves to it.

One indication that the need for repentance played a prominent role in Jesus' preaching is the tenacious tradition of connections between his work and that of John the Baptist. That Jesus himself is said to have received baptism from him is particularly striking in view of the general observation that John preached 'a baptism of repentance for the forgiveness of sins'.[6] With the testimony of John to Jesus' precedence and the voice from heaven praising him the church counters potentially inimical inferences which might be drawn from this account; but the tradition that John baptised Jesus remains.

5. Mark 1: 14–15. Matthew 4: 17 is a close parallel. All quoted passages from the Bible appear in the Revised Standard Version translation.
6. Mark 1: 4. Verses 2–11 describe John's ministry and his baptism of Jesus. Compare Matthew 3: 1–17 and Luke 3: 1–22. In all three Gospels, repentance is central to the description of John's preaching. It is singled out for emphasis in the non-Marcan passage Matthew 3: 7–10; Luke 3: 7–9.

That Jesus himself receives baptism is a dramatic emblem of the persistent theme especially in Matthew and Luke of judgment against those who deny their need for repentance. The parables of the pharisee and the publican in Luke and of the two sons in Matthew state the issue incisively: the only insurmountable obstacle to true righteousness is the refusal to recognize one's need for healing.[7] There are passages particularly in Luke which are still more direct. When bystanders relate the story of 'Galileans whose blood Pilate mingled with their sacrifices', Jesus replies, 'Unless you repent, you will all likewise perish'.[8] Similarly uncompromising is his summary judgment on the pharisees:

You are those who justify yourselves before men, but God knows your hearts; for what is exalted among men is an abomination in the sight of God.[9]

Even that sweeping condemnation is, however, temperate in comparison with Matthew's elaborate recitation of woes against the pharisees and scribes for their alleged self-righteous and hypocritical denial of the need for repentance.[10]

In the dichotomized world of the Synoptics, Jesus' call for repentance is, then, a judgment of condemnation on those Jewish leaders who refuse to acknowledge any need for transformation or renewal. It is, however, a message of hope for those who recognize their need for healing and forgiveness. The positive dimension of Jesus' preaching is of course already evident in such parables as Matthew's about the two sons or Luke's about the pharisee and the publican, even though they appear in a context of reproving spiritual complacency. But the Synoptic accounts also focus more explicitly on this positive dimension of Jesus' message as good news for those open to it. The lines are neatly drawn in the pericope which describes the call of Levi or Matthew: the tax collector responds immediately and then Jesus joins him and his friends in a celebration – to the reported criticism of the pharisees and scribes.[11] Jesus' identification with social

7. Matthew 21: 28–32 and Luke 18: 9–14.
8. Luke 13: 1–5.
9. Luke 16: 14–15.
10. Matthew 23: 1–36. Compare Mark 12: 37b–40 and Luke 11: 37–12: 1; 20: 45–47.
11. Matthew 9: 9–13; Mark 2: 13–17; Luke 5: 27–32. See also the very similar story about Zacchaeus in Luke 19: 1–10.

outcasts is a recurrent theme in the Synoptics. Perhaps the most striking illustration is a passage which has Jesus quote a one sentence characterization of himself: 'Behold a glutton and a drunkard, a friend of tax collectors and sinners!'[12] Jesus' practice of seeking out the rejected is echoed in his teaching, as the parables of the lost sheep, the lost coin, and the prodigal son illustrate.[13] Here too there is an emphasis on rejoicing and celebration in stark contrast to the dire pronouncement of judgment on the self-righteous.

That Jesus' message to the rejected is one of good news rather than condemnation is expressed in summary form in the Synoptic representation of him as forgiving sins. The question of whether Jesus himself pronounced forgiveness of sins is at best an undecided one. The story in which he heals the paralytic would seem to offer evidence that he did; but there are strong critical arguments for the position that the early church elaborated the dialogue about forgiveness of sins to defend its own practice against Jewish opponents.[14] Even if the authoritative pronouncement that sins are forgiven reflects the practice of the church rather than that of Jesus himself, there is, however, continuity with persistent emphases in the Synoptic portrayal as a whole; for the assurance that the repentant sinner is justified and that the Father forgives those who forgive their fellows is central to the good news which Jesus announces.[15] In the Synoptics the authority of Jesus' assurance is evidenced in the power which he exercises in healing the sick, in changing the lives of fraudulent tax collectors and prostitutes, and in engendering joy among the downtrodden. That power is seen as a present reality. It is, however, at the same time placed in an eschatological context.

12. Matthew 11: 19a; Luke 7: 34b.
13. Matthew 18: 12–14 (the lost sheep); Luke 15: 1–32 (all three parables). Luke's introduction to this series of parables sketches their context: 'Now the tax collectors and sinners were all drawing near to him. And the Pharisees and the scribes murmured, saying, "This man receives sinners and eats with them".'
14. Matthew 9: 1–8; Mark 2: 1–12; Luke 5: 17–20. See also Luke 7: 36–50. For a discussion of the possibility that the church inserted the authoritative pronouncement of forgiveness to legitimate its own practice, see, for example: Rudolf Bultmann, *History of the Synoptic Tradition*, J. Marsh, trans. (New York: Harper & Row, 1963), pp. 14–16, 48–48, 212–213 [*Die Geschichte der synoptischen Tradition* (Gottingen: Vandenhoeck & Ruprecht, 1957), pp. 12–14, 49–51, 227]; and Frank W. Beare, *The Earliest Records of Jesus* (Nashville: Abingdon Press, 1962), pp. 76–77.
15. See, for example: Matthew 6: 12, 14–15; 21: 28–32; Mark 4: 11–12; 11: 25–26; Luke 6: 37; 11: 4; 13: 3, 5; 15: 21–24, 31–32; 18: 14; 19: 9–10.

The apocalyptic image of the bridegroom is identified with the person of Jesus to justify the mood of rejoicing among his disciples.[16] And more emphatically, Jesus' healing of the sick and his preaching good news to the poor is interpreted as fulfilling the visions of Isaiah.[17]

In those numerous parables and sayings which refer to the kingdom or rule of God, the eschatological context of Jesus' ministry becomes more explicit. Those who do and do not respond to Jesus' preaching are identified with those who do and do not participate in the kingdom of God. Perhaps the most vivid example is the story about the great banquet where the undeserving and the outcasts receive the king's bounty after the invited guests decline to come and consequently incur the royal wrath.[18] A less vehement portrayal of the issues confronting Jesus in his ministry is the parable of the laborers in the vineyard. There too the apparently undeserving have a full share of compensation – to the consternation and protest of those who see themselves as more deserving.[19]

The kingdom or rule of God is, to be sure, not simply identified with present responses to Jesus' call for repentance and acceptance of the good news. There is a definite future dimension as well: the poor are blessed because theirs is the kingdom; but one measure of their blessing is that the last shall be first.[20] This future dimension is, for example, prominent in the words of Jesus at the last supper, in the second petition of the Lord's Prayer, and in the sayings of the so-called Synoptic apocalypse.[21] But the future realization is nonetheless continuous with the rule of God as it is embodied in Jesus' own life and in the commitment of those who respond to his call. That the parables about the kingdom characteristically reveal patterns

16. Matthew 9: 14–15; Mark 2: 18–20; Luke 5: 33–35.

17. In Matthew 11: 2–6 and Luke 7: 18–23 Jesus is portrayed as responding to the question of John's disciples as to whether he is the Messiah with an allusion to Isaiah 35: 5–6. Luke 4: 17–21 depicts Jesus as claiming to fulfill Isaiah 61: 1–2 in his ministry.

18. Matthew 22: 1–10; Luke 14: 16–24.

19. Matthew 20: 1–16.

20. See Matthew 5: 1–11 and Luke 6: 20–26 as well as the less elaborate but similar *logia* in Matthew 11: 28; 20: 16; 23: 12 and Luke 14: 11; 18: 14. The dialogue about greatness in the kingdom is also relevant; see Matthew 18: 1–5; Mark 9: 33–37; Luke 9: 46–48 and the related verses Matthew 20: 26–27; 23: 11; Mark 10: 43–44; Luke 22: 26.

21. Matthew 6: 10; 24: 4–36; 26: 26–29; Mark 13: 5–37; 14: 22–25; Luke 11: 2; 21: 8–36; 22: 15–20.

parallel to those in Jesus' ministry is one indication of this continuity. Another is such parables as those of the mustard seed and the leaven which testify to the connection between the present and the future even while contrasting the insignificance of the one with the glory of the other.[22]

In Matthew and Luke the present power of the kingdom is explicitly identified with Jesus' authority to exorcize demons:

> If it is by the finger of God that I cast out demons, then the kingdom of God has come upon you.[23]

But that authority is itself exercised only in the context of the radical obedience and trust which characterize the Synoptic portrayal of Jesus' relationship to the Father – an obedience and a trust which are in turn demanded or elicited from those who follow him. The most emphatic representations of Jesus' obedience and reliance on God are the accounts of his temptations and of his prayer in the garden of Gethsemane.[24] But those passages serve only to focus with particular reference to Jesus himself a persistent motif in the Synoptic portrayal of the teaching about the kingdom. Jesus' hearers are enjoined to commit themselves so totally to the kingdom that trust in the Father dispels all anxieties about mundane needs.[25] The kingdom is like a treasure hidden in a field or a pearl of great value for the purchase of which all else must be sold.[26] That unconditional obedience is required is illustrated in the call stories of the first four disciples and Levi and in the encounter with the rich young man.[27] Even more startling are

22. Matthew 13: 31–32; Mark 4: 30–32; Luke 13: 18–19 and Matthew 13: 11; Luke 13: 20–21. See also the related parables about growth and harvest: Matthew 13: 24–30 and Mark 4: 26–29.

23. Luke 11: 20. Matthew 12: 28 is identical, except that 'Spirit' is used instead of 'finger'. The saying occurs in the context of the discussion about the house divided and the conjoined parable of the strong man who must be overcome: Matthew 12: 25–37; Mark 3: 23–30; Luke 11: 17–23. See also Luke 17: 20–21 for a similarly striking reference to the presence of the kingdom and Luke 10: 17–20 for a correlation of power over demons with the fall of Satan.

24. Matthew 4: 1–11; 26: 36–46; Mark 1: 12–13; 14: 32–42; Luke 4: 1–13; 22: 40–46.

25. The most striking passage in this connection is Matthew 6: 25–34; Luke 12: 22–31.

26. Matthew 13: 44–46.

27. Matthew 4: 18–22; 9: 9–13; 19: 16–30; Mark 1: 16–20; 2: 13–17; 10: 17–31; Luke 5: 1–11; 5: 27–32; 18: 18–30.

the isolated discipleship sayings in which Jesus reproves those who put any considerations before the kingdom. His mother and brothers are only those who do the will of God.[28] Not even burial of one's father is ground for delay in following him. [29] As Luke sums up, 'No one who puts his hand to the plow and looks back is fit for the kingdom of God'.[30]

That the kingdom is at hand is, then, proclaimed as good news: God's rule assures ultimate deliverance from sickness and sin and bondage to those who recognize their need and respond to the divine invitation. But in the dichotomized world of the Synoptics, no partial commitment is possible. Those who acknowledge the rule of God receive it with joy, live in obedience to it, and trust in its ultimate power. In contrast, those who rely on their own righteousness incur the judgment of repudiating the good news of deliverance because it makes no special allowance for their own accomplishments.

THE DEATH OF CHRIST IN NEW TESTAMENT THEOLOGY

The motifs which dominate the Synoptic portrayal of Jesus are not, of course, absent from the remainder of the New Testament. The Fourth Gospel, for example, continues and even sharpens the polarity between Jesus and his followers on the one hand and Jewish religious leaders on the other. The words attributed to Jesus after his healing of the 'man blind from birth' epitomize this continuity:

For judgment I came into this world, that those who do not see may see, and that those who see may become blind. Some of the Pharisees near him heard this, and they said to him, 'Are we also blind?' Jesus said to them, 'If you were blind, you would have no guilt; but now that you say, "We see", your guilt remains'.[31]

The same set of issues is also present in the epistles. There the narrative form yields to more directly conceptual expression, as is illustrated in Paul's

28. Matthew 12: 46–50; Mark 3: 31–35; Luke 8: 19–21.
29. Matthew 8: 22; Luke 9: 60.
30. Luke 9: 62.
31. John 9: 39–41.

interpretation of the law as an enslaving power from which men in faith are freed because they are justified or declared righteous before God.[32]

But in addition to reflections which parallel the issues raised in the Synoptic portrayal of Jesus' ministry, there is in the Fourth Gospel, the epistles and the book of Revelation also a more marked tendency to focus on the meaning of Christ's death in particular. This focus is no doubt implicit in the Synoptic tradition. Especially in the case of Mark the crucifixion narrative dominates the Gospel as a whole; and in a passage like the one recounting Jesus' words at the last supper there is an explicit statement that his death is 'for many' or even, as Matthew has it, 'for many for the forgiveness of sins'.[33] But what remains implicit or at most inchoately expressed in the Synoptics is more self-consciously articulated in the Fourth Gospel, the epistles, and the book of Revelation.

The most generalized formulation of the significance of Christ's death in the Pauline and Johannine writings stands in direct continuity with the Synoptic account of Jesus' words at the last supper. It is the simple affirmation that Christ suffered and died 'for us':

God shows his love for us in that while we were yet sinners Christ died for us.[34]

The life I now live in the flesh I live by faith in the Son of God, who loved me and gave himself for me.[35]

For God has not destined us for wrath, but to obtain salvation through our Lord Jesus Christ, who died for us so that whether we wake or sleep we might live with him.[36]

I am the good shepherd. The good shepherd lays down his life for his friends.[37]

By this we know love, that he laid down his life for us.[38]

---

32. Romans 1: 16–17 and 3: 21–26 are classic formulations of Paul's position. It is, however, expressed again and again throughout his epistles and is assumed in his central theological conceptions – faith, sin, righteousness, justification, the law – even when it is not explicitly stated.

33. Matthew 26: 28; Mark 14: 24. Matthew 1: 21 is a general statement that Jesus' destiny is to 'save his people from their sins'. See also Matthew 20: 28 and Mark 10: 45 for the cryptic summary statement that Jesus' destiny is 'to give his life as a ransom for many'.

34. Romans 5: 8.

35. Galatians 2: 20.

36. 1 Thessalonians 5: 9–10. See also Romans 8: 32; 14: 15b; 2 Corinthians 5: 14–15.

37. John 10: 11. See also John 10: 15.

38. John 15: 13. See also John 11: 50 and 18: 14.

Greater love has no man than this, that a man lay down his life for his friends.[39]

As is indicated in the Matthean version of Jesus' words at the last supper, one form of specifying further the vicarious character of the crucifixion is to relate it to the forgiveness of sins. 1 Corinthians 15: 3 is significant in this connection because it refers to a pre-Pauline tradition:

For I delivered to you as of first importance what I also received, that Christ died for our sins in accordance with the Scriptures.[40]

That Christ's death for sins is said to be 'in accordance with the scriptures' in turn suggests Biblical motifs which are elaborated more explicitly in other contexts. One specific example which is very influential in the subsequent history of reflection on the significance of Jesus is Paul's juxtaposition of Adam and Christ in Romans 5 with its emphasis on the contrast between disobedience leading to death and obedience resulting in grace and life 'following many trespasses'.[41] In addition to this distinctive motif of comparing Adam and Christ, there are two general groupings of broadly scriptural thought and imagery which exercise considerable influence. Precisely because they are so pervasive, they may, however, be only provisionally distinguished. First, there is a variety of motifs adapted either from Jewish cultic life or from scriptural conceptions originally derived from sacrificial practices; second, there is the traditional idea of ransom or redemption from debt or from bondage which in combination with apocalyptic motifs is generalized as a theme of deliverance from evil powers.

The influence of sacrificial practices in general and the Jewish Day of Atonement in particular is especially pronounced. Jesus becomes the sacrifice which covers or expiates the sin of all men.[42] It is through his blood that

39. 1 John 3: 16a.
40. For similar formulations of Paul's own, see Romans 4: 25 and Galatians 1: 4.
41. Though the explicit comparison to Adam does not begin until verse 12, the focus on the death of Christ in verses 6–11 underscores the life-death dialectic: not only do the heirs of Christ receive life in contrast to the death meted out to the descendants of Adam; it is also life resulting from obedience even to death itself. The phrase 'even death on a cross' – which is probably Paul's own addition to an already extant liturgical formula – in the 'Christ-hymn' of Philippians 2: 5–11 underscores the same theme of obedience to death.
42. Romans 3: 23–25; Hebrews 2: 17; 1 John 2: 2; 4: 10.

justification or forgiveness or redemption is possible.[43] Especially in Hebrews details of sacrificial practice – ceremonial cleansing, sprinkling with blood, and the disposal of carcasses, for example – accompany the central identification of Jesus with the sacrifice.[44] In addition, the writer of Hebrews portrays Jesus as offering himself: he is not only the sacrificial victim but also the officiating priest.[45] Consequently the writer of Hebrews develops his own distinctive emphases in interpreting the efficacy of Jesus' work. He maintains, for example, that Jesus is able to 'sympathize with our weaknesses' because he too has been tempted 'in every respect ... as we are' – in implied contrast to at least some Levitical priests.[46] Again in contrast to Levitical priests, he asserts that Jesus 'holds his priesthood permanently' and consequently 'always lives to make intercession' for men.[47]

The Day of Atonement is not of course the only paradigm for interpreting the death of Christ in sacrificial imagery. Because of the correlation of the crucifixion with the feast of the Passover, the traditional account of the last supper itself and the communion rituals developing from it already suggest connections with the paschal sacrifice. In one case Paul explicitly identifies Christ with the paschal lamb.[48] The image of the Lamb of God also carries connotations of the Passover sacrifice; but this image is typically combined with other traditions as well. The book of Revelation, for example, fuses the motif of the blood of the Lamb with the motifs of ritual purification and conquering Satan.[49] Similarly, the Fourth Gospel refers to Jesus as the Lamb of God in two instances; but in the first one it combines that appellation with the further phrase 'who takes away the sin of the world'.[50] Since the paschal sacrifice is not a sin offering, the writer either intends only a general parallel to the Passover sacrifice as the sign of deliverance or he is implicitly combining the paschal imagery with other motifs.

Two other closely related traditions in any case are suggested in his

43. Romans 3: 23–25; 5: 9; Ephesians 1: 7; Hebrews 9: 11–12; 13: 20; 1 John 1: 7; Revelation 1: 5; 5: 9; 7: 14; 12: 11.
44. Hebrews 1: 3; 9: 11–14; 10: 22; 12: 24; 13: 11–12. See also 1 Peter 1: 2.
45. Hebrews 7: 27; 9: 14; 9: 26; 10: 10; 12: 14.
46. Hebrews 4: 15. See also Hebrews 2: 18 for another expression of the same theme.
47. Hebrews 7: 23–25. See the related verses Hebrews 6: 20 and 9: 24.
48. 1 Corinthians 5: 7–8.
49. Revelation 7: 14 and 12: 11.
50. John 1: 29, 36.

words. One is the Suffering Servant theme of Isaiah 53 which already informs some details of the Synoptic passion narrative. The other is the ritual transfer of guilt to a scapegoat at the close of the Day of Atonement. The same traditions are echoed in several other New Testament passages on the death of Christ. One instance is the affirmation of First Peter that 'he himself bore our sins in his body on the tree'.[51] More radical still are Paul's formulations: 'God ... made him to be sin who knew no sin'; 'sending his own Son in the likeness of sinful flesh and for sin, he condemned sin in the flesh'; Christ became 'a curse for us'.[52]

In even the most cursory survey of cultic imagery in New Testament reflection on the death of Christ, it is, then, apparent that multiple traditions influence and re-enforce each other. The power of the image 'Lamb of God' epitomizes the possibility of multiple connotations: paschal sacrifice, sin offering, the scapegoat ritual from the Day of Atonement, and the motif of the Suffering Servant all converge. The same difficulties evident in an attempt to isolate different traditions of sacrificial practice recur in the more general differentiation between conceptions or images derived from Jewish cultic life on the one hand and the theme of ransom or redemption from evil powers on the other. The frequent reference to the efficacy of Jesus' blood is an important case in point. Although the idea that shedding of blood is soteriologically effective is intimately related to sacrificial practices, the blood of Christ in some instances is also interpreted as the price which is paid to buy or redeem or ransom man from his bondage to evil powers.[53] This conjunction of the conception of ransom with other motifs is the characteristic pattern. Paul does, to be sure, on occasion refer to redemption or purchase from bondage without immediately relating this conception to other interpretations of Christ's death; but the references are confined to a cryptic 'You were bought with a price'.[54]

That ransom or redemption is from bondage is particularly congenial to the apocalyptic motif of defeat of Satan or of the principalities and powers of the present age. But in the later New Testament writings the theme

51. 1 Peter 2: 24.
52. 2 Corinthians 5: 21; Romans 8: 3; Galatians 3: 13.
53. The clearest examples are 1 Peter 1: 18–19; Revelation 5: 9; 12: 11. More ambiguous but still relevant are Ephesians 1: 7 and Revelation 1: 5.
54. 1 Corinthians 6: 20; 7: 23.

of deliverance from evil powers or defeat of Satan is also correlated with the forgiveness of sins and with a sacrificial interpretation of Christ's death. The Johannine writings, for example, combine their use of sacrificial imagery with a view of Christ's work in general and of his death in particular as the defeat of the ruler of this world or the devil.[55] Even Hebrews combines its dominant emphasis on the sacrificial analogy with commitment to seeing Christ's death as a defeat of the devil.[56] But most striking of all is the tendency of the Deuteropauline epistles to fuse the multiple traditions into single rhetorical passages. Two examples, one from Ephesians and the other from Colossians, may serve to epitomize this exuberant combination of the theme of forgiveness first at least implicitly with sacrifice through the image of blood, then with the conception of ransom or redemption, and finally with the motif of conquering 'the principalities and powers':

In him we have redemption through his blood, the forgiveness of our trespasses, according to the riches of his grace.[57]

And you ... God made alive together with him, having forgiven us all our trespasses, having canceled the bond which stood against us with its legal demands; this he set aside, nailing it to the cross. He disarmed the principalities and powers and made a public example of them, triumphing over them in him.[58]

THE EFFECT OF IMAGES OF CHRIST ON THE RELIGIOUS CONSCIOUSNESS

The conceptions and images which later theories of the Atonement elaborate are at least inchoately expressed in New Testament reflection on Christ's death. In so far as Biblical approaches construe the result of Christ's death as effected in that discrete past event, they parallel Realist-Transactional interpretations in particular. On Nominalist premises this focus on a past event to the at least initial exclusion of attention to its relation to present individuals is, however, not acceptable. Because the Nominalist approach construes claims about the significance of Christ as presupposing the influ-

---

55. John 12: 31–32; 1 John 3: 8.
56. Hebrews 2: 14–15.
57. Ephesians 1: 7.
58. Colossians 1: 13–15. See also Colossians 1: 13–14 for a similar combining of motifs.

ences he exercises on particular individuals in their definite historical contexts, it views theories of the Atonement as the expression of the transformed consciousness of the Christian community rather than as factual accounts of a past transaction. For that reason an interpretation of the significance of Christ on Nominalist premises must explore the effect of the various images of Christ on the religious consciousness before it attempts to understand the force of theories about the relation of the Atonement to mankind or the cosmos as a whole or God.

The most illuminating New Testament precedent for this procedure is Paul's discussion in Romans 6. I have not alluded to it in considering New Testament reflection specifically on the death of Christ because it is in the first instance an interpretation of the believer's religious experience in baptism. That experience is, however, depicted as a dying and rising with Christ:

Do you not know that all of us who have been baptized into Christ Jesus were baptized into his death? We were buried therefore with him by baptism unto death, so that as Christ was raised from the dead by the glory of the Father, we too might walk in newness of life.[59]

Paul does, to be sure, insist on a universal significance for Christ's death and resurrection: 'The death he died he died to sin, once for all, but the life he lives he lives to God'.[60] That he is here presupposing his conception of Christ as a second Adam (which is developed in the preceding chapter of Romans) seems indicated in the immediately following exhortation: 'So you also must consider yourselves dead to sin and alive to God in Christ Jesus'.[61] But the line of argument in this limited context nonetheless proceeds from the concrete experience of believers to the broader claim.

The movement which Paul describes in speaking of dying and rising with Christ is, moreover, a recurrent pattern in the experience of Christ which shapes the Christian religious consciousness. That pattern is a dialectic between judgment and grace or healing, between confession and forgiveness, between bondage and liberation. In the Synoptic portrayal of Jesus' ministry the pattern is expressed in the double-sidedness of his call for repentance

59. Romans 6: 3–4.
60. Romans 6: 10.
61. Romans 6: 11.

and for commitment to the good news of God's rule. Paul's formulation in juridical categories in turn transposes the dialectic into the theological conceptuality of a forensic justification of the man of faith displacing the condemnation of the law under which the sinner stands. The same pattern also informs traditional reflection specifically on the death of Christ and on the resurrection as the sign that his death is ultimately the means to victory and not a defeat. The language of expiatory sacrifice, for example, understands the crucifixion on analogy to the cultic acknowledgement of sin followed by priestly absolution. Similarly, the conception of the scape-goat and the tradition of the Suffering Servant assume a public expression of sinfulness which results in forgiveness through the suffering or death of another. The motifs of ransom or redemption from bondage, of victory over Satan and (at least to some extent) of the paschal sacrifice all stress the positive dimension of liberation; but they patently also presuppose the bondage to the evil powers which are overcome.

In the history of Christian thinking on the Atonement there are, of course, different combinations of motifs and different emphases on either side of the dialectic. Anselm and Calvin, for example, articulate the reality of God's honor or wrath or judgment more powerfully than do many of their ante-cedents and successors. Conversely, in the thought of theologians like Horace Bushnell and Albrecht Ritschl the fact of God's mercy or grace predominates. But the underlying pattern nonetheless remains the same precisely because the concern is always the soteriological one of movement from sin to salvation – a movement which presupposes contrast between the negative and the positive and hence requires both judgment and grace or healing.

The member of the Christian community in particular but also the inter-ested student of the Christian tradition or even simply the man nurtured in a nominally Christian culture is perennially exposed to this Christologi-cally interpreted dialectic between judgment and grace. At least traditionally and for the most part also in the modern period that exposure is, however, most intense for those who belong to the Christian church. The dialectic of judgment and grace is impressed on the believer through his reading of the Bible, through his participation in the liturgy and the sacraments, through sermons and other instruction in Christian doctrine, and through prayer and meditation. His perception of his own sinfulness and his hope for salvation are, moreover, mediated through the image of Christ – and, in Western Christendom, in particular through the image of Christ crucified.

Not infrequently, a definite theory of the Atonement may inform the believer's or a particular community's interpretation of the resolution of judgment into new life. In the West, Anselm's understanding of the transaction effected in the work of Christ is the most conspicuous example. But the image of Christ in the Synoptics or in Paul's epistles or in the Johannine literature or in Hebrews may also serve to focus the believer's religious consciousness. That consciousness is concomitantly re-enforced and shaped further as the believer undertakes his own devotional life and as he participates in the corporate life of the church. The sacraments are especially illuminating examples of this process. Paul's discussion in Romans 6 indicates how baptism may be understood as a ritual action through which the participant appropriates his identity as a believer. In dying and rising with Christ he accepts the judgment of God on the old man of sin and looks toward becoming that new man of fidelity to the rule of God. In the ancient church and in those traditions which continue its practice of adult or believer's baptism, this ritual action has a significance which it cannot, however, have once infant baptism is the norm. Consequently the eucharist or the Lord's Supper becomes all the more central.

In the liturgical life of the church there seems always to have been a recognition of the intimate connection between the cross and the eucharist. Indeed, it could hardly have been otherwise after the first generation of believers in view both of the place of the last supper in the Synoptic tradition and of Paul's commentary on the words of institution ascribed to Jesus. He writes to the Corinthians:

For as often as you eat this bread and drink the cup, you proclaim the Lord's death until he comes.[62]

Like the Pauline understanding of baptism, the eucharist is a ritual action through which the participant's religious consciousness as a believer is shaped and reinforced. Celebration of the sacrament moves from confession through an identification with the brokenness and suffering of Christ represented or embodied in the bread and wine to a response of gratitude for

62. 1 Corinthians 11: 26.

forgiveness and newness of life. In this action the church proclaims dramatically its faith in a loving God who through the very brokenness and suffering of Christ attracts men to the divine rule or kingdom. Hence in participating in the eucharist the believer again experiences the judging and healing God whose rule the Synoptic Jesus announces.

The critical question raised in any such survey of the pattern of judgment and grace informing the various Biblical, doctrinal, and sacramental portrayals of Christ is, of course, that of how these images of him effect change in believers. That they do in fact affect the living of individuals and communities may be stated simply as a matter of empirical observation. But the dynamics of the changes still require further specification.

The question is one of further specification rather than of completely fresh deliberation because the various images of Jesus and in particular of the crucified Christ have the power to effect change in individuals and communities precisely in so far as they mediate the double perception of grace and judgment. For Christian piety the crucified Christ who is finally victorious over evil has become an emblem of that love willing to endure every suffering and humiliation in order to free man from bondage to powers other than the ultimately sovereign rule of God. The communication of divine love through the various images of Christ is itself integral to the process of transforming the self – in the language of Paul, of passing from the old to the new creation.[63] Psychological studies of changes in self-understanding and behavior are instructive in this connection; for there is evidence indicating one ingredient in successful personality change to be the patient's discovery that someone or some others are concerned about his progress because they have genuine affection for him.[64] That assurance

63. 2 Corinthians 5: 17.

64. Especially provocative on this complex of issues is a detailed case study written by Carl R. Rogers about a client whom he counselled at the research clinic of the University of Chicago. See 'The Case of Mrs. Oak: Research Analysis' in C. R. Rogers and R. F. Dymond, eds., *Psychotherapy and Personality Change* (Chicago: University of Chicago Press, 1954), pp. 259–348. Particularly relevant are Rogers' reflections on the possibly essential role which '*caring*' on the part of the therapist plays in facilitating personality change (see pp. 324, 342, 345). For a discussion of the significance of such data for theology which is more detailed than the line of argument in this essay allows, see Daniel D. Williams, *The Minister and the Care of Souls* (New York: Harper & Row, 1961), pp. 52–94. A more expansive but unfortunately less sophisticated attempt to explore the same issues that Williams considers is Don S. Browning. *Atonement and*

of love is integral to healing is, of course, most transparently the case when the individual in question is already oppressed with a sense of guilt or worthlessness. Then perception of inadequacy is already a fact of his experience and the assurance of love and acceptance is what is required. But even for those whose self-esteem precludes any change unless their complacency is called into question, the assurance that criticism is ultimately benevolent in intention may serve to facilitate alteration in self-understanding and behavior.

The effect which the various images of Christ have on the religious consciousness is, then, in part at least derivative from their communication of a love willing to seek out and to suffer with man. That assurance of love cannot, however, be divorced from an awareness of judgment. The good news which the various images of Christ mediate is the promise of healing, of forgiveness, of liberation. But it is both a truism and a profound psychological fact that healing or forgiveness or liberation implies judgment. In traditional theological categories, the experience of salvation presupposes the fact of sin. To accept healing or forgiveness or liberation requires the at least implicit acknowledgement that there is sickness or transgression or bondage to be overcome. Hence one form in which man the sinner receives God's love and grace is as judgment or wrath. In any explication of the significance of Christ and of his death in particular it is, however, of the utmost importance that the fact of judgment retain this status as derivative from the promise of grace. That Christian doctrine may be interpreted so as to leave men in despair is one indication that this subordination of judgment to grace is not always maintained. Indeed, the rhetoric of condemnation can claim ample Biblical legitimation even in the Gospel accounts of Jesus' own preaching. As a result, it is crucial to appreciate the context in which that condemnation occurs.

The admittedly stylized contrast between the pharisees and scribes on the one hand and tax collectors and sinners on the other epitomizes a fundamental distinction in the response which the message of the Synoptic

---

Psychotherapy (Philadelphia: Westminster Press, 1966). Interesting for its attempt to use the categories of orthodox Freudianism, interpreting the efficacy of the cross as an example of transference, is B. G. Sanders, *Christianity After Freud* (London: Geoffrey Bles, 1949). Less enamored with technical psychoanalytic vocabulary and more conversant with theological issues is David E. Roberts, *Psychotherapy and the Christian View of Man* (New York: Charles Scribner's Sons, 1950).

Jesus and also the church's proclamation of Christ evoke. Whereas the one group receives Jesus and his teaching as good news, members of the other group do not acknowledge any need for repentance or renewal. For both the message is perceived as one of judgment as well as grace. Because the tax collectors and sinners know their need, they rejoice in the forgiveness and healing and liberation which are offered. In contrast, the pharisees and scribes reject the loving Father whom Jesus preaches because they cannot accept the implicit judgment on their own efforts to achieve righteousness – and of course the concomitant (and explicit) criticism of the religious status and social power which those efforts confer. The Gospel portrait of Christ is seriously distorted if it is not constantly kept in view that only this latter group is in the end subjected to what in the Biblical tradition at least becomes vituperative judgment and even condemnation. The condemnation is of self-righteousness and hypocrisy – not of personal immorality or social deviance. The Christ of the Gospels is not portrayed as indifferent to immorality or deviance. But his response to it is not condemnation but rather the mediation of healing and forgiveness and liberation. That the Christian proclamation should generate despair is, therefore, the result of a highly paradoxical distortion of the pattern of judgment and grace informing every acceptable image of Christ; for the only human situation for which the goods news of the rule of God is in principle of no avail is that of a self-satisfaction which acknowledges no need for deliverance.[65]

65. Paul Tillich has been the most influential theologian to stress the parallels between the theological and the psychotherapeutic analyses of this complex of issues. He has been especially critical of a moralism which assumes that personality change can be commanded. For a concise statement of his position in reference to the destructive consequences of moralizing in psychoanalytic practice, see *Morality and Beyond* (New York: Harper & Row, 1963), pp. 50–51. Tillich is certainly right in criticizing the tendency to moralize or to command change as in any sense a precondition of acceptance or love. To use the Biblical paradigms, that is to condemn the tax collectors and sinners instead of offering the healing which they know they need. But Tillich is nonetheless too sweeping in his pre-emptory dismissal of what he calls moralistic psychoanalysis or psychotherapy. His own use of the conception of acceptance is susceptible to precisely the dangers which the psychotherapeutic tendencies he criticizes seek to counter. See especially the sermon 'You Are Accepted' in *The Shaking of the Foundations* (New York: Charles Scribner's Sons, 1953), pp. 153–163. In focusing on acceptance – '*Simply accept the fact that you are accepted!*' (p. 162) – Tillich selects a concept which is utterly static. While assurance of acceptance, or better of love, is central to the process of healing, it is not an acceptance or love which is value-free. Tillich does, to be sure, want to speak of the power of grace in the lives of those who accept this acceptance. But in focusing on a category which

CHRIST, THE CHRISTIAN, AND THE KINGDOM

Because it attempts to encompass numerous variations, the foregoing discussion of the effect which images of Christ have on the religious consciousness is highly formal in its analysis. The dialectic between judgment and grace provides a religious impetus for change because it consists in a contrast of at least partially negative actuality with the possibility of the unambiguously positive. To advance beyond merely formal analysis, it is necessary to specify further the conceptions or images of the negative and the positive – of sin and salvation – which are being affirmed. In the foregoing discussion the generalized contrast between judgment, confession, and bondage on the one hand and healing or grace, forgiveness, and liberation on the other, is an attempt to epitomize the most influential Christian traditions of interpretation of this movement from negative to positive. To elaborate any detailed classification of the full diversity of perceptions about the nature of the old and the new man is, however, a major undertaking in its own right. In the following pages I therefore confine myself to sketching what seems to me to be the most promising line of interpretation. At the same time, I address the Realist concern to avoid reducing the Atonement to psychological and ethical changes in particular individuals.

The Synoptic portrayal of Jesus' preaching indicates the positive valence of at least that understanding of the movement from sin to salvation; for central to the good news is the imminence of the kingdom or rule of God to which men are called to commit themselves. Both the life and the teachings which the Synoptics recount are, moreover, metaphorical or parabolic

---

purports to prescind from all evaluation, Tillich is in danger of losing the tension between negative and positive characteristic of Christian soteriology. What is perhaps the most influential collection of tracts of a moralistic psychotherapy, Hobart O. Mowrer's *The Crisis in Psychiatry and Religion* (Princeton: D. Van Nostrand, 1961), provides a(n) (over-) corrective here. In criticizing the tendency of some Freudians to reduce guilt to guilt feelings, Mowrer rightly insists on the unavoidability of value questions. Unfortunately his very liberal attribution of 'evil' and 'perversity' and his eagerness to expose the '*real* misdeed' underlying guilt feelings associated with a trivial act obscure his own theoretical recognition that any such exploration of guilt can occur only in a context which includes 'some new source of strength' enabling the acknowledgement of 'worthelessness' or 'sins' (p. 55). The result is that his writing may serve to support practices which are judgmental in a pejorative sense – namely those which condemn when love is what is required.

intimations of the character of life under that rule of God. However else
it is to be specified, this living in the kingdom requires a radical subordination of all provincial loyalties to an unconditional affirmation of the ultimate sovereignty of him whom Jesus calls Father. The movement of religious transformation – of μετάνοιά or repentance – is, therefore, one of
turning from provincial and finally self-centered preoccupations to a loyalty
which ultimately comprehends the whole of that natural and human order
which the Father loves and which is destined to become the full realization
of the kingdom.

Jesus' life and death dramatize the form and the consequences of utter
commitment to the kingdom. In preaching the good news to the forgotten
and the rejected of his time, the Synoptic Jesus makes the interest of attract-
ing all of life to the rule of God his governing commitment. The result is
his suffering with and for others – a result epitomized in the cross. In contrast
to much theologizing, the fact of this suffering must be taken seriously in
its own right. It is, to be sure, the faith of Christians that the final consequence of suffering with and for others is not defeat, but victory: the kingdom
is indeed imminent and hence the rule of God cannot ultimately be frustrat-
ed. The traditions concerning the resurrection appearances of Christ testify
to this faith. But faith in the ultimate power of the good news which Jesus
announces must not become a facile or premature confidence. The resurrection is after all the sign that what is ultimately victorious is the way of the
cross. It is, therefore, a perversion of the sign itself to allow it to mitigate
the seriousness of continuing evil or to compromise the continuing need
for deliverance from evil through suffering love.

As is argued in its most extreme form by Johannes Weiss and Albert
Schweitzer at the turn of the century, there is in the early church a strong
tradition almost certainly deriving in part from Jesus' own teaching which
sees the coming of God's rule as the imminent ending of the present age.[66]
Whatever one's conclusion as to its form in Jesus' own teaching, consid-

---

66. See Johannes Weiss, *Die Predigt Jesu vom Reiche Gottes* (Göttingen: Vandenhoeck
& Ruprecht, 1900); Albert Schweitzer, *The Quest of the Historical Jesus*, pp. 328–401
(327–401). Also relevant, though far less influential, is Schweitzer's posthumously pub-
lished *The Kingdom of God and Primitive Christianity*, L. A. Garrard, trans. (New York:
Seabury Press, 1968), pp. 68–183 [*Reich Gottes und Christentum* (Tübingen: J. C. B.
Mohr – Paul Siebeck, 1967), pp. 74–204].

erable apocalyptic imagery is in any case evident in the Synoptics, in the Fourth Gospel, in the epistles, and, of course, very dramatically in the book of Revelation. Apocalyptic motifs in the different documents are, to be sure, not simply identical or interchangeable; but despite variations, there is a common vision of the imminent coming of the Son or the Son of Man or the Lord or the Lamb in power and glory to judge the present corrupt age. That variations between the New Testament documents are not insignificant is indicated in differences on the critical question of timing. The Johannine writings in particular reveal a definite pattern of accentuating the tendency already present in the Synoptics to identify apocalyptic imagery with Jesus' ministry.[67] In spite of this movement away from not only a cosmological dualism of heaven and earth but also a temporal dualism of future and present, there is, however, still a radical discontinuity between the two realms, between darkness and light, between false and fallen existence and the new spiritual life and truth. For much of the history of Christian piety that contrast has simply been appropriated to the pattern of heaven *vs.* earth and future *vs.* present more directly expressed in the apocalyptic imagery of the Synoptics or the epistles or the book of Revelation. The result is that all of the apocalyptic themes of the New Testament have served to support those interpretations of Christian faith which construe the kingdom of God or the final realization of the divine purpose for creation as fundamentally discontinuous with natural and cultural life in its historical development.

The various Transactional interpretations of the significance of Christ are, of course, illustrations of this pattern. The connection is most transparent in those instances when the fruits of his work are identified centrally with the promise of heavenly fulfillment for the faithful. But even when they are not overtly 'otherworldly' in orientation, Transactional approaches to the significance of Christ still in effect isolate the efficacy of his work from the course of ordinary historical events. That is self-consciously the case

---

67. For an interpretation of the Johannine writings as emphasizing the present reality of the 'eschatological occurrence', see Rudolf Bultmann, *Theology of the New Testament*, vol. 2, K. Grobel, trans. (New York: Charles Scribner's Sons, 1955), esp. pp. 9–10, 17–21, 25–26, 31–32, 33–40, 49, 56–59, 66–69, 78–92 [*Theologie des Neuen Testaments* (Tübingen: J. C. B. Mohr–Paul Siebeck, 1953), pp. 356, 364–367, 372, 378–379, 379–386, 396, 402–406, 413–416, 424–439].

in Nominalist-Transactional interpretations like that of Kant or Kierkegaard or Bultmann, since the ethical or religious encounter or transformation is programmatically distinguished from the causal nexus of the spatial-
temporal continuum. Realist-Transactional interpretations provide a provisional contrast in so far as they affirm that the work of Christ is effected in
a particular historical event; but in maintaining that this transaction is universally efficacious in principle independent of its influence as historically
mediated, they too assert a fundamental discontinuity between the divine
work of reconciliation and historical development.

One of the merits of Hegel's thought from a theological perspective is
that he rejects every form of cosmological dualism or otherworldliness
while nonetheless attempting systematically to reformulate the central
affirmations of the Christian faith. That reformulation is Processive: it
construes Christian symbols as providing a comprehensive interpretation
of the whole scope of historical development. Instead of attempting to
provide a secure shelter for religious truth outside of space and time,
Hegel argues that every truth can refer only to some dimension of an
ultimately unified spiritual process. This Hegelian perspective is remarkably
congenial to twentieth-century man's conception of himself and his world,
especially once the contrast between 'material' and 'spiritual' is recognized
as a useful distinction only on a macroscopic scale. The Darwinian revolution in the life sciences and the twentieth-century transformation of
Newtonian mechanics into sub-atomic physics illustrate the pervasive
preoccupation with development and process in the natural sciences. And
the very existence of the social sciences testifies to the interest particularly
from the Enlightenment on to understand man as interacting with his
personal, social, and cultural environments. As Hegel himself consistently
maintains, his position is, however, also significantly parallel to traditional
Christian commitments.

The parallels may be illustrated in comparing Hegel's conception of
spirit with the Synoptic portrayal of Jesus' preaching of the kingdom.
Neither Hegel's spirit nor the Synoptic kingdom is simply a present fact;
yet both impinge on the present and connect the present to its coming fulfillment. Hegel's repudiation of the Enlightenment's absolutizing of the
individual is, moreover, analogous to the Gospels' condemnation of self-
righteousness and pride. Finally, for both the Synoptic tradition and for

Hegel, the result of religious transformation is the acknowledgement that one's living is a participation in the rule of God or the infinite process of spirit. The movement of the religious life is, then, in both cases from an affirmation of the self as an autonomous and independently valuable existent to a recognition of its integral relation to a comprehensive spiritual order to which is owed loyalty and faithfulness and from which is derived not only the sustenance and structure of life but also the significance or value that accrues from participation in the realization of the goals or ends of spirit or God.

There is no disputing the contention that Hegel's systematic rejection of any form of metaphysical dualism does represent a significant departure from the prevailing worldview of both the New Testament documents and the history of Christian thought. That the Biblical writers and the Christian tradition see the kingdom of God not only as the ultimate goal of the Christian life but also as intimately related to the response which is made to Jesus' ministry is, however, an indication of a definite tendency to qualify any complete dualism. This tendency is, of course, also expressed in the doctrines of the incarnation of God in the world and of the church as the continuation of that incarnation. What Hegel does is to pursue to one possible logical extreme the implications of the tendency to qualify dualism inherent in the Christological dogma. The result is his conclusion that there is no final destiny for man or the cosmos which is discontinuous with the present. Christian theologians who propound a consistently Processive interpretation of the significance of Christ at least implicitly agree with this conclusion. The kingdom or rule of God not only impinges on the present life of man; it is also the destiny of that definite historical existence. There are, to be sure, potentially serious deficiencies in Hegel's system when it is viewed from a theological and ethical perspective. But nothing is gained in formulating those issues so that disagreement with Hegel implies a commitment to some sphere or realm of spiritual existence in principle discontinuous with man's natural and cultural life.

The question of the continuing power of evil is a central example of the need to reject theologically and ethically unacceptable inferences which may be drawn from Hegel's thought. To avoid those implications through the reaffirmation of any form of metaphysical dualism is, however, to exchange a morally unacceptable reading of Hegel for an intellectually untenable position. In criticizing the spurious infinite of Kant and Fichte and in speaking of the capacity of thought to overcome time, Hegel does provide formulations of his position which may be interpreted as simply legitimating whatever is the prevailing state of affairs. But the structure of his thought nonetheless does not require any such uncritical legitimation of the *status quo*. To agree with Hegel in repudiating the so-called spurious infinite need entail only the affirmation that the kingdom is in some measure a present reality as well as a future goal – that man's obedience to the rule of God is continuous with the ultimate establishment of the universal divine sovereignty. This affirmation imbues man's present existence with significance in its own right rather than making whatever value it has dependent on and derivative from the attainment of a future goal. It does not, however, require the elimination of tension or contrast between the present and not yet fully actualized ideals. Similarly, Hegel's position that thought transcends or annuls or overcomes time need not entail the legitimation of any present state of affairs. In so far as absolute knowledge is construed as an ideal and universals are recognized to be human constructions elaborated in order to interpret man's natural and cultural environments, thought is seen to be in reciprocal relation to the processes it grasps or comprehends. Abstracted from experience, universals do in turn have a normative status; and in that sense they transcend or overcome temporal particularity. But precisely this normative status renders possible a critical judgment of every present state of affairs falling short of the ideal which human imagination and reason construct.[68]

It is, then, possible to concur with Hegel in rejecting every form of metaphysical dualism without collapsing the critical tension between present actuality and the fulfilled future which is the realized kingdom or rule of God. In so far as that contrast is the underlying religious import of traditional apocalypticism or other-worldliness, the intention of that imagery is preserved. But because the contrast is between different historical states of affairs rather than between different metaphysical orders, the movement

68. For an incisive and influential statement of the critical power of Hegel's thought, see Herbert Marcuse, *Reason and Revolution: Hegel and the Rise of Social Theory* (Boston: Beacon Press, 1966), especially the introduction, pp. 1–29. See also Marcuse, *One Dimensional Man: Studies in the Ideology of Advanced Industrial Society* (Boston: Beacon Press, 1964), esp. pp. 119–120, 123–124, 133–134, 140–143.

or transformation from the negative to the positive is the summation of temporal development, not a contradiction or repudiation of it. Hence the Atonement is that comprehensive process through which the kingdom of God is actualized. As a theological category, the Atonement or the process of reconciliation thus encompasses the whole of traditional systematic theology from the doctrinal divisions of creation and providence through redemption to eschatology.

The focus is, to be sure, on redemption. Specifically, such Processive interpretations of the Atonement in any case attend to the influence which Jesus is portrayed as having on his hearers and which the Christ of faith continues to exercise on believers. But attention exclusively to this transformation in individuals is a limiting case. It is exemplified in those highly individualistic forms of pietism which combine concern for sanctification in this life with an almost total disinterest in the social and cultural implications and presuppositions of that individual sanctification. More characteristic of especially the relatively more traditional interpretations of the actualization of redemption is a combination of this attention to change effected in individuals with a complementary attempt to elucidate the social forms and the historical continuity which are at least implicitly presupposed. Conceptions of the church and of the Holy Spirit are central to articulating such additional concerns.

This study is not, of course, the appropriate context for elaborating all the implications which a Processive approach to the Atonement has for systematic theological reflection. It may, however, be instructive to review the extent to which the foregoing analysis does adumbrate the multiple issues which a Processive approach to the doctrinal division of redemption confronts. In surveying the various images of Christ elaborated in the New Testament in particular and then in exploring their influence on the religious consciousness, I attempt to elucidate the process through which change is effected in individuals. That the church as a particular institution is indispensable for the historical mediation of this change in individuals is assumed throughout my consideration of its images, its theological reflection, and its ritual patterns. Finally, my summary comparison of Hegel's concept of spirit and the Biblical image of the kingdom of God indicates my understanding of the Holy Spirit as yet another traditional designation for that comprehensive spiritual order to which man gives his ultimate allegiance when he turns from a preoccupation with self-centered concerns and attempts instead to integrate his personal aims and interests into the more inclusive goals of the multiple communities to which he belongs as a not uncritical member.

The connections between an approach to the Atonement like the one I am commending and the doctrinal divisions of creation, providence, and eschatology are, not surprisingly, less immediately evident than are the connections to the doctrinal concerns addressed under the rubric of redemption. A consistently Processive approach to those further doctrinal commitments may, however, interpret them as implying or affirming that the process of Atonement or reconciliation both antecedes the ministry of Jesus and ultimately transcends the church.

That the goal actualized through the process of Atonement – the rule or kingdom of God – is finally more comprehensive than the life of the church is a view acceptable to even the most traditional theology, especially if 'church' is taken to refer to the empirical institution rather than to the total body of the faithful. But this affirmation becomes more problematical if the kingdom or rule of God is construed as the destiny of historical existence and therefore as finally also an empirical state of affairs. As Hegel points out in a variety of contexts, the affirmation that the kingdom of God is more comprehensive than the church then means specifically that the goal of reconciliation is the transformation of the whole of social and cultural life – which he identifies as the state – and not simply either the perfection of the church or the final ascendency of the church. In Hegel's thought this subordination of the church to the state not infrequently conveys the impression of premature acquiescence. Here again an insistence on the apocalyptic motif of contrast between what is and what ought ultimately to be is necessary. In this view the church not only performs the crucial historical function of mediating the influence of Christ on believers through its scripture and its doctrines and its sacraments; it is in addition called to be self-conscious about its critical or prophetic role in initiating change within its non-ecclesiastical context. Hence the church in so far as it fulfills its double function continues to stand over against the secular order as a critical counter-institution. Since the ideal of the church as a community of love ultimately loyal to the rule of God is also the model for creation as a whole, the church should, however, only be gratified to see its traditional ministry, for example to the poor and the infirm, progressively recognized as a responsibility of the state. The tasks of criticism and further initiation which remain are in any case enormous. Consequently the church should concentrate its limited energies on this role of initiator and critic. For its aim should be to dramatize continued callousness and to broaden the culture's acknowledgement of responsibility for its members and finally for all of life to the end that the ultimate spiritual community or the rule of God may be realized.[69]

To speak of reconciliation or Atonement as a process through which not only the individual self but also finally the whole of human society and culture are transformed is still to confine it to change conceivable on Nominalist premises. It is, in short, possible to conceive of social and cultural development as simply the cumulative product of change in individuals. The doctrines of creation and providence are, however, indications that the universality which Realist interpretations of the Atonement affirm is more integral to Christian faith than the Nominalist approach to the significance of Christ acknowledges. Nominalist interpretations can, to be sure, affirm processes of reconciliation analogous to the effect of Christ on Christians in individuals and communities before the ministry of Jesus or even in cultural traditions more or less divorced from Christendom. But the

69. My summary comments are, of course, a reiteration of a recurrent perspective in Christian theology. One very influential example of a similar approach on the modern American scene is Walter Rauschenbusch's well-known *A Theology for the Social Gospel* (Nashville: Abingdon Press, 1954). I note this book in particular not only because it may serve to epitomize an entire tradition but also because it is in what I consider undeserved bad repute among many theologians and churchmen. A more recent and equally straightforward exposition of this perspective is Wolfhart Pannenberg's *Theology and the Kingdom of God* (Philadelphia: Westminster Press, 1969), especially chapters 2 and 3 on the church and ethics. These essays are popular rather than technically theological; but they are as a result also refreshingly direct. Another very provocative example of recent reflection on this set of issues is Wolf-Dieter Marsch, *Gegenwart Christi in der Gesellschaft: Eine Studie zu Hegel's Dialektik* (München: Chr. Kaiser Verlag, 1965). It is, I think, more than coincidence that both Pannenberg and Marsch are very much influenced by Hegel. Marsch finally qualifies the Hegelian position of continuity between empirical history and ultimate fulfillment (see esp. pp. 265–268). But his analysis of the issues is nonetheless precise and relatively free from theological obfuscation. Any consideration of even only the most recent theological literature on the question of the relationship between the church and the secular order would, of course, also require discussion of the writings of Harvey Cox, Jürgen Moltmann, Gerhard Sauter, and Johannes B. Metz, to mention only the best known of the self-consciously theological studies.

Christian doctrines of creation and providence affirm in addition that this process of Atonement is in some sense ontologically grounded in the very structure and development of the cosmos itself: the kingdom of God is the goal or τέλος of creation. The transformed life of faithfulness and loyalty to the rule of God is, therefore, seen as the expression of a more fundamental nisus or intentionality not only in all of human life but also in the natural environment from which it emerges and on which it depends.

This Realist affirmation that change in human selves and communities is grounded in the physical (φύσις) or ontological order which historical particulars presuppose may find support in a number of prominent scientific hypotheses. Evolutionary theory is of course the most immediately suggestive example of confirmation that social and cultural development is continuous with and integrally related to biological or physical adaptation. But the inter-relation between social and cultural change on the one hand and natural or physical tendencies on the other is more generally supported in the recognition that the distinction between matter and mind or spirit becomes untenable if it is pressed into service as more than a useful shorthand for designating levels of complexity in processes ultimately composed of the same energy impulses. Among the earliest thinkers to appreciate the implications of this dynamic worldview for Christian theology is Jonathan Edwards; as his early essays indicate, even Newtonian physics already suggested to him the possibilities of a thoroughly wholistic and processive theology.[70] As Edwards' thought also illustrates, there are similarities between a wholistic or Realist perspective and not only the Greek fathers but also such prototypically Western thinkers as Augustine and Calvin. What is needed in contemporary theology is, however, a more explicit acknowledgement that the church's mediation of change in individuals and communities participates in, interprets, and in turn shapes an ultimately universal teleological process which Christian thought has no compelling doctrinal grounds for viewing as restricted to one particular tradition.

70. See my 'The "Idealism" of Jonathan Edwards', *Harvard Theological Review*, 62 (1969), 209–226.

GOD AND THE KINGDOM OF GOD

The most promising Western resources available to contemporary theology for conceptualizing that universal teleological process are the philosophies of Hegel and Whitehead. Both philosophers self-consciously attempt to incorporate theological commitments into their systems; yet they nonetheless end in rendering the traditional Christian affirmation of God highly problematical. Though the two formulations of the issue are certainly not interchangeable, the Hegelian version may serve to illustrate the difficulty. The issue is already articulated in the disagreements between the right and left-wing Hegelians. Whereas the former insist on continuing to speak of God as self-conscious apart from the world, the latter insist that the only consistent understanding of Hegel's thought is to repudiate any such transcendent God. Hegel's own writings are not without ambiguous formulations, though his consistent position that infinite spirit knows itself through finite spirit and that God without the world is not God support the left-wing alternative.[71] But whatever Hegel's own position, the question remains as to whether or not God is affirmed as self-conscious independently of those finite centers of consciousness which are in any case integral to the cosmic process.

It may be useful to point out how extremely speculative this issue is. What practical difference results from choosing one or the other alternative? If in either case it is affirmed that there is a teleological order sustaining and structuring the development of the cosmos toward that comprehensive spiritual community traditionally termed the kingdom of God, then how does the additional assertion or denial of a God self-conscious apart from

---

71. For a convenient summary of Hegel's position on this set of issues in particular, see his review of the later right-wing Hegelian Carl Friedrich Göschel's 1829 book entitled *Aphorismen über Nichtwissen und absolutes Wissen im Verhältnis zur christlichen Glaubensbekenntnis* in Hegel, *Berliner Schriften, 1818–1831*, J. Hoffmeister, ed. (Hamburg: Verlag von Felix Meiner, 1956), pp. 295–339. Hegel praises Göschel for trying to reconcile faith and knowledge (pp. 324–329). But he also rejects Göschel's *reductio ad absurdum* that to say God knows himself in man is to equate man with God; all that follows, Hegel maintains instead, is 'that *man is in God*, not that man is God' (p. 311). Hence Hegel reaffirms his position that God knows himself in man. Hegel also insists that God is 'the truth of the world' and that 'only he who apprehends the world apprehends God' (p. 324). He then offers an aphorism of his own: 'It is on the contentless supernatural that rationalism works away' (p. 324).

that process qualify this common position? One answer is that it makes an enormous difference to Christian piety. A rhetorical question of the right-wing Hegelian Georg Andreas Gabler may serve to epitomize this concern: 'For what solace [Trost] is there in one who merely "grounds" the world [ein der Welt bloss "zu Grunde liegender"]?'[72] But unless one frames the alternatives in reference to a God who intervenes in the natural or historical order in answer to particular supplications, it is difficult to see how this argument from piety is very forceful. To deny purpose or teleological development in the cosmos as a whole is, to be sure, to call into question whether or not man can ever be at home in or trust his multiple environments. But on the ultimate trustworthiness of man's most comprehensive ontological context, both alternatives agree. Both responses also concur in seeing ultimate reality or the end toward which the teleological process moves as inclusive of that complexity of organization which in men is termed personality – even though they disagree as to the existence of such personality temporally prior to its emergence in the process of evolution. Finally, both alternatives agree in rejecting those species of atheism which exalt individual men as the ultimate attainment of cosmic process; instead both responses insist on the religiously necessary view that the individual man is integral and finally subordinate to a universal process to which he owes loyalty and faithfulness.

That empirical data are not relevant to adjudicating the question of whether or not there exists a God who is self-conscious apart from the world is not, of course, surprising; for the issue is defined so as to exclude any such data as soon as one focuses on God conceived as independent of the world. Since it is in any case not adjudicable and since there are no compelling practical implications resulting from choosing one or the other response, it is, however, at least questionable that this issue should remain a focus for theological controversy. There are other critical issues which do have definite practical consequences. The question of whether or not the cosmos is a teleological order is a case in point. The answer to this question is, to be sure, far from self-evident. But at least it is patent what sorts of empirical data count as evidence for and against either position.

In traditional theological categories, the question of whether or not there

---

72. *Die Hegelsche Philosophie* (Berlin: Verlag von Alexander Duncker, 1843), p. 214.

exists a God who is self-conscious apart from the world may be formulated as the question of whether or not one can speak of God as independent of the kingdom of God. That the theological tradition has tended to do so is indisputable. But if the kingdom of God is that divine order which governs and sustains the world conceived as teleological process, then the need to speak of God as distinguished from the rule or kingdom of God is at least very questionable. Wolfhart Pannenberg is among the few theologians who states this view explicitly:

Thus it may be asserted that God, as identical with the coming of his imminent Kingdom, is the concrete embodiment of the good.... The key to understanding the inextricable connection between love for God and love for fellowmen is the identity of God's *being* with the coming of his Kingdom.[73]

Pannenberg does, to be sure, also maintain that because of 'the ontological priority of the future', 'what turns out to be true in the future will then be evident as having been true all along'.[74] This position is in effect a conception of eternity as comprehending temporal development – a conception which is of course also expressed in Hegel's system, though his emphasis on the metaphor of presence is more easily subverted to a static understanding than is Pannenberg's focus on the future.[75] From the temporal perspective of finite man, the kingdom or rule of God is, however, in any case in the

73. *Theology and the Kingdom of God*, pp. 111–112. See also 'Der Gott der Hoffnung' in *Grundfragen systematischer Theologie: Gesammelte Aufsätze* (Göttingen: Vandenhoeck & Ruprecht, 1967), p. 391. This essay is reprinted from *Ernst Bloch zu ehren*, S. Unseld, ed. Frankfurt/Main: Suhrkamp Verlag, 1965; the corresponding passage is on p. 215. Richard R. Niebuhr also views the conceptions of God and the kingdom of God as interchangeable, though he has not explicitly argued for that identity in his published writings. And in *Religion in the Making* (Cambridge: Cambridge University Press, 1927), p. 138, Alfred North Whitehead equates 'the kingdom of heaven' with God. Finally, Royce's line of argument throughout *The Problem of Christianity* identifies God and the 'Universal Community' or the 'Beloved Community'. See esp. vol. 1, pp. 405–409 and vol. 2, pp. 361–379, 423–432.
74. *Theology and the Kingdom of God*, pp. 62–63. See also 'Der Gott der Hoffnung' in *Grundfragen systematischer Theologie...*, p. 394; the corresponding passage in *Ernst Bloch zu ehren* is on p. 219.
75. For a concise formulation of Pannenberg's own view of his relation to Hegel on this issue, see 'Was ist Wahrheit?' in his *Grundfragen systematischer Theologie...*, pp. 218–222. Pannenberg focuses in particular on what he considers to be Hegel's loss of any genuinely significant future. See also 'Der Gott der Hoffnung', p. 391; the corresponding passage in *Ernst Bloch zu ehren* is on p. 215.

process of actualization. Only this affirmation allows the ethical seriousness with which Christian theology imbues the task of transforming the created order into that ultimate spiritual community which expresses the kingdom or rule of God. The kingdom does, to be sure, exist as a nisus or a potentiality as soon as the cosmos itself comes into being. There is, moreover, no compelling reason to restrict the kingdom or rule of God to this particular planet or solar system. But in reference to life on earth the kingdom or rule of God and therefore God himself is a yet to be fully attained destiny.

9

Christology and Non-Christian Traditions

In this and the following chapter I explore the mutual implications between the various Christological types and a number of alternative approaches to interpreting the fact of religious pluralism. In the present chapter I attempt to demonstrate the systematic relations between these two sets of issues. My procedure is first to argue for the inadequacy of interpretations of religious pluralism in so far as they reflect the affirmation of one or another form of Transactional Christology. I focus on the very influential thought of the contemporary theologians Karl Rahner and Schubert Ogden in this connection. I then contend that Processive commitments may result in a more adequate formulation of the issues which the fact of religious pluralism raises. I refer to the writings of Ernst Troeltsch in illustrating this contention because I view engagement with his formulation of the issues as an inescapable ingredient in any contemporary attempt to state a systematically Processive approach to the fact of religious pluralism. Finally, after establishing this context for the discussion, the tenth and last chapter elaborates an approach to pluralism consistent with the Christological commitments outlined in the chapter preceding this one. My intention is to develop a position more adequate than the ones which Rahner and Ogden espouse but at the same time also less problematical than that of Troeltsch.

In so far as the connections between the questions of Christology dominating the preceding eight chapters and the fact of religious pluralism are not self-evident, it may be helpful to amplify the reasons indicated in the Introduction for exploring the mutual relations between the two sets of issues. There are at least two such reasons.

The first and most important one is already adumbrated in the foregoing summary of my procedure in this chapter. This reason is simply that the two sets of issues are systematically inter-dependent. To underscore the mutual implications, the question which the existence of other traditions poses for Christian theology may be formulated specifically as how the work or efficacy of Christ is related to those traditions. It is then evident not only that a given Christian theological approach to interpreting the fact of religious pluralism is correlative with definite Christological commitments but also that a theologian's evaluation of other traditions in turn has implications for his understanding of the significance of Christ.

The systematic inter-dependence of Christological commitments and interpretations of the fact of religious pluralism is central to the argument developed in the remainder of this study. In the pages that follow it is, therefore, examined in some detail. In addition to the fact of this systematic inter-dependence there is, however, a second reason for exploring the mutual relations between Christology and the existence of other religious traditions. This second reason is that interpreting the fact of religious pluralism is itself a pressing theological task and as such may serve to illustrate the relative viability of the various Christological positions through an examination of their systematic implications with reference to a specific question confronting contemporary theology. This further reason of course presupposes the inter-dependence of the two sets of issues. Consequently a more detailed and systematic statement of that inter-dependence is the first oder of business.

THE CHRISTOLOGICAL TYPES AND APPROACHES TO RELIGIOUS PLURALISM

To argue that interpreting the fact of religious pluralism is for the Christian theologian an undertaking correlative with his understanding of the significance of Christ is not of course to maintain that the issues raised by the fact of religious pluralism are simply and exclusively Christological. But if one accept the argument advanced throughout this study that Christological commitments may be elaborated into a comprehensive religious worldview, then questions analogous to the epistemological, metaphysical, and ethical issues involved in the fact of religious pluralism are also implied in the various approaches to interpreting the significance of Christ. It is, therefore, feasible to differentiate Christian interpretations of religious pluralism with reference to variables in Christologies.

In so far as the work of Christ is construed as effecting once for all a transformation in mankind as a whole or in the governance of the cosmos or in God himself, that work is as a matter of definition of direct significance for all men regardless of their particular social or cultural contexts. Consequently this Realist-Transactional approach cannot consistently entertain even the possibility of salvation apart from Christ. From this restriction, it does not necessarily follow that all men ignorant of the Christian proclamation about Jesus are without any hope of deliverance. Indeed, for those programmatically Realist and Transactional theories which radically subordinate the question of appropriating the benefits of Christ's work to the fact that the work itself is completed, the more consistent conclusion is that all men are saved whether they know it or not. Even this commitment to universal salvation is, however, illustrative of the characteristic Realist-Transactional response to the fact of religious pluralism: while all men are saved, none of them attains that salvation apart from Christ. In contrast to the limiting case of commitment to universal salvation already effected through Christ's past or eternally completed work, the more typical Realist-Transactional position combines exclusive Christological claims with derivatively exclusive claims in reference to the means through which his work is appropriated. Though universal in principle, that work effects salvation only for those receiving its benefits. The result is an exclusivism of the church or at least of the Christian message over against all other traditions and, of course, a correlative exclusivism of Christians over against adherents of other traditions.

Because the Realist-Transactional position is that of the various interpretations of the significance of Christ traditionally accepted as orthodox, the exclusivist approach to non-Christian traditions which it implies has also been the dominant tendency of official ecclesiastical Christianity. Other approaches have, however, not been lacking. Perhaps the most sharply defined alternative is that which conceives of Christianity as communicating timeless truths in principle independent of the particular tradition in which they arise. The significance of Christ is in this view inseparable from the influence of his teachings or of the truths which he comes to represent in Christian doctrine. Strauss' Christology is of course one highly self-conscious articulation of this position. But the implications for understanding the fact of religious pluralism are more central in the writing of an Enlightenment thinker like Matthew Tindal; in his *Christianity as Old as the Creation* (1730) he sees Christianity as the republication of a natural religion available to all men at all times and in all places. A similar concern to establish conti-

202 *Christologies and Cultures*

nuities with other traditions is evident in the Logos Christologies of the second-century Apologists and of Clement of Alexandria. For them focusing on Christ as the incarnate Logos who teaches mankind also allows the elaboration of parallels to other traditions – in this case that of Greek philosophy in particular.

Despite its emphasis on universally valid truths, this tendency to focus on Christ as teacher and as example is an interpretation on Nominalist premises because it locates the significance of his work in the influence he has on individual believers. A central concern with change in individuals renders exclusivist claims extremely difficult to support because of the need to demonstrate the impossibility of analogous change in other traditions. It is not, therefore, surprising that this approach frequently is combined with a programmatic denial of exclusivism. That denial is, of course, a rejection of the Realist-Transactional position. This antithesis should not, however, obscure an important parallel between the two perspectives: both are Transactional in the sense of ascribing to historical mediation only an incidental or at least only a secondary significance. The Realist-Transactional type purports to take history seriously while ascribing universal significance to the work of Christ as in principle complete even apart from its temporal appropriation. The Nominalist-Transactional type focuses on truths allegedly available to all men without attending specifically to the question of the historical mediation of those teachings or conceptions. Hence both the radical exclusivism of the Realist-Transactional position and the programmatic Nominalist-Transactional acceptance of the value in other traditions fail to do justice to the thoroughly historical character of man's existence.

The various Processive interpretations offer a contrast to both forms of Transactional perspective in their concern with temporal development and historical mediation. The recognition that religious systems are in constant interaction with the cultural and even the natural context in which they are affirmed no doubt complicates any theological appraisal of the fact of religious pluralism. Combined with detailed scholarship on the diverse and even contradictory patterns in religious phenomena, it may result in an uncritical acceptance of the different traditions and subtraditions as internally coherent even if in some cases mutually exclusive perspectives. That form of final relativism is one possible correlate of a position which is both Processive and Nominalist. Indeed, it is the only consistent view for an uncompromising Nominalism. Even those Processive interpretations which focus exclusively on change in individuals and their communities may, however, formulate criteria for differentiating relative value in different traditions. Schleiermacher and Ritschl are influential examples of this tendency. In contrast, the typically Realist-Processive position not only makes normative judgments but also attempts to see the various traditions as the more or less adequate expression of a single ultimately unified development. Those Logos Christologies which share the emphasis of Irenaeus on an ever more comprehensive realization of spirit and theologies of evolution like that of Teilhard which view not only all religious traditions but also all of life as finally integral to a single process exemplify this position.

My constructive proposal for interpreting the significance of Christ indicates that I view the Processive approach to interpreting Christian faith as the most promising theological program because it allows the combining of Realist and Nominalist commitments. As the following chapter argues in detail, the greater adequacy which I claim for the Processive position extends to the question of appraising the fact of religious pluralism. This greater adequacy may be summarized succinctly: in contrast to theological interpretations of religious pluralism which presuppose Transactional Christologies, the various Processive approaches are in principle committed to grounding their evaluation on concrete data about the different traditions in their respective historical contexts. That commitment to focusing on the historical particularity of religious traditions does in fact provide a contrast to Transactional interpretations follows from the very definition of the category 'Transactional' as abstracting the change which Christ effects from dependence on mediation through time. But it may still be useful to focus specifically on examples of the line of argument through which both Realist-Transactional and Nominalist-Transactional Christologies programmatically exclude any requirement for detailed consideration of the various religious traditions in their appraisal of the fact of religious pluralism.

Examination of the positions of the contemporary theologians Karl Rahner and Schubert Ogden may serve to epitomize the inadequacies of the Transactional approach with particular force because each of them combines a Transactional Christology with considerable emphasis on development in other dimensions of his thought. Though Rahner's interpretation of the work of Christ is Realist-Transactional, he also makes prominent use of evolutionary conceptuality. Similarly, Ogden appropriates the resource of process philosophy while also arguing for a Nominalist-Transactional interpretation of the significance of Christ and correlatively of religious pluralism. The result is that their respective approaches to non-Christian traditions along with the Christologies which those approaches presuppose not only are inadequate in their own right but also stand in tension with other tendencies in each of their theologies. Their positions are, in short, striking illustrations of the inadequacy of Transactional approaches to the fact of religious pluralism because the deficiencies in their interpretations derive directly from Christological commitments even though other tendencies in their thinking would counsel a more direct and explicit consideration of historical particularity and hence a more adequate appraisal of the various traditions. If Rahner and Ogden as individuals were peripheral figures on the contemporary theological scene or if the positions which they exemplify were simply isolated idiosyncrasies, a summary dismissing of their views as utterly abstract and lacking reference to concrete data would suffice. But because Rahner and Ogden exert considerable influence with their respective liberal Roman Catholic and liberal Protestant constituencies and because their positions do illustrate dominant lines of interpretation in the past and into the present, it is necessary to examine them in some detail in order both to indicate the grounds for their widespread appeal and to underscore their deficiencies.

KARL RAHNER'S 'ANONYMOUS CHRISTIANITY'

Karl Rahner's conception of anonymous Christianity is an influential and representative formulation of the attempt of liberal Roman Catholic theologians to affirm traditional exlusivism in a form as inoffensive as possible to those outside the institutional church. As Rahner sees it, the Roman Catholic finds himself committed to two propositions which require some such conception to avoid contradicting each other. On the one hand, the Catholic is required to affirm that 'in order to attain salvation man must believe in God – and not only in God: in Christ'.[1] Or, to take the ecclesiological correlate of this Christocentrism, he must be willing to subscribe to the position that 'outside the church there is no salvation'.[2] On the other hand, 'it is part of the Catholic statement of Faith that the supernatural saving purpose of God extends to all men in all ages and places in history'.[3] Rahner summarizes the dilemma:

The only question here is how the Catholic, who believes the Church to be the universal path to salvation for everyone and who at the same time holds fast both in theory *and* in his practical hope to the certainty of God's *universal* salvific will, can come to terms with ... the existence of the pluralism of worldviews, a pluralism which cannot be overcome in the forseeable future.[4]

He also indicates his intention to affirm both exclusivism and universalism:

If, on the one hand, we conceive salvation as something specifically *Christian*, if there is no salvation apart from Christ ...; and if, on the other hand, God has

1. 'Die anonymen Christen' in *Schriften zur Theologie* (Einsiedeln: Benziger Verlag, 1954–1970), vol. 6, p. 545. Volumes 6–9 have not yet been published in the English translation. Volumes 1–5 have been issued as *Theological Investigations*, C. Ernst, B. Kruger, K. Kruger, and K. Smyth, trans. (Baltimore: Helicon Press, 1961–1967). Subsequent references to this multiple volume collection of Rahner's writings indicate only the title of the specific essay and then the volume and page numbers in the series. The volume numbers in the English and German are the same. For similar statements that the necessity of Christ for salvation is one of the dogmatic assumptions with which the Christian approaches the fact of pluralism, see: 'Christianity and the Non-Christian Religions', vol. 5, pp. 118–121 [139–143]; '"Ich Glaube an Jesus Christus",' vol. 8, p. 216; 'Der eine Mittler und die Vielfalt der Vermittlungen', vol. 8, pp. 232, 235; 'Kirche, Kirchen, und Religionen', vol. 8, pp. 355–356, 362, 371–372.
2. 'Dogmatic Notes on "Ecclesiological Piety",' vol. 5, p. 353 [397]. For similarly exclusivist ecclesiological formulations, see: 'Christianity and the Non-Christian Religions', vol. 5, p. 132 [155]; 'Die anonymen Christen', vol. 6, pp. 545–546; 'Kirche, Kirchen, und Religionen', vol. 8, pp. 355–356, 365. Also relevant is the full discussion in 'Membership of the Church according to the Teaching of Pius XII's Encyclical *Mystici Corporis Christi*', vol. 2, pp. 1–88 [7–94].
3. 'History of the World and Salvation History', vol. 5, p. 103 [121]. See also: 'Thoughts on the Possibility of Belief Today', vol. 5, p. 11 [19–20]; 'Christianity and the Non-Christian Religions', vol. 5, p. 122 [144]; 'Die anonymen Christen', vol. 6, p. 546; 'Der eine Mittler und die Vielfalt der Vermittlungen', vol. 8, p. 230; 'Kirche, Kirchen, und Religionen', vol. 8, pp. 357–359; 'Theologische Überlegungen zu Säkularisation und Atheismus', vol. 9, p. 187.
4. 'Dogmatic Notes on "Ecclesiological Piety"', vol. 5, p. 356 [400].

really, truly and seriously intended this salvation for all men – then these two aspects cannot be reconciled in any other way then [*sic*] by stating that every human being is really and truly exposed to the influence of divine supernatural grace.[5]

As his posing of the theological problem suggests, Rahner's proposed solution entails a sufficiently comprehensive interpretation of the conceptions 'church' and 'grace' to allow universal reference for salvation in Christ.

Rahner's approach to the ecclesiological issue is indicated in his detailed analysis of the 1943 papal encyclical *Mystici Corpus Christi*. One of the three questions on which he focuses in that essay is, 'What does it say about the possibility of union with Christ through grace for those who... are not members of the Church in the sense in which the encyclical defines membership?'[6] Interpreting the encyclical to employ 'Church' only in the sense of an established organization, Rahner argues that its rigid requirement for membership (baptism, profession of true faith, continued attachment to the corporate institution) need not be construed as applying to every ecclesiological conception:

The Church, as something visible and as sign of the union with God by grace, must itself be composed of a further twofold reality, viz. Church as an established juridical organization in the sacred order and 'Church as humanity consecrated by the Incarnation'.[7]

Rahner insists that this second conception of the church is 'no mere abstract idea' but rather a definite historical reality resulting from the Incarnation:

By the fact that God the Son became man of the Virgin Mary, a member of this one human race, the Word of God became himself a member of this one Adamite humanity and, conversely, the one human race became thereby fundamentally and radically called to share the life of God supernaturally. This calling to share supernaturally in the life of the triune God is fundamentally already given as a real fact in the world (and not merely as God's 'intention' and 'law'), by the

5. 'Christianity and the Non-Christian Religions', vol. 5, p. 123 [145].
6. 'Membership of the Church', vol. 2, p. 3 [9]. The entire essay is relevant, since this second of Rahner's three questions presupposes the first question, namely, 'What does the Encyclical say about the conditions for membership of the Church?' But Rahner explicitly treats the second question on pp. 34–69 [40–75] and 76–88 [83–94].
7. 'Membership of the Church. . .', vol. 2, p. 86 [93].

simple fact of the Incarnation of the Word. . . . Because it is a reality accomplished by the fact that the Word of God became *flesh*, it is a reality which belongs to the historical and visible dimension and a reality which, as a factual determination of the human race as a whole, is also a real ontological determination of the nature of each human being.[8]

Rahner's conception of 'the people of God' or 'humanity consecrated by the Incarnation' is, then, in effect a universalizing of the conception of the church so as to include all men. In his thought, the conception of grace is similarly universalized. Especially after the condemnation of the so-called *nouvelle théologie* in the encyclical *Humani Generis*, Rahner is, to be sure, careful to formulate his position so as to avoid implying that ordination toward grace is both fully natural and unconditional. Instead he distinguishes between man's 'essential quiddity' or his 'pure nature' and his 'existential' or 'concrete quiddity'. Only the latter is endowed with the 'supernatural existential' which determines man as destined for grace or salvation. But he also readily admits that the concept of 'pure nature' is a limiting concept (*Restbegriff*) or 'an essentially formal doctrine' which 'is not even necessary' for normal discourse in as much as the supernatural existential is 'always' present in 'man as he really is'.[9] The result is that all men are viewed as in fact ordained toward grace – a position which reiterates or provides an alternative formulation of the assertion that they belong to the people of God. Although Rahner typically focuses his reflection about Christology on the fact of the Incarnation itself, he also in several

8. 'Membership of the Church. . .', vol. 2, p. 81 [87–88]. The insistence that this 'humanity consecrated in the Incarnation' or 'people of God' is no mere abstract idea is on p. 83 [89]. The essay 'Christology Within an Evolutionary View of the World' has a similar focus on the fact of the Incarnation itself. Rahner suggests that the achievement of the Hypostatic Union may be conceptualized as a decisive advance in the evolutionary process. See vol. 5, esp. pp. 160–161, 176–184 [186–187, 203–212]. For a more systematic theological analysis of the significance of the Incarnation, see 'On the Theology of the Incarnation', vol. 4, pp. 105–120 [137–155].

9. See 'Concerning the Relationship between Nature and Grace', vol. 1, esp. pp. 311–317 [338–345]; 'The Dignity and Freedom of Man', vol. 2, pp. 240, 243 [252–253, 256]; 'Nature and Grace', vol. 4, pp. 181–187 [229–235]; 'Die anonymen Christen', vol. 6, pp. 549–550; 'Atheismus und Implizites Christentum', vol. 8, p. 188; 'Kirche, Kirchen, und Religionen', vol. 8, pp. 359–360. See also Rahner's entry on the supernatural existential in J. Höfer and K. Rahner, eds., *Lexikon für Theologie und Kirche*, (Freiburg: Herder, 1957–1965), vol. 3, p. 1301.

instances correlates the supernatural existential with the death of Christ in particular:

> Prior to any subjective appropriation of salvation, man is inwardly determined by a supernatural existential, which consists of the fact that Christ in his death 'justified' sinful man before the all-holy God.... This ... can be simply called the supernatural existential of being (objectively) redeemed or of being (objectively) justified.[10]

But whether he refers specifically to Christ's death or more generally to the Incarnation, the affirmation that the supernatural existential informs the life of every man agrees with the inclusion of all men in the people of God in expressing the conviction that the work of Christ effected a transformation in the situation of mankind as a whole.

Despite his explicit references to the life and death of Christ and despite his not infrequent use of evolutionary categories to speak of a decisive advance achieved in the Incarnation, Rahner nonetheless insists on an uncompromising universalism which encompasses even those living before the first century. That his essay on justification is a symphatetic treatment of Hans Küng's delineation of parallels between Barth's doctrine of reconciliation and Roman Catholic views is one indication of this subordination of the entire created order to the Incarnation. But Rahner is also explicit in at least tentatively aligning himself with this Scotist tradition: 'The *possibility* of the Creation depends on the possibility of the Incarnation'.[11] He

10. 'Controversial Theology on Justification', vol. 4, p. 200 [250]. See also the entry for the supernatural existential in the *Lexikon für Theologie und Kirche*, vol. 3, p. 1301; in that entry Rahner identifies the supernatural existential with '"objective justification" as distinguished from its subjective appropriation through sanctification'. The same equation is made in 'Atheismus und Implizites Christentum', vol. 8, p. 188. In his essay *On the Theology of Death*, C. H. Henkey, trans. (New York: Herder and Herder, 1961) [*Zur Theologie des Todes* (Freiburg: Herder, 1958), pp. 58–61], Rahner also correlates the creation of new possibilities with Christ's death: 'Possibilities of a real ontological nature were opened up for the personal action of all other men which would not have existed without the death of our Lord' (pp. 65–66 [60]). Rahner relates his remarks about the crucifixion to his more characteristic focus on the Incarnation as such through the contention 'that it is in death, and only in death, that man enters into an open unrestricted relationship to the cosmos as a whole' (p. 63 [58]).

11. 'Nature and Grace', vol. 4, pp. 176–177 [221–223]. See also 'Christology within an Evolutionary View of the World', vol. 5, pp. 184–187 [213–216].

repeatedly relates this position specifically to the question of other religious traditions:

In so far as every movement toward a *telos* is always carried by the goal or high-point of the movement, the whole universal *and* explicit-official salvation and reve-lation history is carried by Jesus Christ, even already where that history does not yet in its explicit thought and institutions know anything of Jesus Christ.[12]

'Grace', 'faith', 'spirit', 'justification' were also effective before Christ and became evident in the whole length and breadth of history, even where the explicit preach-ing of the Gospel was not present.[13]

Rahner's position is, then, that because of the Incarnation all men are or-dained toward grace and as such are members of the church in the sense of the people of God. He does not, however, maintain that all men are anony-mous Christians:

One should not go so far as to declare everyone an 'anonymous Christian' whether or not he accepts grace.[14]

That this grace is not explicitly accepted and that the corresponding faith is judged to be not fully or even adequately articulated is, of course, the defining characteristic of anonymous or implicit Christianity. Yet acceptance and rejection of grace can in Rahner's view nonetheless be distinguished. This contention follows from his understanding of the Incarnation:

The Incarnation of God is therefore the unique, *supreme*, case of the total actuali-zation of human reality, which consists of the fact that man *is* in so far as he gives himself up.... The *potentia oboedientialis* ... for the hypostatic union ... is objectively identical with the essence of man.[15]

12. 'Kirche, Kirchen, und Religionen', vol. 8, p. 362. See aslo p. 360: 'The "supernatural existential" has its history throughout the length and breadth of the historical life of man'.
13. 'Der eine Mittler und die Vielfalt der Vermittlungen', vol. 8, p. 230. See also the entire discussion of his 'second thesis' in 'Christianity and the Non-Christian Religions', vol. 5, pp. 121–131 [143–154].
14. 'Die anonymen Christen', vol. 6, p. 550. See also 'Atheismus und implizites Chris-tentum', vol. 8, p. 188 and 'Kirche, Kirchen, und Religionen', vol. 8, p. 359.
15. 'On the Theology of the Incarnation', vol. 4, p. 110 [142]. The most direct corre-lation of this theological anthropology with the possibility of anonymous Christianity is in 'Die anonymen Christen', vol. 6, pp. 548–550. See also 'Current Problems in Chris-tology', vol. 1, pp. 183–184 [204–205].

Because the Incarnation is itself the consummate actualization of human existence, man is said to affirm God and his grace in Christ wherever he fully accepts himself and his fellows:

Anyone who accepts his own humanity in full – and how immeasurably hard that is, how doubtful whether we really do it! – has accepted the Son of Man, because God has accepted man in him. When we read in Scripture that he who loves his neighbours has fulfilled the law, this is the ultimate truth, because God himself has become this neighbour.[16]

This confidence that in fully affirming himself man implicitly affirms the reality of God underlies Rahner's exuberant embrace of 'everything in the way of truth and love which exists or could exist anywhere in the world'.[17] Because the very possibility of man's fully affirming himself and thereby opening himself to God implies his ordination to salvation which in turn presupposes the Incarnation, the man who in fully accepting himself implicitly accepts grace is, moreover, not only an anonymous theist but also an anonymous Christian.[18]

CRITIQUE OF THE REALIST-TRANSACTIONAL DIMENSION OF RAHNER'S POSITION

There are significant emphases in Rahner's thought toward a Processive understanding of traditional Christian affirmations. This tendency is perhaps most evident in the essay 'Christology within an Evolutionary View of the

16. 'On the Theology of the Incarnation', vol. 4, p. 119 [154]. Consistent with this position is Rahner's contention that actions and attitudes are more reliable indicators of the acceptance of grace than are verbal affirmations. See 'The Christian Among Unbelieving Relations', vol. 3, pp. 356–366 [430–432]; 'What is Heresy?', vol. 5, pp. 475, 479 [534–535, 539].

17. 'Thoughts on the Possibility of Belief Today', vol. 5, p. 9 [18]. Similar summary comments as well as occasional references to more specific virtues abound throughout Rahner's essays. For a striking example of the latter, see 'The Order of Creation within the Order of Redemption' in *The Christian Commitment*, C. Hastings, trans. (New York: Sheed and Ward, 1963), p. 42 [*Sendung und Gnade* (Innsbruck: Tyrolia-Verlag, 1959:, p. 56].

18. 'Christianity and the Non-Christian Religions', vol. 5, p. 132 [155]; 'Die anonymen Christen', vol. 6, pp. 546–547, 550; 'Atheismus und implizites Christentum', vol. 8,p. 208; 'Anonymes Christentum und Missionsauftrag der Kirche', vol. 9, pp. 502, 503.

World'. But it also informs his persective in virtually every other of his essays as well. In view of this attraction to evolutionary and development categories, it is, therefore, particularly noteworthy that his conception of anonymous Christianity presupposes a Realist-Transactional Christology.

Because he is committed to the proposition that God's grace is universally active, Rahner insists that genuine spiritual value is possible at all times and in all places. But because he also believes that all spiritual value is dependent on the Incarnation, he can affirm the universality of grace at least in the first instance only in abstraction from the question of historical mediation. Rahner does, to be sure, acknowledge that religious systems inevitably find expression in concrete historical forms. That recognition is most explicit in the essays 'Christianity and Non-Christian Religions' and 'Church, Churches, and Religions' because of their direct concern with institutionalized religious traditions. But even those passages which affirm the need for historical mediation most emphatically nonetheless construe social institutionalization or reflective articulation as the expression of that membership in the people of God or (more frequently) that supernatural existential which derives from the transhistorically effective work of Christ. In 'Christianity and Non-Christian Religions', for example, Rahner states that even though Christianity is 'the absolute religion', it 'must come in a historical way to men'.[19] He observes, moreover, that 'religion can exist only in a social form'.[20] Yet those statements in no way qualify his grounding of everything of value in all traditions on the efficacy of Christ's work:

Until the moment when the gospel really enters into the historical situation of an individual, a non-Christian religion (even outside the Mosaic religion) does not merely contain elements of a natural knowledge of God, elements, moreover, mixed up with human depravity which is the result of original sin and later aberrations. It contains also supernatural elements arising out of the grace which is given to men as a gratuitous gift on account of Christ.[21]

'Church, Churches, and Religions' makes this double affirmation more systematically in that it distinguishes two dimensions of God's communi-

19. 'Christianity...', vol. 5, p. 119 [140].
20. 'Christianity...', vol. 5, p. 120 [142].
21. 'Christianity...', vol. 5, p. 121 [143].

cation or impartation of himself to his creatures. The first dimension is the supernatural existential which is 'always and everywhere active' as a divinely bestowed 'moment' of man's spiritual existence.[22] This ever-present 'transcendental consciousness' or 'spiritual transcendentality' of man is then in turn realized or expressed in concrete historical life – which is the second dimension of God's self-communication.[23]

The discussion in 'Church, Churches, and Religions' is especially revealing because it indicates the extent to which the commitments informing Rahner's interpretation are anthropological and theological rather than directly Christological. His definition of the absoluteness of Christianity is particularly striking in this connection:

> *Absoluteness* of Christianity indicates in the first instance ... that the whole of humanity's salvation and revelation history, which is co-existent with its spiritual-personal and ethically good history and, in so far as it is so, is carried by that gracious transcendental self-communication of God which attains its highest, irreversible historical appearance and free human acceptance in the God-man Jesus Christ.[24]

Even this passage does continue Rahner's consistent Christocentrism. The immediate context reenforces the commitment to the centrality of Christ in its contention that he is the τέλος who carries or supports the whole of human salvation and revelation history. Yet this formulation

22. 'Kirche, Kirchen, und Religionen', vol. 8, p. 359.
23. 'Kirche...', vol. 8, p. 360. Since pure human nature apart from the supernatural existential is only a hypothetical construct, Rahner's anthropology consistently assumes this transcendental or supernatural 'horizon'. For summary formulations of this anthropological analysis, see: 'Atheismus und Implizites Christentum', vol. 8, p. 209; 'Anonymes Christentum und Missionsauftrag der Kirche', vol. 9, pp. 502–503. Of course, the most extended exposition of Rahner's theological anthropology is *Hearers of the Word*, M. Richards, trans. (New York: Herder and Herder, 1969) [*Hörer des Wortes*, J. B. Metz, ed. (München: Kösel-Verlag, 1963)]. This essay first appeared in 1941. It is, I think, significant that although Rahner describes man as open to God's self-communication, he sees no need for the supernatural existential or an analogous conception at the time of his writing this essay. Because it is an argument from silence it cannot in itself carry much weight; but the absence of any such conception nonetheless may be interpreted as providing indirect support for those who consider (as I do) the supernatural existential superfluous. That *Hearers of the Word* antedates the papal condemnation of the *nouvelle théologie* for compromising the gratuity of grace is not irrelevant in this connection.
24. 'Kirche...', vol. 8, p. 363.

nonetheless indicates the extent to which Rahner sees the significance of Christ in his exemplification of God's gracious giving of himself and in his paradigmatic actualization of man's potential for response.

That Rahner on successive pages speaks not only of God but also of Christ as supporting or carrying the whole of salvation history is, however, not simply the result of an identification of God and Christ. Instead this double emphasis reflects his consistent concern to avoid grounding the universal possibility of salvation exclusively in the divine intention. The ideas of the people of God and of the supernatural existential as the equivalent of objective justification represent his attempts to conceptualize an ontological correlate of that divine intention. A footnote in one of his discussions of the supernatural existential registers this concern concisely:

The decisive argument for the existence of the supernatural existential is that ... even prior to grace man's binding, indissoluble ordination to the supernatural end is a real determination of man himself, and not merely a divine intention, a decree 'in God's will'. To make of this a purely 'juridical', a purely 'moral' entity is nothing but a nominalism which has not taken cognisance of itself.[25]

But even for those who agree with Rahner's concern to conceive of the possibility of salvation as ontologically grounded, the question unavoidably arises as to whether the affirmation that this grounding is dependent on or derivative from the historical Incarnation is at all plausible apart from a prior commitment to the universal efficacy of that historical work of Christ. Rahner himself is, of course, content to present his reflections as an attempt to reconcile Christian commitments to both exclusivism and universalism. Hence the supernatural existential is conceived so as to avoid the position that nature is unconditionally ordained to grace and, correlatively, to preserve a need for the traditional affirmation of objective justification. Similarly, the conception of the people of God or of humanity consecrated in the Incarnation is commended because it allows assent to the proposition that outside the church there is no salvation. For a theological method which does not begin with unquestionable dogmas or even for reflection committed to the principle of economy, Rahner's case for the conceptions of the people of God and the supernatural existential as he interprets and

25. 'Concerning the Relationship between Nature and Grace', vol. 1, p. 312 [339]. See also pp. 302–303 [328–329].

214 <i>Christologies and Cultures</i>

defends them is, however, less than convincing. Indeed, it is difficult to avoid the conclusion that these conceptions are superfluous except as *ad hoc* attempts to preserve prior affirmations.

To eliminate the supernatural existential and the equation between mankind and the church is to focus unambiguously on the conceptions of God and man – that is, on the conceptions which in any case underlie Rahner's position. The systematic theological consequences of this exercise of the principle of conceptual economy are theocentrism and grace in creation which is not dependent on or derivative from the historical Incarnation of Christ as the God-man. Even with this modification of his position, one can agree with Rahner that 'pure nature' is not unconditionally ordained toward grace. But since 'pure nature' is in any case a limiting concept, there is also agreement that all men are in fact ordained toward God's giving of himself. The disagreement is only as to whether that ordination results from the grace of the Incarnation or from the divine grace active in the creative process as such. Similarly, there may be agreement that the universal possibility of salvation is ontologically grounded. Disagreement arises only over whether that grounding derives from the historical work of Christ or from the divine intention as it is expressed in the ongoing process of creation.

If this line of modification of Rahner's position is accepted, then the focus of any consideration of religious pluralism is unambiguously on the historical traditions which purport to mediate spiritual value. For the Christian perspective the possibility of universal salvation is assured in so far as God is believed to be gracious not only in intention but also in actuality and man is understood to be ordained toward grace in spite of his sinfulness. The question is, therefore, whether or not this universal possibility is in fact realized historically. The Christian of course affirm that it is realized in the community of those who follow Christ; for that reason Jesus is praised as the mediator of God's grace. Hence for the Christian the question which the fact of religious pluralism raises is whether or not other individuals or other institutions or other convictions – whether, in short, other traditions – in fact similarly mediate the grace which he both experiences and affirms as a universal possibility for all men.

NOMINALIST-TRANSACTIONAL TENDENCIES IN SCHUBERT OGDEN'S APPROACH TO PLURALISM

Schubert Ogden agrees with Karl Rahner in attempting to interpret traditional Christian affirmations as consistent with 'an evolutionary view of the world'. For Ogden the specific form of that attempt is an interest in appropriating the conceptuality of process philosophy for constructive theological purposes; *The Reality of God and Other Essays* (1966) testifies to this project. But Ogden and Rahner also share definite Transactional tendencies in their respective Christologies. While Rahner's position seeks to incorporate the formulations of orthodoxy, Ogden self-consciously aligns himself with the Enlightenment and nineteenth-century liberal critiques of that orthodoxy. The result is a Nominalist-Transactional approach which parallels the Realist-Transactional dimension of Rahner's Christology in its contrast with an otherwise Processive perspective.

As is characteristic of the thought of his predecessors in the tradition of Western religious liberalism, Ogden's interpretation of the significance of Jesus is critical of the absolute claims traditionally advanced in his name. Indeed, the central argument of *Christ Without Myth* is, first, that Christocentric exclusivism as it is expressed in the theology of Rudolf Bultmann is incoherent and, second, that the various attempts to criticize this position while nonetheless maintaining an analogous exclusivism (the program of the 'right' in Ogden's analysis) are untenable. The extent to which the question of exclusivism underlies his study becomes most explicit in Ogden's concluding chapter.[26] But he also relates the question of exclusivist claims directly to the problematic of demythologizing which is the focus of his discussion of Bultmann's thought:

When it is viewed from the standpoint of modern man's picture of himself and his world, his [Bultmann's] claim that authentic historicity is possible only in Jesus Christ must be regarded as just as incredible and irrelevant as the other myths with which it properly belongs.[27]

26. *Christ Without Myth* (New York: Harper & Row, 1961), pp. 133, 143–145, 156–158. The note on p. 133 is particularly striking in that it uses the criterion of non-exclusivism to adjudicate similarities in British and American theology to the 'left' position of Fritz Buri. The result is that he sees significant parallels in the thought of both Reinhold and H. Richard Niebuhr, Paul Tillich, and John Baillie.
27. *Christ Without Myth*, p. 120.

In summarizing this section of *Christ Without Myth* in the essay 'What Sense Does It Make to Say, "God Acts in History"?' Ogden is more specific:

By saying that God acts to redeem mankind *only* in the history of Jesus Christ, he [Bultmann] subjects God's action as the Redeemer to the objectifying categories of space and time and thus mythologizes it.[28]

In Ogden's view exclusivist claims are, then, unavoidably mythological and consequently untenable in a consistently demythologized Christology. To appraise the conception of myth which Ogden employs in making this judgment would, of course, be essential in any systematic evaluation of his position. Because that undertaking is a considerable task in its own right, it is, however, fortunate that his position on the question of exclusivism is also formulated without direct reference to the program of demythologizing. Ogden details how Bultmann's Christocentrism leads him to argue that although authentic existence is a 'possibility in principle' for all men, it is in fact realized only through encounter with Christ.[29] In contrast, Ogden insists that authentic existence is a 'possibility in fact' as well as a 'possibility in principle':

Christian existence is always a 'possibility in fact' as well as a 'possibility in principle'. This may also be expressed by saying that the specific possibility of faith in Jesus Christ is one and the same with a general ontological possibility belonging to man simply as such.... This possibility is not man's own inalienable possession, but rather is constantly *being made possible for him* by virtue of his inescapable relation to the ultimate source of his existence. To be human means to stand *coram deo* and, by reason of such standing, to be continually confronted with the gift and demand of authentic human existence.[30]

Even this summary statement of his position indicates the extent to which Ogden's thought cannot accurately be classified as simply Nominalist and

28. *The Reality of God and Other Essays* (New York: Harper & Row, 1966), p. 173.
29. See *Christ Without Myth*, pp. 111–126 for Ogden's summary presentation of Bultmann's position.
30. *Christ Without Myth*, p. 140. For Ogden's exposition and defense of this position, see pp. 146–164. Not surprisingly, Paul's discussion of 'natural' knowledge of God in Romans 1: 18*ff.* is a Biblical text which Ogden cites in support of his view. See esp. pp. 154–155.

Transactional. In addition to the non-Transactional emphases which his commitment to process philosophy represents, there are Realist implications in his references to the ontological grounding of the possibility of authentic existence in God. But on the specific issue of soteriology, Ogden's analysis is nonetheless Nominalist and Transactional in the sense that he conceives of faith or authentic existence as an 'original' human possibility universally available to every individual without attending to the question of how that possibility is mediated to men in their diverse historical contexts. Ogden maintains that 'what faith means by "Christ" ... is not one historical event alongside others, but rather the *eschatological* event, or *eternal* word of God's unconditioned love, which is the ground and end of all historical events whatever'.[31] While he defends the claim of the Christian church to finality, he also contends that its particular word is addressed to man in his every experience:

To be sure, the church stands by the claim that the decisive manifestation of this divine word is none other than the human word of Jesus of Nazareth and thence of its own authentic proclamation. But the point of this claim is not that the Christ is manifest only in Jesus and nowhere else, but that the word addressed to men *everywhere*, in all the events of their lives, is none other than the word spoken in Jesus and in the preaching and sacraments of the church.[32]

The difficulty with this position is, of course, that it is not self-evident how all events communicate this eternal or eschatological word. Indeed, in so far as events cannot communicate at all apart from the system of symbols through which they are interpreted, the claim that all events convey the same word is at the very least premature prior to careful comparative study of 'the various mythologies, philosophies, and religions in which the perennial question of human existence and its equally perennial answer have found expression'.[33]

As is indicated in several contexts including the paragraph from which the foregoing phrase about the variety of worldviews is taken, Ogden is not unaware of this complex of issues. That awareness does not, however,

31. *Christ Without Myth*, p. 156.
32. *Christ Without Myth*, p. 156.
33. *Christ Without Myth*, pp. 156–157.

inform his line of argument as a whole. Both the awareness and the limitations in its influence on Ogden's overall analysis are perhaps most evident in his attempt to reject the suggestion that he sees in Christ only the exemplification of 'timeless truths'. At one point he articulates his disagreement with Bultmann so as to allow that his rejection of Christocentric exclusivism nonetheless recognizes the need for at least some particular form of historical mediation:

> Although we may agree that faith must indeed be an event of *existentiell* decision, rather than the intellection of timeless truths, Bultmann completely fails to show that such a requirement has any necessary connection with what he takes to be the distinctive Christian claim. So far as his argument goes, all that is required is *some* event in which God's grace becomes a concrete occurrence and is received by a decision of faith.[34]

But this apparent suggestion of the necessity for some particular event or complex of events interpreted so as to communicate 'God's grace' is not developed. Instead there is simply the assertion that all events address this word to men.

Ogden differentiates his position from one which interprets the Christian message as 'a body of timeless truths' only in distinguishing between 'knowledge about' and 'knowledge of' – between *existential* and *existentiell* understanding. To use his own contrast, for the Enlightenment conception of Jesus as mankind's teacher, Ogden substitutes humanity's preacher. But in both cases the significance of Jesus is conceived as the 're-presentation of the truth of man's existence'.[35] In his radical emphasis on the responsibility of every individual to actualize the original possibility of human authenticity, Ogden affirms his continuity with the existentialist tradition. His insistence on the model of personal encounter rather than objectivizing knowledge does not, however, result in increased attention to historical mediation or the social and cultural conditioning of every self-understanding. Because his criticism of Bultmann's exclusivism focuses on precisely what particularity there is in that approach, eschatological encounter with the word becomes if anything an even more completely formal possibility.

34. *Christ Without Myth*, p. 123. See also p. 139.
35. *Christ Without Myth*, pp. 162–163. See also p. 123.

Such abstraction is, to be sure, potentially useful. It can illuminate parallels which are not at first obvious. But to realize that potential it is necessary to examine the concrete patterns and expressions in which the formal possibility of authentic existence is institutionalized and interpreted. His references to the church's word and sacraments and his occasional comments about Jesus' ministry implicitly acknowledge this need. So too does his recognition of his own intellectual debt to the philosophical traditions of Heidegger and Hartshorne. At the same time Ogden's programmatic commitment to seeing authentic existence as a factual possibility for all men simply as individual men with its correlative affirmation that any and every event communicates this possibility is, however, an indication of indifference to cultural, social and even personal particularity which in effect pronounces the question of historical mediation superfluous. This latter dimension of his thought is Nominalist and Transactional – and inadequate.

THE ROLE OF HISTORICAL MEDIATION: RETURN TO ERNST TROELTSCH

The contrast between the perspectives of Rahner and of Ogden recapitulates motifs evident throughout the debates between orthodoxy and its critics during the modern period. The contrast is of special interest because it persists despite very considerable commonality in the commitments of the two positions. Most striking in this regard is the shared concern to conceptualize a universally available possibility of salvation. For both Ogden and Rahner this concern is articulated in the context of a more comprehensive commitment to evolutionary or developmental categories. Yet despite this commitment, the contrast between their respective positions remains the familiar one of a truth or a self-understanding present to all men everywhere *vs.* an already accomplished transformation in the situation of mankind as a whole from which the appropriation of salvation is in turn derivative. Consideration of the thought of Ernst Troeltsch may serve to underscore the inadequacies of both alternatives which this formulation of the issue allows while at the same time establishing the context for a more viable approach to interpreting the fact of religious pluralism.

Unlike Ogden and Rahner, Troeltsch focuses unambiguously on the particularity of historical phenomena: 'My eagerness to acquire knowledge was directed toward the historical world from early youth on'.[36] He is not unaware of the potentially revolutionary implications for Christian faith of a thoroughly historicized theological method:

Once it is applied to Biblical scholarship and to church history, historical method is a yeast which transforms everything and finally explodes the whole hitherto existing form of theological methods.[37]

But despite the threat to the credibility of traditional Christian doctrinal formulations, Troeltsch insists there is no alternative to forging a theology which accepts the historical relativity of every religious affirmation.

The implications of Troeltsch's approach to theological reflection are illustrated in his essay on the significance of the historicity of Jesus for Christian faith. At the outset Troeltsch acknowledges that interest in his formulation of the question already excludes two positions. On the one hand, for an ecclesiastical orthodoxy committed to a once for all historical work of redemption, the very raising of the question of the significance of Jesus' historical existence in so far as it is raised as an open question can be perceived only as 'a death notice for the whole of Christianity'.[38] On the other hand, such theologians as Strauss and Biedermann in effect eliminate any significance of the historicity of Jesus independent of the speculative validity of Christianity.[39] Troeltsch considers this speculative position as an unambiguous formulation of what is perhaps the dominant tendency in distinctively modern Christian thought. Hence he adumbrates its antecedents in the piety of seventeenth-century spiritualists like Sebastian Francke and in the mysticism of a Meister Eckhart; and he also refers to the tradition of Schleiermacher, Ritschl, and Herrmann as an example of a mixed genre (*Mischform*) because it attempts to retain definite historical reference for

36. 'Meine Bücher' in *Gesammelte Schriften*, vol. 4, H. Baron, ed. (Tübingen: J. C. B. Mohr – Paul Siebeck, 1925), p. 3.
37. 'Über historische und dogmatische Methode in der Theologie' in *Gesammelte Schriften*, vol. 2 (Tübingen: J. C. B. Mohr – Paul Siebeck, 1913), p. 730. See also 'Geschichte und Metaphysik', *Zeitschrift für Theologie und Kirche* VIII (1898), p. 69 for his discussion of an emerging though still latent 'theology of historicism'.
38. *Die Bedeutung der Geschichtlichkeit Jesus für den Glauben* (Tübingen: J. C. B. Mohr – Paul Siebeck, 1911), p. 5.
39. ...*Geschichtlichkeit Jesus*..., pp. 9–10.

its affirmations about Jesus while nonetheless declining to observe the strictures of critical historical method.[40]

Troeltsch's constructive position is in effect an attempt to reform this Schleiermacher-Ritschl-Herrmann tradition so that it is more consistently historized. He maintains that 'the actual inner necessity of the historical person of Christ for salvation' is established only in the orthodox doctrine of a once for all redemption wrought through him and accepted on ecclesiastical authority. In so far as other approaches attempt to affirm a similar necessity, they at least implicitly rely on conceptions incompatible with their own premises. Here Troeltsch agrees with Strauss' criticism of Schleiermacher's portrayal of Christ as a sinless second Adam and the attack of the history of religions school on Ritschl's picture of Jesus because both interpretations present dogmatic traditions as historical facts. Similarly, he notes sardonically that Herrmann's 'fact of Christ' is not like other facts in that it can be perceived only in faith. In each case, Troeltsch argues, affirmations are grounded on the authority either of traditional doctrines or of Christ as he is experienced rather than on defensible historical judgments. Hence he proposes his alternative of focusing on 'social-psychological necessities' rather than on requirements of dogma in an attempt to elucidate the significance of the historical Jesus for faith.[41]

Troeltsch contends that the single most powerful source of resistance to the approach he represents is the commitment of non-historicized interpretations to viewing Christ as the absolute center of salvation for all men. This commitment is, of course, least ambiguously affirmed in ecclesiastical orthodoxy. But Troeltsch sees the same tendency in Schleiermacher's conception of Christ as the second Adam or in Ritschl's identification of God's ultimate end for the world with the destiny of Christ and his church. For any such quasi-historicized Christocentrism, Troeltsch has a summary judgment: 'One can naturally say nothing certain about that, but it is not probable'.[42] Against the attempt to construe Jesus as the center of a universal history Troeltsch insists that the available data in fact attest only to his centrality for Christian faith. More specifically, his concern with 'social-

40. ...*Geschichtlichkeit Jesu...*, pp. 8–9, 10–17.
41. ...*Geschichtlichkeit Jesu...*, pp. 19–23, 40–51.
42. ...*Geschichtlichkeit Jesu...*, p. 15. See also pp. 13–16, 47–51.

psychological necessities' leads to a focus on Christian worship and fellowship or community:

It is one of the clearest results of all history of religion and psychology of religion that what is essential in all religion is not dogma and idea but rather cult and community.[43]

Troeltsch acknowledges that Schleiermacher, Ritschl, and Herrmann share this focus on cult and community; but he thinks they fail to appreciate fully the extent to which the centrality of Christ is an instance of a general pattern of historical development and as a result do not confine their interpretations of the significance of Jesus to what is consistent with this perspective.

Troeltsch's own conclusion is in any case consistent with the strictures of the historical method which he commends. The centrality of the person of Jesus for Christian faith is understood not as a testament to his uniqueness but rather as fulfilling a general requirement of the development of all traditions:

Decisive for the appraisal of the significance of Jesus is, therefore, not the unavailability of salvation for non-Christians but rather the need of the religious community for a support, a center, and a symbol of its religious life.[44]

Because of this need, Troeltsch rejects the speculative position that the truth of faith is not dependent on its historical origins. He is, moreover, persuaded that the outlines of Jesus' life and at least something of his teaching are recoverable through Biblical scholarship. But Troeltsch's focus on the centrality of Christ in Christian piety requires no restriction of faith to this recoverable residue. Instead his perspective demands only that any claims made for the significance of Jesus be defensible with reference to the historical influence exercised through the community which centers its life on his person. Troeltsch himself expresses confidence that a genuinely communal Christian faith will again emerge from the ruins of modern individualism – 'either within our present churches or next to them'. But he also maintains that 'in view of the possibility of a human future of many hundreds

---

43. ...*Geschichtlichkeit Jesu*..., p. 25. See pp. 25–31.
44. ...*Geschichtlichkeit Jesu*..., p. 42. See also 'Geschichte und Metaphysik', pp. 7, 59–62.

of thousands of years', no one can say with certainty that a Christianity focusing its worship and fellowship on the historical personality of Jesus is destined for 'eternal duration'.[45]

Troeltsch's programmatic restriction of Christological affirmations to what is consistent with general 'social-psychological necessities' for the development of any tradition is of course illustrative of his commitment to viewing Christianity as one historically relative tradition among others. Troeltsch unambiguously subscribes to this position in *The Absoluteness of Christianity and the History of Religions:*

In all moments of its history Christianity is a purely historical phenomenon with all the conditionedness of an individual historical phenomenon just like the other great religions.[46]

At the same time, however, Troeltsch maintains that an acknowledgment of historical relativity does not require 'unlimited relativism'. Instead, the norms or criteria for evaluating the 'depth, the power, and the clarity' of the various traditions are themselves articulated in the course of the historical process as its 'ideals and goals'. Consequently 'the historical mode of thinking' does not in principle preclude the judgment that Christianity is the highest religion.[47]

In *The Absoluteness of Christianity* Troeltsch argues that Christianity is 'the highest and most consistently developed religious *milieu* that we know'. Though in Troeltsch's view any such judgment is finally a matter of personal conviction (*persönliche Überzeugung*), it is not simply a private decision; rather it can and should be supported through comparative study of historical traditions. Central to his elaboration of this comparative argument is the contention that Christianity (including Judaic and Hellenistic roots as well as European developments) is the most deeply personal of the religions which at the same time has great social and cultural power because its denial of the world as it is occurs in the context of ultimately affirming it

---

45. ...*Geschichtlichkeit Jesu...*, pp. 46–47, 49.
46. *Die Absolutheit der Christentums und die Religionsgeschichte* (Tübingen: J. C. B. Mohr – Paul Siebeck, 1912), p. 51. See the whole line of argument, pp. 25–51. This book was first published in 1902. In 'Meine Bücher', *Gesammelte Schriften*, vol. 4, p. 9, Troeltsch describes it as the 'germ' of all his subsequent writings. See also 'Geschichte und Metaphysik', pp. 3–5, 16–19.
47. *Die Absolutheit...*, esp. pp. 57–58, 64–65, 78–80. All of pp. 51–80 argue this point.

as God's creation.[48] Troeltsch distinguishes his argument, with its attention to comparative appraisal in addition to personal conviction or decision, both from the 'naive' claims which all traditions make to absoluteness and from the 'artificial, apologetic' contentions of the ecclesiastical tradition and of those rationalistic-evolutionary theories which understand Christianity as realizing the concept or essence of all religion.[49] In contrast to such untenable claims to absoluteness, Troeltsch does consider it a viable approach to argue that Christianity is the most adequate of the religious alternatives available – as long as this argument for its greater 'depth, power, and clarity' does not attempt artificially to avoid the undeniable historical fact that Christianity is one religious tradition among others.

This assertion of the finality of Christianity in *The Absoluteness of Christianity* is not, however, Troeltsch's last pronouncement on the question of the relationship between Christianity and other religious traditions. In a lecture written for delivery in England just before his death, Troeltsch reviews his analysis in *The Absoluteness of Christianity* and then indicates some revisions which he feels constrained to make. He offers his own summary:

The individual character of European civilization, and of the Christian religion which is intimately connected with it, receives now much greater emphasis, whilst the somewhat rationalistic concept of validity, and specifically of *supreme validity* falls considerably into the background.[50]

Especially in view of Baron von Hügel's potentially misleading introductory comments about Troeltsch's 'excessive individualism' toward the end of his life, it is important to appreciate the comprehensive cultural reference of the characterization of European civilization and Christianity as 'individual'. In this lecture Troeltsch himself indicates that his modifications of the perspective articulated in *The Absoluteness of Christianity* result from his studies in writing *The Social Teachings of the Christian Churches* and

48. *Die Absolutheit*..., pp. 80–91, esp. 86–87. See also the summary on p. 92.
49. *Die Absolutheit*..., pp. 107–150.
50. 'The Place of Christianity among the World Religions' in *Christian Thought: Its History and Application*, F. von Hügel, ed. (London: University of London Press, 1923), p. 24. A German edition appeared subsequently under the dubious title (not Troeltsch's) *Der Historismus und seine Überwindung* (Berlin: Pan Verlag Rolf Heise, 1924); the quoted passage is on p. 76.

Historicism and its Problems. First in examining Christian social and ethical doctrines and then in pursuing that study to the development of political, social, ethical, aesthetic, and scientific ideas, Troeltsch reports that he became more and more convinced of the thorough relativity of all such commitments to the historical context in which they arise.[51] Hence he uses the concept 'individuality' to refer to that cultural whole or that 'totality of meaning' which is presupposed in the articulation of particular views or commitments and in the development of specific institutions. The concepts 'Renaissance' or 'Reformation' exemplify individuality in this sense.[52] To characterize Christianity as 'individual' is, then, to focus on its integration not only into one cultural whole but rather into a variety of totalities of meaning in relation to which a diversity of interpretations of Christian faith appears.

In combination with his discovery that 'Buddhism and Brahminism especially' are 'humane and spiritual religions', the result is that Troeltsch no longer advances any claim for the absolute validity of Christianity. Instead his emphasis falls on the extent to which its significance is inextricably involved with the development and the destiny of Western civilization:

Its primary claim to validity is thus the fact that only through it have we become what we are, and that only in it can we preserve the religious forces that we need.[53]

Christianity is still believed to 'possess a mighty spiritual power and truth' and to be, 'in some degree, a manifestation of the Divine Life itself'; but the 'criterion of its validity' is now 'the evidence of a profound inner experience' – and that criterion is 'be it noted, only of its validity *for us*'.[54] In the context of recognizing this integrity of the various traditions, Troeltsch sees the possibility of fruitful further contacts between them:

In relation to the great world-religions we need to recognize that they are expressions of the religious consciousness corresponding to certain definite types of

51. 'The Place of Christianity...', pp. 21–24 (74–76).
52. For a summary characterization of his use of the concept of individuality, see *Der Historismus und seine Probleme* in *Gesammelte Schriften*, vol. 3 (Tübingen: J. C. B. Mohr – Paul Siebeck, 1922), p. 54. All of pp. 111–220 develop the implications of this conception.
53. 'The Place of Christianity...', p. 25 [77].
54. 'The Place of Christianity...,' p. 26 [77–78]. The emphasis on 'for us' is absent in the German.

culture, and that it is their duty to increase in depth and purity by means of their own interior impulses, a task in which the contact with Christianity may prove helpful, to them as to us, in such process of development from within.[55]

Troeltsch then concludes with an insistence that this recognition of cultural relativity does not succumb to 'any spirit of scepticism':

A truth which in the first instance is a truth for us is nevertheless still truth and life.... If all of us in every group seek to develop what is highest and deepest, then we may hope to meet one another.... In our earthly experience the divine life is not one but many. To apprehend the one in the many – that is, however, the special character of love.[56]

HEGEL, TROELTSCH, AND RELIGIOUS PLURALISM

Troeltsch's relation to the thought of Hegel is a complex one.[57] On the one hand, he indicates great respect both for Hegel's apprehension of values or ideals and for his insight into particular historical facts and developments. Troeltsch also recognizes that Hegel exerted 'an enormous influence on historical thought – or better still, on the historicizing of the thought of an entire generation, yes even until today'.[58] On the other hand, Troeltsch repeatedly and emphatically criticizes Hegel's 'monistic metaphysicizing of history' which is, he observes laconically, 'nothing but Spinoza's philosophy of identity set into motion and put into contact with concrete life'.[59] When he scrutinizes Hegel's thought more systematically, Troeltsch focuses on

55. 'The Place of Christianity...', p. 29 [80]. As the reference to Brahminism and Buddhism on p. 23 [75] indicates, Troeltsch does not intend to exclude 'historical, geographical, and social conditions' in this reference to 'types of culture'. He even alludes to the possibility of correlating the various religious traditions with the 'biological and anthropological forms' of the different racial groups. See pp. 29–30 [80].

56. 'The Place of Christianity...', pp. 34–35 [83]. Because the published translation of this passage is indefensibly interpretive, I have modified it to conform more closely to the German. (Despite its earlier publication in English, Troeltsch wrote the lecture in German and sent it to England for translation.)

57. For Troeltsch's most concise, incisive, and systematic appraisal of Hegel's thought, see *Der Historismus und seine Probleme*, pp. 130–133. For more details, see pp. 243–277.

58. *Der Historismus und seine Probleme*, p. 253.

59. *Der Historismus und seine Probleme*, pp. 274, 370; pp. 274–277 summarize this criticism.

what he sees as two specific deficiencies. The first is that Hegel's ascription of inherent value to the individual as 'a concretion of the absolute' is qualified and finally negated in his relegation of man to the 'abstract isolation of a point in a process'. The second inadequacy is that Hegel's thought cannot accommodate a genuine future because of its emphasis on attaining the absolute standpoint which encompasses all time and all individuals.[60]

The force of Troeltsch's criticism of Hegel is, then, to argue for an at least provisional pluralism and for a genuinely open future which allows for continued development. His rejection of the rationalistic-evolutionary defense of the absoluteness of Christianity on the grounds that it fulfills or sums up the concept or essence of all religions is consistent with this line of criticism.[61] But Troeltsch's dissatisfaction with Hegel's system should not obscure the considerable similarities in the two positions. Perhaps the most striking illustration of those similarities is the relatively early essay 'Methapysics and History'. In this essay Troeltsch aligns himself with the attempt to formulate an idealism based on the philosophy of history (*geschichtsphilosophischer Idealismus*) or a developmental-historical idealism (*entwicklungsgeschichtlicher Idealismus*). He maintains that commitment to any particular conception of the unity or the teological nisus of the historical process is a matter of faith rather than knowledge.[62] But he nonetheless recognizes the importance of elaborating an interpretation of history and the metaphysics which it implies.[63] Troeltsch conceives of this enterprise as more in the tradition of Schleiermacher than of Hegel precisely because it is not in his view in the first instance a 'methaphysics of the Absolute' but rather a 'metaphysics of history' or a 'metaphysics of spirit'. Yet he acknowledges continuities between this metaphysics of history and 'the further circles of metaphysics'.[64] Finally, he concludes his essay with a reference to 'a latent theology of historicism' which requires a metaphysics of history to ground its faith:

60. *Der Historismus und seine Probleme*, pp. 132–133.
61. See, for example: *Die Absolutheit...*, pp. 6–8, 42, 135–136, 141–144; 'Geschichte und Metaphysik', pp. 54, 64–65; 'The Place of Christianity...', pp. 10–13 [67–69].
62. 'Geschichte und Metaphysik', pp. 32–34, 46.
63. 'Geschichte und Metaphysik', pp. 40–41.
64. 'Geschichte und Metaphysik', pp. 40, 41–47. The reference to circles invokes Troeltsch's image of concentric circles of metaphysical analysis beginning with anthropological concerns and moving progressively toward the inclusion of man's various environments. See especially p. 45.

In the face of nothing but historical analyses and portrayals we no longer know how to formulate and support what we ourselves believe. Here again that cannot be helped through a repudiation of history and a return to supernaturalism. Here again that difficulty can be resolved only through a metaphysics of history which ... discerns Christian truth as the core and goal of history and knows how in clear and compelling fashion to exhibit this core in its relation to the metaphysics of nature and the metaphysics of the Absolute.[65]

In the last years of his life Troeltsch does not, to be sure, speak as positively about metaphysics. But the problems entailed in elaborating a universal history nonetheless still preoccupy him in his later writings. In its final formulation, his position continues to strive for comprehensiveness without denying pluralism. Hence he concludes that philosophy of history can emerge only from the 'correlation' of a definite cultural perspective and the data of history as a whole:

The result is a universal history which is organized from the perspective of the idea of a contemporary synthesis of culture and a contemporary synthesis of culture which is extracted from the whole of our developing historical life.[66]

In so far as one construes Hegel's 'absolute knowledge' as an ideal rather than as the content of his own system, the measure of commonality between his thought and this Troeltschian conception of a metaphysics of history or a universal history is, of course, increased. Indeed, the two approaches are then sufficiently similar in intention that they may be interpreted so as to provide a mutual corrective for each other's deficiencies. The result is the possibility of a position more consistently and explicitly aware of its historical relativity than is Hegel's thought while at the same time less inclined toward an uncritical relativism than is Troeltsch's perspective.

That serious attention to the historicism of Troeltsch may serve to underscore and to systematize Hegel's occasionally explicit recognition of the cultural relativity of his own system need not be belabored. But Hegel's philosophy provides an equally significant corrective to the thought of Troeltsch. Even after it is granted that Hegel's system is one attempt among others to interpret and organize the whole of human experience, the ideal of absolute knowledge remains as a judgment against every uncritical

65. 'Geschichte und Metaphysik', p. 69.
66. *Der Historismus und seine Probleme*, p. 692.

relativism. Hegel's own procedure in the *Phenomenology* establishes the precedent that the question of adequacy to the real is a legitimate question with respect to any and every claim to knowledge. The affirmation that the truth is the whole requires the pursuit of this question toward the ideal of total explanation of every datum of experience. The result is that no privatizing of perspectives is permissible either on the personal or on the cultural level. In so far as a tradition purports to interpret the whole of experience, it cannot avoid the requirement to indicate its approach to whatever data may be proposed for consideration. Because the experience of mankind is increasingly becoming a common one, the question of adequacy to that common experience is, moreover, a question which the various traditions confront together. Troeltsch was, to be sure, not unaware of this fact. There is after all only a tendency toward uncritical relativism in his thought. In the end he insists he is not a sceptic and speaks of seeing the one in the many. But he never pursues the question of relations between disparate cultural syntheses in satisfactory detail. The following chapter attempts in a preliminary way to address this complex of issues from the perspective of the Realist-Nominalist-Processive position which I advocate throughout this study.

10

Christian Theology in a Pluralistic World Culture

In completing my analysis of religious pluralism as a theological issue, this chapter also concludes the study as a whole because the constructive position here outlined is presented as the correlate of the Realist-Nominalist-Processive approach to the significance of Christ which I advance as the most adequate of the Christological alternatives. Indeed, from within the Christian perspective the commonality between this chapter and my constructive remarks on interpreting the significance of Christ may be stated more forcefully: for a Realist-Nominalist-Processive Christian theology, the interaction between religious traditions which this chapter describes and analyzes may itself be viewed as integral to the process of reconciliation which constitutes the work of Christ. My procedure in this chapter is not, however, simply to deduce an approach to non-Christian traditions from a Realist-Nominalist-Processive Christology. Instead, after some initial systematic comments I examine in cursory fashion one other tradition – that of Buddhism – so that the subsequent analysis of interaction between traditions may have at least the specificity of one extended illustration. That further analysis is also descriptive and systematic in its approach rather than theological in a doctrinal or dogmatic sense. Consequently the process of interaction among traditions in general and of dialogue in particular is analyzed without explicitly interpreting this process as parallel to and even potentially ingredient in reconciliation understood Christologically. The parallelism is, however, present and is expressed in the concluding remarks at the very end of the chapter.

THE POSSIBILITY OF A PLURALIZED VERSION OF HEGEL'S APPROACH

That Troeltsch does not systematically relate the different religious perspectives to each other is, of course, in large measure the result of his programmatic insistence on at least in the first instance viewing each tradition in the context of its own historical particularity. Hegel too is committed to elucidating concrete historical data. That commitment is evident throughout his philosophical treatment not only of social and cultural history but also of the data of the natural sciences. It is, therefore, only consistent with his philosophical program as a whole that his *Lectures on the Philosophy of Religion* attempt to organize and interpret whatever information about religious life is available to him. But in contrast to Troeltsch, Hegel also attends more directly and centrally to the question of relations among traditions. This focus is in part simply a consequence of Hegel's more pronounced interest in systematizing and synthesizing initially discrete and even contrary tendencies. That Hegel sees the various religious traditions as stages in a single line of historical development is, however, also in some measure a function of the available historical and comparative studies. To be sure, Hegel in any case indicates his willingness to declare entire geographical areas and civilizations as irrelevant to the development of world history in specified periods. But the complexity and variety within each tradition which is evidenced in the enormous accumulation of historical and comparative data during the latter half of the nineteenth and the twentieth centuries nonetheless argue forcefully against Hegel's procedure of first reducing a tradition to a single characteristic position and then integrating it as a single stage in a unilinear historical process. The fact of very considerable pluralism even within a single tradition along with the capacity for development through interaction with changing historical circumstances are, in short, more critical data for interpreting the relations among traditions than Hegel's approach to the question suggests.

The advent of detailed and sophisticated study of non-Christian traditions has not, of course, in itself rendered Hegel's line of interpretation untenable. Positions analogous both to his philosophical legitimation of Christianity as absolute because it realizes the very idea or concept of religion and to his understanding of Western civilization as the historical heir of all other traditions continue to have their advocates. Paul Tillich's argument that Christ is the final revelation illustrates the approach of determining unqualified validity through the elaboration of a criterion in reference to which a claim for complete fulfillment is then advanced.[1] And Arend

1. *Systematic Theology*, vol. 1 (Chicago: University of Chicago Press, 1951), pp. 132–155, esp. 133, 135–136.

Theodoor van Leeuwen's interpretation in *Christianity in World History* is in effect a restatement of Hegel's view of Christianity as central to history conceived as a single line of development.[2]

While Tillich and van Leeuwen may be taken to represent the continuing influence of broadly Hegelian defenses of Christian preminence even after the availability of reliable historical and comparative data on the various religious traditions, their positions do not require systematic consideration of that data. Indeed Tillich and van Leeuwen each in his own way abstracts his apologetic for Christianity from the context of religious pluralism as such.

Tillich's highly formal analysis prescinds from any specific attention to possible alternative claims for finality and instead constructs an argument centering on the problematic of Christian revelation. Tillich himself indicates that his personal encounter with the Buddhist tradition in Japan, and his joint seminars with Mircea Eliade at the University of Chicago in the years immediately before his death, impressed on him the need for theological reflection more self-consciously in conversation with the history of religions than in his own *Systematic Theology*. The meeting of that need is, however, a 'hope for the future of theology' – not a task which Tillich claims to have undertaken.[3]

Despite the cosmopolitan scope of his perspective, van Leeuwen similarly confines direct appraisal of the various religious traditions to the periphery

---

2. *Christianity in World History*, H. H. Hoskins, trans. (New York: Charles Scribner's Sons, n. d.), esp. pp. 13–45, 399–439. The Dutch copyright is registered in 1965. I think the book was not first published in Dutch. In any case, I have not been able to procure a Dutch text and therefore do not include the usual reference between brackets to corresponding pages in the original. See also van Leeuwen's *Prophecy in a Technocratic Era* (New York: Charles Scribner's Sons, 1968), pp. 56–67, 83–103, and *Development Through Revolution* (New York: Charles Scribner's Sons, 1970), pp. 253–304. Both of these latter books were originally published in English.

3. See 'The Significance of the History of Religions for the Systematic Theologian' in *The Future of Religions*, J. C. Brauer, ed. (New York: Harper & Row, 1966), pp. 80–94, esp. 91–94. This lecture is Tillich's last public presentation prior to his death. For reflections related more specifically to his trip to Japan, see *Christianity and the Encounter of the World Religions* (New York: Columbia University Press, 1964), esp. pp. 53–75. Also revealing is his 'Informal Report on Lecture Trip to Japan – Summer 1960' prepared in mimeographed form for distribution to friends and colleagues. See especially his concluding comment (p. 15): 'No Western provincialism of which I am aware will be tolerated by me from now on in my thought and work.'

of his study. He defines the issues which he analyzes so as to isolate the Christian Gospel from the fact of religious pluralism. In celebrating the 'technological revolution' effected in the West, van Leeuwen does maintain that the 'technocratic pattern' which is displacing its 'ontocratic' predecessor on a global scale is intimately related to Jewish and Christian religious commitments. But he also insists that this process of secularization relegates religion as such to the status of an anachronism. In so far as Christianity pursues the ideal of a *Corpus Christianum* encompassing all of society and culture, it too falls under this judgment:

One thing is certain: in no circumstances whatever could this new revolution mean returning to the age of 'religion' – and that applies as much to Christianity as to the other religions.[4]

Because van Leeuwen adopts the Barthian distinction between Christianity and the Gospel, he is able to avoid a complete condemnation of Christian faith along with the other traditions as '*nihil*' or 'nothingness':

In the secularized situation of the twentieth-century West we need to clear away, once and for all, any false idea of the Gospel of the crucified and risen Lord as having the character of a religious message.[5]

The result is that the Gospel continues to have some measure of significance in relation to the process of secularization. At the same time this line of argument obviates the need for any detailed and explicit attention to the question of religious pluralism.

Although there are Hegelian precedents for both the philosophical and the historical apologetic for Christianity, Hegel's recognition that conceptual analysis entails a process of abstraction from concrete historical data means the historical line of argument is the fundamental one. For the purpose of exploring contemporary formulations of a broadly Hegelian perspective on the question of religious pluralism, the approach of van Leeuwen is, therefore, a more relevant focus of attention than is that of Tillich.

The indisputable strength of van Leeuwen's interpretation is its unambiguous recognition of the extent to which the context for appraising the contemporary role of Christianity and other religious traditions is the in-

---

4. *Christianity in World History*, p. 410.
5. *Christianity in World History*, p. 417.

cipient world culture emerging under the impetus of those processes of modernization which arose initially in the West. That virtue is, however, compromised through deficiencies in his analysis of religious phenomena themselves. Disagreement with van Leeuwen's approach unavoidably ends in focusing on the question of whether or not the religious dimension of human culture is as readily dispensable as he suggests. But even apart from this fundamental issue, van Leeuwen is liable to criticism for his dichotomizing of all religious perspectives into Western and non-Western patterns without attending sufficiently either to the multiple variations discernible in even ostensibly unfied traditions or to the capacities for adaptation and further development which the East as well as the West evidences.

Because it shares neither van Leeuwen's negative judgment on religious phenomena as such nor his preoccupation with contrasting Jewish-Christian commitments to all other traditions, Robert Bellah's recent article on religious evolution provides a corrective to the inadequacies of van Leeuwen's analysis. Bellah agrees with van Leeuwen in stressing the significance of the historical development moving from modern Western civilization toward a world culture. In this sense he too exemplifies a broadly Hegelian perspective. Indeed, there are striking parallels between Bellah's evolutionary typology and the overall progression of Hegel's philosophy of history. Like Hegel, Bellah sees a movement in human religious history from a monistic metaphysics combined with a religious system relatively undifferentiated from other forms of social organization and cultural life through a more or less radical metaphysical dualism in conjunction with increased differentiation of religious institutions from other social and cultural forms to the collapse of that metaphysical dualism and a correlative reintegration of religious and secular concerns which nonetheless preserves and even increases the complexity and plurality developed in the intervening process of differentiation.[6] Bellah's primitive and archaic ideal types specify the

---

6. See 'Religious Evolution', in *Reader in Comparative Religion: An Anthropological Approach*, W. A. Lessa and E. Z. Vogt, eds. (New York: Harper & Row, 1965), pp. 73–87. For summary references to this overall three-fold pattern, see esp. pp. 74–75, 86–87. Originally published in the *American Sociological Review*, XXIX (1964), pp. 358–374, this essay is also reprinted in Bellah's *Beyond Belief: Essays on Religion in a Post-Traditional World* (New York: Harper & Row, 1970). The passages referred to in this note are on pp. 20–50, esp. 22–24, 44–45. In subsequent references to this article, the page numbers between brackets indicate the location of the same passages in *Beyond Belief* .. .

first pattern, the historic stage focuses the movement toward dualism and differentiation, and the early modern and modern types exemplify the development first only inchoately but then fully and self-consciously beyond dualism.

In spite of the parallels between their positions Bellah's article is not, however, simply a restatement of Hegel's view in the conceptuality of contemporary social science. Instead, Bellah's analysis can claim greater adequacy because it is more aware than is either Hegel or van Leeuwen of both the variety and the capacity for further development in non-Western as well as Western traditions. In contrast to Hegel's virtually exclusive focus on Jewish, Greek, Roman, and then European traditions for his documentation of the development of an increasingly self-conscious individualism, Bellah correlates the emergence of a 'clearly structured conception of the self' with the widespread phenomenon of 'world rejection':

Only by withdrawing cathexis from the myriad objects of empirical reality could consciousness of a centered self in relation to an encompassing reality emerge.[7]

In Bellah's view the emergence of this dualistic devaluation of the phenomenal world is among the critical 'massive facts of human religious history':

The first of these facts is the emergence in the first millenium B. C. all across the Old World, at least in centers of high culture, of the phenomenon of religious rejection of the world characterized by an extremely negative evaluation of man and society and the exaltation of another realm of reality as alone true and infinitely valuable.[8]

Bellah sees direct continuity between this historic type and the further development to early modern and modern perspectives. He does, to be sure, elaborate his early modern stage as an ideal type through exclusive reference

---

7. 'Religious Evolution', p. 87 [45]. See also pp. 80–81 [33–34].
8. 'Religious Evolution', p. 74 [22]. Van Leeuwen is, of course, familiar with the similar thesis of Karl Jaspers that there is in this period a time of axis (*Achsenzeit*) in man's religious development. But he rejects this argument for parallels between the West and India and China on the grounds that the failure of the Orient to initiate the second time of axis which Jaspers sees in the present demonstrates the illusion of ascribing participation in a first time of axis to it. See *Christianity in World History*, pp. 26, 157, 404. The result is that all religious traditions other than the Judeo-Christian one remain hopelessly 'ontocratic'.

to the Protestant Reformation. Because he agrees with 'Weber, Merton, *et al.*, in attributing very great significance to the Reformation, especially in its Calvinistic wing, in a whole series of developments from economics to science, from education to law', Bellah's modern type is also described in the context of Western history.[9] But the widespread exemplification of the historic type nonetheless results in tendencies in other traditions analogous to the early modern and modern types as they develop and are more 'successfully institutionalized' in the West.[10]

In as much as his article is only an article, Bellah's reference to non-Western parallels to the early modern and modern types are oblique to the point of being cryptic. He notes in particular Shinran Shonin's version of Pure Land Buddhism and other reform movements in Buddhism as well as in Islam, Taoism and Confucianism as incipient parallels to the early modern type.[11] Similarly, he tentatively suggests that 'highly "modern" implications exist in more than one strand of Mahāyāna Buddhism and perhaps several of the other great traditions as well'. As Bellah himself observes, even inchoate or incipient parallels may, however, be highly significant not so much for understanding the past but rather for shaping the future:

Although in my opinion these implications were never developed sufficiently to dominate a historical epoch as they did in the West in the last two centuries, they may well prove decisive in the future of these religions.[12]

In contrast to van Leeuwen, Bellah does, then, allow for the possibility that extant tendencies combined with significant capacities for development provide resources through which non-Western religious traditions can interpret and in turn shape even the radically novel facets of their emerging 'planetary world'. It is, moreover, arguable that this possibility is not in principle incompatible with the interpretation of Hegel proposed in this study.

9. 'Religious Evolution', p. 83 [38]. All of pp. 82–86 [36–44] is relevant.
10. 'Religious Evolution', pp. 82, 83, 85 [36–37, 37–38, 41]. That the West did in fact more successfully institutionalize the early modern and modern types is, of course, a very significant fact. Bellah in no way denies this significance. In his 'Reflections on the Protestant Ethic Analogy in Asia' in *Beyond Belief...* Bellah is especially unambiguous on this point. See p. 57 in particular.
11. 'Religious Evolution', p. 82 [36–37].
12. 'Religious Evolution', p. 85 [41].

The judgment that a pluralized version of Hegel is conceivable is, to be sure, untenable if one accepts the popular caricature of Hegel as deducing from ideas the course of development both of human culture and even of nature itself. But this caricature is after all – a caricature. Even in the *Logic* Hegel's elaboration of a normative conceptual structure is not divorced from the concrete particularity of empirical phenomena. The *Logic* is not only incidentally but programmatically abstract; it is, however, abstracted from precisely that empirical order which it in turn interprets. The resultant system of concepts does not simply reflect the world as it is: Hegel is not a positivist. Instead it provides a teleological structure, a systematizing of ends or ideals, which transcends the given and therefore serves to criticize and modify what is interpreted: Hegel is in this sense an idealist. But this form of idealism cannot legitimately be characterized as a deducing of reality from ideas. The dynamic interaction between conceptions and empirical data is of course more directly evident in the *Phenomenology* or the *Philosophy of History* or the *Philosophy of Right* or the *Lectures on the Philosophy of Religion* than it is in the *Logic*. The dynamic itself is, however, the same. Philosophy is normative but not inventive. Abstract though its reflection may be, it requires particular data from which to generalize its universal conceptions. Hegel's philosophical method is, in short, in principle committed to interpreting every new datum which experience provides.

If an awareness of this programmatic empiricism in Hegel's thought is combined with an interpretation of absolute knowledge as an ideal rather than as the content of his own system, then a pluralizing of Hegel's position so as to allow a continuing validity for multiple traditions of interpretation of man's developing experience is entirely conceivable. This modified version of Hegel's approach need not deny that developments in particular traditions shape the course of world history as a whole. More specifically, it is able to acknowledge the extent to which the results of modern Western thought and action inform the context within which the various traditions interpret their experience in the present. But that acknowledgment does not in principle preclude the possibility that multiple religious systems interpret an increasingly common experience with reference to the symbolic resources of their particular traditions.

As Hegel maintains in the *Phenomenology* with reference to any claim to possess knowledge or truth, each such perspective at least implicitly aspires to the goal of absolute knowledge – of a fully adequate comprehension of the total experience of mankind. Pursuit of that end in an increasingly unified world unavoidably entails interaction among the various traditions as they attempt to interpret the whole of experience including the existence of religious perspectives other than their own. This interaction may, however, itself be conceived as integral to the process of criticism and modification in the direction of greater adequacy which constitutes the development of human knowledge as Hegel portrays it in the *Phenomenology*. This approach differs from Hegel's position only in that it allows the at least provisional possibility of multiple contemporary, world-historically relevant movements toward greater comprehensiveness rather than insisting on the view that significant world history is a single line of development.

That a pluralized version of Hegel's thought is conceivable does not, of course, itself decide the question of the continuing vitality and viability of any particular tradition. Adjudication of that question is not possible apart from attention to empirical data about the tradition under scrutiny. Any appraisal which results from such scrutiny is, moreover, itself not exempt from the historical conditionedness of its particular perspective. In the case of this study, the perspective is that of the Realist-Nominalist-Processive type of Christian theological position which I advocate. But from that particular perspective one approach to the fact of religious pluralism which commends itself is to begin with an exploration of the extent to which other traditions address questions analogous to those informing the Christological types employed throughout this study. A comprehensive analysis would require detailed consideration of religious and also avowedly secular perspectives at least representative of the full variety of traditions. That is, however, impossible in the very limited scope of this chapter. Consequently I propose instead to focus on the Buddhist tradition in the hope of providing some measure of specificity to the enquiry – an enquiry which in any case remains very tentative and attempts only to suggest an approach to other traditions which is consistent with and congenial to my argument for a Realist-Nominalist-Processive interpretation of the Atonement or the significance of Christ.

Two Recurrent Types of Buddhist Worldview

Even to raise the question of parallels in Buddhist thought and action to types developed with reference to Christological issues is a highly problematical line of enquiry. The difficulty is especially pronounced in the case of the category 'Transactional', since that designation derives in the first instance from Christian preoccupation with the claim that the work of Christ is effective once for all. But already with respect to Western thinkers this classification requires considerable generalization if it is to serve effectively in discerning not only differences but also similarities between what at first seem disparate views. Hence Transactional as a variable in the typology comes to refer to interpretations which in some sense abstract the realization of salvation from the continuities of historical development. Because the categories 'Processive', 'Realist', and 'Nominalist' are similarly formalized in their use for classifying even Christian alternatives, there is along with the risks of distortion the possibility that they may serve to illuminate very general and necessarily abstract parallels and divergences between the various Christian and Buddhist views.

The least problematical parallel is to the alternatives which the Realist-Nominalist contrast distinguishes. Despite considerable variation within each tradition, differences between the soteriological focus of the Mahāyāna and the Theravāda in general correspond to the differentiation between Realists and Nominalists respectively. Both traditions are, to be sure, committed to a concern for the ultimate salvation of all beings. But the typical Theravāda focus is on the disciplines required for the individual to advance toward that ultimate goal of *nirvāṇa* summarily characterized as the extinction of the greed, hatred, and delusion which constitute attachment to phenomenal existence (*saṃsāra*). *Nirvāṇa* is, therefore, conceived as the antithesis to *saṃsāra* – as a critical ideal toward which the individual strives, an absolute norm against which phenomenal existence is measured and judged as inadequate, as unsatisfactory, indeed, ultimately, as undesirable.[13]

---

13. Despite differences in emphasis, virtually all Therevādins would assent to this general formulation. For representative exegetical and systematic discussions both by Theravādins themselves and by Western scholars, see: Edward Conze, *Buddhism: Its Essence and Development* (New York: Harper & Brothers – Torchbooks, 1959), pp. 93–95; *Buddhist Thought in India* (Ann Arbor: University of Michigan Press, 1967), pp.

Many Mahāyāna schools also emphasize personal discipline especially in the form of meditational exercises. There is, however, at the same time a central tendency perhaps most directly expressed in the Mādhyamika and the Yogācārin schools and in Zen to affirm a universal reference for the salvation which is realized: when the disciple attains enlightenment, he sees that the whole of phenomenal existence (*saṃsāra*) is in truth ultimate reality itself (*nirvāṇa, dharmakāya, tattva*).[14]

The contrast between radically individual and universal reference on the question of salvation has its parallel in Buddhological conceptions. Whereas Mahāyāna devotion affirms myriad celestial Buddhas and *bodhisattvas* and some of its philosophical schools assent to a universal Buddhahood inform-

69–79, esp. 75–76; T. W. Rhys Davids, *Buddhism: Its History and Literature* (New York: G. P. Putnam's Sons, 1896), p. 151; I. B. Horner, *The Early Buddhist Theory of Man Perfected: A Study of the Arahan* (London: Williams and Norgate, 1936), esp. 103, 106, 128; K. N. Jayatilleke, "Nirvāṇa", mimeographed lecture, pp. 1–4; Étienne Lamotte, *Historie du Bouddhisme Indien* (Louvain: Institut Orientaliste, 1958), pp. 43–45; Trevor Ling, 'Buddhist Mysticism', *Religious Studies*, I (1966), 163–175; Nyanaponika Thera, 'Anatta and Nibbana', *The Wheel*, number 11 (Kandy, Ceylon: The Buddhist Publication Society, 1959), pp. 25–28; Hermann Oldenberg, *Buddha: His Life, His Doctrine, His Order*, W. Hoey, trans. (London: Williams and Norgate, 1882), pp. 263–267 [*Buddha: sein Leben, siene Lehre, seine Gemeinde* (Berlin: Verlag von Wilhelm Hertz, 1881), pp. 269–273]; Piyadassi Thera. *The Buddha's Ancient Path* (London: Rider, 1964), pp. 67–76; James Bissett Pratt, *The Pligrimage of Buddhism* (London: McMillan, 1928), pp. 64–70; Walpola Rahula, *What the Buddha Taught* (Bedford, England: Gordon Fraser, 1967), pp. 35–44; U. Thittila, 'The Fundamental Principles of Theravada Buddhism', in *The Path of the Buddha*, K. W. Morgan, ed. (New York: Ronald Press, 1956), pp. 111–112; E. J. Thomas, *A History of Buddhist Thought* (London: Routledge and Kegan Paul, 1951), pp. 119–132.

14. For discussion of this view including references to the relevant passages of Buddhist scriptures and commentaries, see: Conze, *Buddhism*..., pp. 135–140; *Buddhist Thought*..., pp. 198, 228–232, 242–249, 263–264; T. R. V. Murti, *The Central Philosophy of Buddhism* (London: George Allen & Unwin, 1960), pp. 232–233, 271–275; Pratt, *Pilgrimage*..., pp. 265–268, 406–407, 642–645; Richard H. Robinson, *Early Mādhyamika in India and China* (Madison: University of Wisconsi Press, 1967), pp. 40, 46–47, 118–119 121, 132, 200–203; F. Th. Stcherbatsky, *Buddhist Logic* (New York: Dover Publications, 1962), vol. 1, pp. 7–14, 47–52; *The Conception of Buddhist Nirvāṇa* (The Hague: Mouton, 1965), esp. pp. 45–48, 60–62; Frederick J. Streng, *Emptiness: A Study in Religious Meaning* (Nashville: Abingdon Press, 1967), pp. 69–81; D. T. Suzuki, *Essays in Zen Buddhism – First Series* (London: Rider, 1958), pp. 48–59, 85, 90–92, 229–232; *Introduction to Zen Buddhism* (Kyoto, Japan: Eastern Buddhist Society, 1943), pp. 91–103; *Outline to Mahāyā Buddhism* (New York: Schoken Books, 1963), pp. 331–371, esp. 352–357; *Studies in the Lankavatara Sutra* (London: Routledge and Kegan Paul, 1930), pp. 96–99, 127–129; Thomas, *History of Buddhist Thought*, pp. 224–225, 235.

ing the whole of existence, the Theravādins insist that their thought and piety in the last analysis focus on and derive from the historical individual Gautama. The analogy to Western disagreements over the relative importance of the Jesus of history and the Christ of faith need not be belabored. That there is even a partial analogy is, however, noteworthy because the existence of a tradition of criticism of Mahāyāna innovations on the grounds that they are not historically attested indicates the only partial accuracy of any facile generalization to the effect that Indians or even all Asians have no sense of history. It is, moreover, an interesting coincidence that when Conze discusses this complex of issues, he characterizes the disagreement between the Mahāyānists and their critics as 'a philosophical difference which corresponds to the age-old cleavage between "Nominalism" and "Realism".'[15]

As is the case in discriminating among Western thinkers, the Transactional and Processive variables may be correlated with the Realist-Nominalist distinction.

Because the Theravāda perspective focuses on the need for definite spiritual and ethical attainments normally acquired gradually and over a long period of time, its radical Nominalism is typically Processive in character. Those interpretations which maintain that the sole legitimate use of the term *nirvāṇa* is to designate an ethical and psychological state are, moreover, consistently Processive in the sense that they do not affirm a transhistorical state as the goal of salvation. Perhaps the most influential modern formulation of this position is (somewhat ironically) the definition of *nirvāṇa* in the Pali Text Society's *Pali-English Dictionary:* 'Nibbāna is purely and solely an *ethical* state, to be reached in this birth by ethical practices, contemplation

---

15. *Buddhism...*, p. 150. Pp. 147–152 offer a convenient summary of the Buddhological contrast. Conze gives his own concise definition of the distinction as he uses it: 'To the Nominalist only the individual has real existence, to the Realist the universal'. I should perhaps note that both Conze's use and my own differ from Stcherbatsky's references to Realism and Nominalism in his *Buddhist Logic*, vol. 1, pp. 47–52, 444–456. While Conze and I focus on soteriological questions, Stcherbatsky examines the epistemological issues with reference to which the distinction is originally developed in the West. His use is, however, problematical in any case, since he considers 'Nominalist' and 'Idealist' interchangeable with the consequence that Mahāyānists and even Vedāntins are classified as Nominalist – though, he acknowledges, not as extreme in their Nominalism as the Hīnayānists or Theravādins. See esp. pp. 444–451.

and insight'.[16] In this view those renderings of *nirvāṇa* which appear to designate a place or even an objective metaphysical entity are at least in origin simply metaphorical descriptions of the psychological state of the Buddhist saint or *arhat*. A very thorough and competent elaboration of this position is available in a recent essay by the Swedish scholar Rune Johansson. He restricts his study to the *Sutta Pitaka* of the Pāli Canon. He recognizes that even within that body of discourses there are occasional references which appear to view *nirvāṇa* as a 'metaphysical substance, transcending space, time and causality, a supramundane reality with independent existence'. The most striking example is the well-known passage in the *Udāna* which seems to assert that *nirvāṇa* is not only a condition or state of affairs that is not born, not become, not made, not compounded, but also a sphere utterly divorced from the elements of phenomenal existence. In Johansson's judgment the rare 'traces' of this tendency in the Pāli Nikāyas refer to the '*experienced world* projected as a real world' and then hypostatized as an independent entity. Consequently they do not vitiate the claim that 'the *nibbāna* of the Nikāyas is ... a transformed state of personality and consciousness'.[17] Though relatively few of them would accept the argument that the tendency to interpret *nirvāṇa* as a metaphysical entity is simply the result of projection and hypostatization of psychological states or experiences, many Buddhist intellectuals nonetheless do insist on the attainability of *nirvāṇa* as an ethical and spiritual achievement here and now.[18] As the anthropologists Gananath Obeyesekere and Michael Ames document in the case of Ceylon, there is, to be sure, also a widespread conviction among less formally educated contemporary Theravāda Buddhists that attaining *nirvāṇa* has become all but impossible in any time before the distant

16. T. W. Rhys Davids and William Stede, eds., *The Pali Text Society's Pali-English Dictionary* (London: Luzac & Co., 1959 [first edition, 1921–25]), p. 362a.

17. Rune Johansson, *The Psychology of Nirvana* (London: George Allen & Unwin, 1969), pp. 51–57, 111–112, 131–137. See also I. B. Horner's similar line of argument in reference to the term 'beyond' in *The Early Buddhist Theory of Man Perfected...*, pp. 282–312.

18. See, for example, Jayatilleke, 'Nirvāṇa', pp. 3–4; Nyanaponika, 'Anatta and Nibanna', pp. 25–28; Piyadassi, *The Buddha's Ancient Path*, esp. pp. 68–69, 72; Rahula, *What the Buddha Taught*, pp. 35, 41, 43–44; Thittila, '...Theravada Buddhism' in *The Path of the Buddha*, K. W. Morgan, ed., pp. 111–112. Among Buddhist students and faculty with whom I conversed in Ceylon there was virtual unanimity in affirming the possibility of attaining *nirvāṇa* here and now.

future after innumerable future births.[19] But even when the goal of salvation is conceived or imaged as a future state radically discontinuous with phenomenal existence, the Theravāda position is still Processive in the sense that the means through which the individual reaches that transcendent end is spiritual and ethical improvement in the course of time.

In contrast to the characteristically Nominalist and Processive tendency of the Theravādins, the Realism of the Mahāyāna tradition is typically Transactional in its soteriology. Among the various Mahāyāna schools there is, to be sure, no equivalent for the Christian commitment to a once for all redemption in the historical work of Christ. In his essay 'Passivity in the Buddhist Life' D. T. Suzuki does argue that the Mahāyāna interprets *karma* 'cosmologically' with the result that a single act like that of the Buddha's enlightenment may be construed as imbuing the whole universe with his wisdom and virtue.[20] But as Suzuki's willingness to apply the conception of cosmic *karma* to all action indicates, this line of interpretation cannot plausibly be construed as a systematic parallel to the paradigmatically Transactional position in the Christian tradition. Despite the absence of commitment to a once for all historical effecting of universal salvation, there are, however, significant parallels between Mahāyāna tendencies and the approach of those Christian theologians who interpret the significance of Christ as his manifesting or communicating the reality of a salvation or reconciliation eternally and in principle universally achieved and transhistorically available to all men.

In the Buddhist as in the Christian case actualization of salvation in the context of this approach is a matter of knowledge or insight or spiritual apprehension about an already existing state of affairs which is normally misperceived or rejected. Several emphatic statements from the writings of D. T. Suzuki and T. R. V. Murti may serve to epitomize the formulation of this position. Murti's description of the Mādhyamika perspective is very explicit in this connection. There is, to be sure, repeated reference to the preliminary role of morality and spiritual discipline. But from the ultimate

19. Michael McClean Ames, *Religious Syncretism in Buddhist Ceylon* (Harvard University Ph.D. dissertation, 1962), pp. 1–45, 224–270; Gananath Obeyesekere, 'Theodicy, Sin and Salvation in a Sociology of Buddhism', in *Dialectic in Practical Religion*, M. Fortes, J. R. Boody, and E. R. Leach, eds., Cambridge Papers in Social Anthropology, no. 5 (Cambridge: University Press, 1968), pp. 7–40.

20. *Essays in Zen Buddhism – Second Series* (London: Rider, 1958), pp. 262–264.

perspective which the Mādhyamika dialectic reveals, the defilements and evils and dualities against which moral and meditational disciplines are directed prove to be completely unreal. They must be so, since otherwise the absolute character of *nirvāṇa* would be compromised:

The Absolute as Nirvāₙa is conceived by some as the cessation of all desires and aversions. This implies that it was not existent before the destruction.... This is wrong according to the Mādhyamika. There has been no initial fall, and there is no need for re-transformation. Nirvāna, says Nāgārjuna, is non-ceasing, un-achieved. There is only the dissolution of false views (kalpanāksaya), but no becoming in the real.[21]

Even more unambiguous is Murti's explicit differentiation of the Mādhya-mika conception of *nirvāṇa* from those which maintlan that 'discrete exist-ences (saṁskṛta dharmas) are really changed into another state':

The Mādhyamika brings out by his criticism that there is no change in things; if the kleśas were real, they could not be reduced to nothing. There is only change in our outlook, not in reality. Nirvāna is 'what is not abandoned nor acquired....' The function of prajñā is not to transform the real, but only to create a change in our attitude towards it. The change is epistemic (subjective), not ontological (objective). The real is as it has ever been.[22]

Suzuki repeatedly advances the same argument. Perhaps his most striking formulation is his insistence that affirmation of what is characterizes the very nature of religion:

Whatever we may say about moral ideals of perfection, religion is after all the acceptance of things as they are, things evil together with things good.... 'You are all right as you are', or 'to be well with God and the world', or 'don't think of the morrow' – this is the final word of all religion.... To strive, which means to 'negate', is, according to Buddhist phraseology, eternally to transmigrate in the ocean of birth and death.[23]

In this interpretation as in its Christian analogues there is, of course, a

21. *The Central Philosophy of Buddhism*, pp. 229, 233.
22. *The Central Philosophy of Buddhism*, pp. 273–274.
23. *Essays... Second Series*, p. 283. For a similarly striking but more extended discus-sion, see Suzuki's *Introduction to Zen Buddhism*, pp. 91–103.

recognition of the need to realize or to appropriate enlightenment or salvation. But the position is nonetheless both Realist and Transactional in that all of phenomenal existence is said 'already' or eternally to be reconciled with or essentially to be identical with that ultimate reality to which sinners or the unenlightened take it to be opposed.

INCIPIENT MERGING OF THE WHOLISTIC AND PROCESSIVE MOTIFS

Even so cursory a survey of the contrasting emphases in typical Theravāda and Mahāyāna approaches to the central religious question of salvation or emancipation suggests the possibility of a parallel to the Christian attempt at combining Realist and Nominalist commitments in a consistently Processive interpretation of the significance of Christ. Because the Theravāda and the Mahāyāna traditions have the complementary characteristics of the Nominalists and Realists respectively, it is difficult to escape the impression that each of them has definite strengths from which the other could benefit. In the Theravāda case, there is the manifest asset of a full appreciation that the religious task entails a straightforward confrontation with moral limitations and a concerted effort to overcome them – an effort, that is, to change the existing state of affairs. The result is a conception of *nirvāṇa* which emphasizes differences from and consequently the need for changes in the prevailing patterns of phenomenal existence or *saṃsāra*. The strength of the Mahāyāna lies in a different direction. Its insistence that *nirvāṇa* and *saṃsāra* are ultimately one constitutes an at least potentially positive valuation of the whole of being. Hence the concern of the Mahāyāna Buddhist is with all of reality. All beings participate in the Buddha-nature; all are already ingredient in *nirvāṇa*. That this broader concern is not simply an abstraction is evident in the ideals and practice which have characterized the Mahāyāna. It is indeed the more comprehensive path. From its inception, laymen as well as monks have been more integral to its program than in the typical Theravāda position. And the *bodhisattva* ideal articulates explicitly an active concern with the destiny of all beings, a concern which often remains only implicit when the ideal of the *arhat* is dominant.

Mahāyāna and Theravāda Buddhists have not been unaware of the strengths of each other's perspective. On the Mahāyāna side this recognition of the value of the Theravāda concern with moral and meditational discipline is evident in the not infrequently emphatic inclusion of those dimensions in its own conception of spiritual discipline. Similarly, on the Theravāda side, there have been growing numbers of twentieth-century devotees who appreciate the Mahāyāna insistence on a connection between *nirvāṇa* and *saṃsāra*. Typically, this tendency is allied with a conviction that the Buddhist way must address social and political issues. Not surprisingly, the vigorous polemical writings of men like Anagarika Dharmapala and D. C. Vijaya-vardhana thus demand a positive and even this-worldly interpretation of *nirvāṇa*.[24] In spite of some measure of mutual appreciation, the dominant tone of evaluation is, however, critical. The consistent Mahāyāna position that a preoccupation with overcoming defilements or attachments represents only a provisional discipline still captive to the illusion that such obstacles are real illustrates the criticism implicit even in praise for the Theravāda moral vigor. Conversely, the typical Theravāda appraisal of the Mahāyāna – usually oral, since few Theravāda writers have addressed themselves to questions relating to the Mahāyāna – is that it underestimates the seriousness of moral evil or that it makes the attainment of *nirvāṇa* too easy.[25]

One can only hope that a spirit of mutual appreciation and criticism may lead to a more comprehensive interpretation combining the strengths of both positions. The outlines of at least one version of this more inclusive interpretation are discernible. It employs the resources which the Mahāyāna offers for ascribing a positive status to the phenomenal world: the whole of *saṃsāra* is potentially *nirvāṇa*. In this way it generates a soteriological concern with all of reality. But in contrast to many formulations of the traditional Mahāyāna position, this synthesis is not committed to the conception of an eternal and unchanging Absolute. Instead it recognizes the necessity for real development and consequently views the whole of being as in process – as temporal. In this way the Theravāda appreciation of the fact of ethical and psychological change is fully appropriated and in turn

24. Anagarika Dharmapala, *Return to Righteousness*, Ananda Guruge, ed. (Colombo, Ceylon: The Government Press, 1965), pp. 313, 807; D. C. Vijayavardhana, *The Revolt in the Temple* (Colombo, Ceylon: Sinha Publications, 1953), p. 586.

25. See, for example, the short essay of Bhikkhu Ananda, *Theravada and Zen* (Colombo, Ceylon: M. D. Gunasena, 1962), especially pp. 18, 19, 21. See also K. N. Jayatilleke, 'Buddhist Relativity and the One-World Concept', in *Religious Pluralism and World Community*, E. J. Jurji, ed. (Leiden: E. J. Brill, 1969), pp. 50–51, 59–60.

applied to reality in its totality. The whole of being is developing toward its ultimate realization; it is in the process of its transformation from *saṃsāra* into *nirvāṇa*.

There are occasional indications especially among Mahāyāna Buddhists that the interpretation of the relation between *nirvāṇa* and *saṃsāra* is developing in some such fashion. Kenneth K. Inada, for example, construes the equation of *nirvāṇa* and *saṃsāra* to mean that 'this mundane empirical world has all the makings or ingredients whereby the pure enlightened world can be realized'.[26] Similarly, Susumu Yamaguchi observes that 'the fundamental notion of the Mahāyāna doctrines was that our actual and empirical world is nothing other than the basis for the realization of the negative and absolute world'.[27] Interpreting the relationship of *nirvāṇa* to *saṃsāra* as that of actuality to potentiality rather than as that of reality to illusion does, to be sure, entail a positive valuation of development which is absent from many Mahāyāna metaphysical systems. But such positive valuation of change is nonetheless very congenial to Mahāyāna spiritual ideals. The *bodhisattva* is committed to relentless efforts to bring happiness and deliverance from suffering to all beings. The very purpose of his existence is to foster change in the world of *saṃsāra*. To interpret the relationship between *nirvāṇa* and *saṃsāra* as one of actuality to potentiality is, then, to construe such change as ultimately significant. It is not an apparent change which is finally illusory because the Absolute is eternally the same; instead it constitutes a change, a transformation, in the real itself.

Insofar as religious systems offer symbolic interpretations of man's experience, such a modification in emphasis is not surprising. For man's experience is in fact changing. Twentieth-century man is becoming increasingly persuaded that he can in fact influence the course of his history not only in trivial matters but also on profound and ultimately significant issues for which he must assume responsibility. A remarkable growth of social and

26. 'Some Basic Misconceptions of Buddhism', *International Philosophical Quarterly*, IX (1969), 119. See also Inada's more general observation in 'Toward a Re-orientation of Buddhist Thought', *Japanese Religions*, IV/2 (March, 1966), p. 10: 'My personal opinion about Buddhism is that the various organizations must now take a step forward in reorienting and reorganizing themselves to meet the demands and spirit of the times'.
27. 'Development of Mahayana Buddhist Beliefs', in *The Path of the Buddha*, K. W. Morgan, ed. (New York: Ronald Press, 1956), p. 171.

political self-consciousness and the correlative awareness of the innovative capacities of human technology have become critical dimensions of man's experience. That the Mahāyāna tradition is able to appropriate, illumine, and in turn shape even what is novel in that experience testifies to the vitality and the viability of its central symbols.

There seems to be less indication that the Theravāda interpretation of the relationship between *nirvāṇa* and *saṃsāra* is evolving in a similar direction. The traditional emphasis on the distinction between *nirvāṇa* and *saṃsāra* with its recognition of the need for moral and psychological change in order to attain the 'other shore' is of course highly conducive to a dynamic and critical ethic. But there seems to be little inclination to forge a position which systematically ascribes a positive status to phenomenal existence. Although traditional social virtues and lay ethics are extolled, the ultimate aim of the Buddhist life is still concieved as escape from *saṃsāra* – *saṃsāra* conceived in total contrast to *nirvāṇa*. Hence the dominant theoretical judgment of phenomenal existence is one of sweeping rejection.

This pattern is evident in the hierarchy of religious roles characteristic of Theravāda Buddhist communities. The order of value begins with the ordinary layman, proceeds to the lay disciple and the monk with temple duties, and culminates with the monk who has retreated to an isolated hermitage in order to devote himself completely to mediation. The measure of status is inversely proportional to the measure of involvement with worldly tasks.[28] The ideal of mediational and spiritual discipline is, of course, the common heritage of all streams in the Buddhist tradition. But the Theravāda exemplifies it in particularly striking form because it has only a very subdued emphasis on the role of the *arhat* after he attains enlightenment. Indeed, among that very large proportion of Theravāda Buddhists who believe that it is virtually impossible to attain arhatship in the present degenerate age, the question of a saint's post-enlightenment role is all but irrelevant. As a result, the task of promoting the happiness or alleviating the suffering of beings within the context of phenomenal existence is of decidedly secondary importance; and the question of directing or influencing the course of human history can have only a very limited and indirect religious significance.

28. See Gananath Obeyesekere, 'Theodicy, Sin and Salvation in a Sociology of Buddhism', pp. 31–38.

Within the Theravāda community of interpretation there are, of course, also indications of change. That increasing numbers of university-educated believers are rejecting the popular view of the unattainability of *nirvāṇa* and insisting on understanding the goal of the Buddhist life as capable of realization here and now is one illustration of the attempt to relate the tradition to present concerns. With the support of university faculty in departments of Buddhist civilization, philosophy, and Pāli, this growing stratum of intellectuals can marshal overwhelming textual support for its position. The question is, however, more serious when it is not one of documenting textual support but rather that of enriching or even modifying traditional interpretations. And this is what a rethinking of the traditional Theravāda conception of the relationship between *nirvāṇa* and *saṃsāra* would require. Among those Buddhist thinkers actively engaged in political life, there seems to be some inclination to move in this direction. They constitute only a very small minority; buth they are, in effect, raising the crucial question of whether or not a religious system is viable in the twentieth century if it declines to interpret as religiously significant man's increasing capacity to shape his personal and corporate life within the sphere of phenomenal existence. To that question Theravāda as well as Mahāyāna communities will be responding in one way or another during the coming decades.

INTERACTION BETWEEN TRADITIONS TODAY

The possibility of a type or multiple types of Buddhist worldview which combine the strengths of Theravāda and Mahāyāna perspectives is not, of course, simply the product of mutual enrichment among the various Buddhist communities. Instead a significant impetus toward reinterpreting traditional commitments so as to allow a more positive appraisal of man's active role in historical development is attributable to the impact of Western expansion into Asia. Both the self-conscious movement toward reformulating traditional conceptions and the acknowledgment among Buddhists themselves of the influence of Western incursions are probably most advanced in Japan. One striking indication of this double awareness is a recent essay of Masao Abe, a Japanese Buddhist professor of philosophy. Originally written as a lecture in Japanese for Japanese hearers but then also published in an English translation, Abe's article calls for a break with 'traditional patterns' so that Buddhism and Christianity can be studied 'in the context of world history' and 'with reference to our vital concern for the future – how can we attain the truly human life and being, and how can we establish a perfect world order'.[29] Abe's two part essay plus a response to friendly critics explores numerous similarities and differences between Christians and Buddhists and notes what he sees as the particular problems confronting each tradition. Significantly, the difficulty confronting Buddhism on which he focuses particular attention is 'that of ethical and historic action'. While acknowledging that Western personalism and theism are able to stress man's moral activity and responsibility, he does not, however, recommend adopting or imitating this perspective because its dualistic implications are incompatible with modern science. Instead he tentatively proposes a greater emphasis on the Buddhist conception of *karma* and on the *bodhisattva* ideal.[30]

Abe's article may serve to epitomize what is almost certainly the dominant response to the expansion of Western influence which van Leeuwen celebrates in *Christianity in World History*. That response is to reject any uncritical identification of modernization and Westernization (or Christianization). The exigencies of the former are accepted, while the latter is subjected to critical evaluation. The two are, to be sure, not readily separable, as is evident from even a casual acquaintance with the Third World in transition. Even so sympathetic an interpreter of non-Western cultures as Wilfred Cantwell Smith observes that 'the concept "modern" involves a sense that history is moving in a particular direction':

To be modern ... means to live in the environment that one's society has deliberately chosen to construct (or accept); and to do so rationally, self-consciously.... The knowledge of what is possible – an ever-widening knowledge of ever new possibilities – and the techniques of implementing these, this is modernity.[31]

29. Masao Abe, 'Buddhism and Christianity as a Problem Today, Part I'. *Japanese Religions*, III, 2 (summer, 1963), pp. 15–16.
30. 'Buddhism and Christianity..., Part II'. *Japanese Religions*, III, 3 (autumn, 1963), esp. p. 30 .
31. *Modernisation of a Traditional Society* (New York: Asia Publishing House, 1965), pp. 19, 20. See also Smith's 'Traditional Religions and Modern Culture', an address presented at the XIth Congress of the International Association for the History of Reli-

Not only the requisite technological innovations but also the pervasive sense of a directionality to history are in significant measure offspring of the West. Yet despite the undeniable dependence of the modernizing process on the West not only historically but also to some extent still technologically and even ideologically, non-Western cultures nonetheless seek to interpret this at least partially novel dimension of their experience with reference to the symbolic resources of their particular traditions.

As numerous studies since Max Weber's pioneer work *The Protestant Ethic and the Spirit of Capitalism* (1904–1905) have documented, not only Western science and technology but also its political and economic systems are in their origins and their development intimately and reciprocally related to Jewish and Christian religious commitments. Similarly, the integration of the modernizing process into non-Western cultures requires a mutual adaptation between the novel ingredients and traditional beliefs and practices. As a result, the contemporary movement toward a world civilization involves not only technical, economic, and political exchange but also at least implicit interaction between religious traditions. To recognize this interaction as an instance of contemporary encounter between contrasting religious perspectives is a potent reminder that no such contact occurs in isolation from correlative social and cultural movements. Useful though this recognition may be, it is, however, misleading in so far as it suggests that the process of interaction between religious traditions moves in only one direction. That is of course not the case.

As Abe rightly avers, Christianity also has its difficulties – difficulties with which the Buddhist perspective is not beset.[32] The intelligibility of its traditionally highly anthropomorphic conceptions and images of God is only one example. The question of immortality and the perhaps excessive individualism which it implies is another. Less perennial but particularly pressing on the contemporary scene is the whole complex of issues involved in conceiving or imaging man's relationship to his natural environment. Like the interaction resulting from the modernization process, each such

---

gions, Claremont, California, September 9, 1965, pp. 22–23 of the mimeographed copy, for his observation that 'the whole religious (and indeed cultural) history of mankind is entering a seriously new phase' – 'largely as a result of the spread throughout the world of a dynamic movement originating in the West by which man is transforming mundane life'.

32. 'Buddhism and Christianity..., Part II'. esp. p. 30.

problem is, of course, not independent of correlative developments in human culture and in nature itself. Even direct interest in other religious traditions like that increasingly expressed by Westerners disenchanted with or alienated from their own multiple traditions patently does not illustrate attention to religious questions in isolation from other social and cultural issues. But precisely because the issues at stake are not only personal but also social and cultural, another religious perspective may be able to offer resources not otherwise readily available.

If to abstract religious interaction from its relatedness to multiple cultural and even natural environments is to oversimplify the complexities of reciprocal influence, to ignore the religious dimension of such interaction in favor of focusing exclusively on technical, economic, and political issues is similarly to indulge in oversimplification and distortion. The successes and failures of myriad governmental aid programs or business investments in the Third World testify eloquently to the accuracy of this truism. It is, therefore, ironical that a book like van Leeuwen's *Christianity in World History*, with its sweeping and frequently insightful cross-cultural analysis, should conclude with a virtual elimination of overtly religious concerns except as 'treasures' from the past to serve as 'ornaments' for the technocratic civilization of the emerging planetary world.[33]

Van Leeuwen's most categorically negative judgments are not surprisingly reserved for non-Christian traditions. But Christianity *qua* religion is also included.[34] The uncompromisingly critical character of his position is in large measure a function of his identification of religion with a comprehensive legitimation of the traditional social and cultural *status quo*.[35] Alternative tendencies are simply excluded from the category 'religion'. Van Leeuwen's programmatically negative judgment on religion is, of course, very much under the influence of Karl Barth's attempt to distinguish the Christian Gospel from all religion and Dietrich Bonhoeffer's references to a 'religionless Christianity'. The question is, however, unavoidable as to whether it is not more adequate to the historical experience of the various traditions including the Jewish-Christian one to see criticism of religious practices and institutions as a dynamic within religious life. Certainly the

33. *Christianity in World History*, esp. pp. 401–404, 410–427.
34. *Christianity in World History*, pp. 410–411 is very explicit on this point.
35. *Christianity in World History*, esp. pp. 401–404, 410–411, 416–417, 422.

traditions which Bellah classifies as illustrating the historic type offer numerous parallels to the prophetic criticism of established religious patterns which van Leeuwen celebrates in the Jewish and Christian case. That Gautama the Buddha exemplifies such criticism of existing practices through reference to an ideal or norm which transcends them suffices to indicate that this tendency is not simply a peripheral aberration in non-Western traditions. It is no doubt true that the tension between the ideal and the actual which the dualistic tendency of Bellah's historic type entails is not as successfully institutionalized elsewhere as it is in the West. But that fact does not justify defining religion so as to exclude all such prophetic or critical motifs.

If one rejects van Leeuwen's polemically restrictive definition of religion, then the tenability of his conclusion that specifically religious concerns are dispensable also becomes very doubtful. As van Leeuwen himself readily acknowledges, the existence of recognizably analogous religious traditions is in any case a universal fact of man's past. The contemporary situation especially in the West of radical pluralism and of widespread disenchantment with overtly religious institutions does, to be sure, make any extrapolation to the future on the basis of the past a highly precarious enterprise. But there is nonetheless every indication first, that man will continue to raise questions about the ultimate meaning of his personal and social life and also of cosmic history as a whole and second, that his responses to such questions will employ concepts, images, and practices not completely discontinuous with presently extant religious and quasi-religious traditions. In so far as or as long as this double judgment proves accurate, the possibility of increasing contact between religious traditions is, then, of interest and significance in its own right and not simply as an implicate of other forms of cross-cultural interaction.

DIALOGUE AS A PROCESS OF MUTUAL EVALUATION

To speak seriously of dialogue between adherents of different religious traditions is to concur in the judgment of Troeltsch and of virtually all contemporary anthropologists, sociologists, and historians of religion that the various religious faiths and traditions perform significantly analogous functions in their respective cultures or subcultures. In each case the religious system is a complex of ethical norms, rituals, institutional patterns, and literary and doctrinal formulations which provides a comprehensive frame of reference for interpreting and in turn responding to or shaping the conditions of human living. This position is, of course, relativistic. That it need not subscribe to an uncritical relativism is, however, evident from the process of dialogue itself.

The very fact that adherents of different traditions engage in dialogue already belies any resignation to an unqualified relativism. For the process of dialogue is not only an attempt to achieve mutual understanding but also, to use an increasingly uncommon phrase, a quest for truth. Interaction between religious traditions is not of course confined to the situation of direct conversation between believers or devotees of the various traditions. Instead it occurs whenever a man who self-consciously subscribes to definite values or beliefs or patterns of action appraises a perspective other than his own. The printed word and, in pluralistic cultures, direct observation are, therefore, widespread media for such interaction. It may nonetheless still be instructive to consider the paradigm of personal conversation between adherents of different traditions in order to indicate the multiple directions from which the question of truth is in practice raised.

Dialogue is an inherently critical enterprise because it unavoidably entails a process of mutual appraisal. Though understanding and conse-quent appreciation are not absent, evaluation is not normally positive without qualification. Perhaps the most frequent form of initial dissatis-faction is expressed as an appeal to ostensibly shared premises. The conten-tion that certain beliefs – in a transcendent personal deity or in transmigration, for example – are simply inconceivable if one accepts generally established scientific hypotheses illustrates this appeal. So too does questioning the ethical implications of a belief or a complex of beliefs and practices because they seem to violate universally accepted values or norms. Any such appeal to allegedly shared premises may, however, be premature if it is made with reference to a particular commitment abstracted from the religious system as a whole. This possibility is most readily apparent in the second line of criticism. A Buddhist may, for example, argue that the substantial and immortal soul in which at least some Christians believe unavoidably entails a preoccupation with the self and its eternal destiny – a self-preoccupation which is held to be destructive of genuine spirituality. Or a Muslim may charge that the Hindu view of phenomenal existence as ultimately illusory undermines any serious concern with concrete social and ethical problems. The initial criticism is, in short, on a pragmatic level: a belief or a practice is appraised negatively because it at least seems to conflict with values which the critic espouses. But in examining the ramifications of any specific criticism, it is quickly apparent that there are numerous interconnections between the particular point at issue and other commitments of the religious system. Hence the initial use of what is in effect a pragmatic criterion of truth results in a systematic evaluation of the dialogue partner's position as a unified religious perspective.

Evaluation at this level is, then, a combining of the initial pragmatic criterion with judgments about the coherence of the system as a whole. In this process of appraisal one way in which further interconnections among the beliefs and practices constituting the religious system become evident is in response to questions about experiences which seem to contradict the religious commitments under scrutiny. In that sense a correspondence theory of truth is operative: the critic indicates data of experience which seem to conflict with the religious tenet in question. But the response to such queries typically is an argument to the effect that further resources in the religious tradition can account for the apparent difficulty. As a result, the criterion of correspondence functions in the first instance only to provide the impetus for elaborating the full complexity of the religious system. Once that system is articulated in some detail, the criterion of correspondence may again be employed. But at this level, the correspondence theory no longer conforms to the paradigm of perception of an empirical object – verification of whether the pole in the water is in fact bent, for example. Instead the question of correspondence has reference to wholes of experience. Hence the truth question becomes an appraisal of the degree to which the religious system offers a coherent interpretation of the whole of human experience and thereby effectively shapes man's thoughts, affections, and actions in what is deemed a constructive direction. Any such evaluation unavoidably requires the application of criteria which themselves are not exempt from criticism. But that requirement only makes the process of evaluation mutual and therefore more complex; it does not invalidate the process itself.

Assessment of religious systems ranging from the most primitive to the most complex of contemporary world traditions may be construed as conforming to this pattern. To take a very general and simplistic example, the fact that matriarchally structured agricultural societies frequently conceive of ultimate principles as feminine in character while patriarchally organized pastoral cultures affirm masculine deities renders highly dubious a claim that either view offers a literal formulation of absolute truth. Yet both types of religious system nonetheless serve to interpret the world which their adherents experience. In this sense they have reference to the facts of particular forms of social and personal life. Hence they may legitimately claim some measure of validity, even if it is limited in scope.

But at precisely this point the situation of contemporary religious traditions contrasts with the past to a degree not yet fully appreciated. The contrast may be stated succinctly: despite the continued applicability of this pattern of appraising the adequacy of a tradition, any such provincial validity is no longer viable. Because twentieth-century men are increasingly aware of each other's experience on a global scale, religious systems cannot simply claim relevance to a particular cultural tradition or limited geographical area. Instead they must interpret or in principle allow for the possibility of interpreting the total variegated experience of mankind; for it is in this context of an emerging global consciousness that contemporary religious perspectives affirm the apprehension of experience to which they are committed.

Religious Affirmation and the Systematic Appraisal of Alternatives

In so far as the process of appraisal involved in dialogue is applicable to any religious position, one's own tradition is, of course, included. The parallels to the situation of dialogue are, moreover, especially marked when that tradition itself is seen to encompass multiple perspectives within it. In this case, the relationship which the reflective believer or devotee has to his own religious community is significantly analogous to the not uncritical encounter which dialogue between traditions represents. In affirming commitment to a particular tradition the believer or devotee acknowledges and assents to images, patterns of action, and conceptions which inform or structure his awareness of himself and his role in the world. Typically those institutional forms, ritual actions, images, and ideas pervade at least a significant dimension of his culture or subculture in addition to influencing the formation of a set of personal commitments. Consequently the particular symbolic resources of the tradition in question possess a power or an authority which an abstractly articulated series of various alternative worldviews cannot convey. Though this evocative power is no doubt possible apart from social and cultural reinforcement and repeated exposure from an early age on, this possibility is something of a limiting case rather than the norm in as much as it seems to require an extraordinarily independent individual and/or an unusual combination of circumstances and influences. In so far as even a typical adherent becomes aware that there is a plurality of possible interpretations not only of peripheral beliefs and practices but also of the central commitments of his own tradition, he is, however, confronted with the responsibility of making judgments of relative adequacy even if he maintains his loyalty to its particular symbols. Once this awareness of multiple possibilities arises he is, therefore, engaged in a process of dialogue with his own tradition – at least he is so to the extent that his affirmation is not simply uncritical acceptance.

The very existence of multiple types of worldview within a single line of historical continuity in turn supports the prospect of fruitful dialogue between different communities because it underscores the developmental character of all still dynamic religious traditions. Inherent in this fact of development is the responsibility which adherents have to interpret or even to modify accepted formulations so that they become sufficiently comprehensive to incorporate new perceptions. Hence dialogue between religious traditions is not only an academic exercise in mutual understanding. It is also a process through which constructive change can occur in each participant's interpretation of his own position as he attempts to respond to the critical appraisal which his partner offers. That result may at first seem to be quite contrary to what is generally taken to be the purpose of contact between traditions, since it emphasizes modification in one's own position rather than in that of one's partner. But apart from the extreme policy of forced conversion, change in religious consciousness can in any case occur only through altered conviction or awareness. That a description of the process of dialogue recognizes this fact need not be construed as a frustration of evangelicals in all traditions for two reasons. First, the possibility that a modification of position may occur through the interchange is in any case mutual; and second, an endorsement of dialogue does not in itself preclude the view that traditional evangelism is appropriate in at least some contexts.

Such missionary activity must, however, be differentiated from the program of dialogue; for there is a significant difference between the intentions of the two enterprises. That difference may be epitomized in the observation that the purpose of dialogue is not conversion of the partner from his tradition to one's own. Participants in dialogue need not of course abandon a conviction that all men must be converted – that all men must experience a radical reorientation of their self-understanding, their values, their manner of living. But the intention of dialogue between religious traditions is not to effect that transformation by a transfer of allegiance from one tradition to another. It is instead to understand, to appreciate, and to evaluate critically both traditions to the end that they become more adequate to the total experience of their adherents. Although no definitive judgments on such matters are possible, this process of modifying existing commitments in the direction of greater adequacy may well be more influential as a mode of interaction between traditions for at least the foreseeable future than will be the attempt to effect conversion from one tradition to another. In any case, there is every indication that such interaction will continue and almost certainly increase in seriousness. It is, therefore, legitimate and even imperative to formulate the intentions of the undertaking as explicitly and forthrightly as possible.

To construe the purpose of dialogue as the achievement of more adequate religious systems no doubt places a positive valuation on the possibility of modifications in each participant's self-understanding. This emphasis should not, however, be confused with a policy of syncretism. Dialogue does, to be sure, presuppose that each partner in principle recognizes that he can benefit from conversation with the other. One can also assume that alterations in the direction of greater comprehensiveness will increase the measure of common ground which different traditions share. But in contrast to the product resulting from a process of syncretism, each tradition will continue to exemplify an integrity of its own because any modifications are reinterpretations or adaptions of its own images, conceptions, and practices. The result is not an incongruous combination of incompatible elements but a new synthesis which is continuous with a living and therefore developing tradition.

The figures of Mahatma Gandhi and Martin Luther King provide vivid twentieth-century illustrations of this synthetic power – and also of the cumulative effect of interaction between religious traditions. In neither case is there an attempt to integrate all the commitments of a number of different systems. Instead both men appropriate insights or emphases complementary to their own particular convictions from one or more other traditions; in the process they fashion a richer though nonetheless still unified religious worldview which stands in direct (even if frequently critical) relation to the tradition in which it is nurtured. Dialogue will not of course create a Gandhi or a King. But their lives and thought nonetheless exemplify in striking form the potential for increasing the depth and power of one religious tradition through creative interaction with another. To judge the realization of this potential as generally desirable assumes that no tradition has an interest in celebrating or perpetuating inadequacies in any other religious system. Those who seek deficiencies in other traditions in order to confirm their belief in the superiority of their own may dispute this assumption. But one can hope that this tendency will be one of the first casualities of genuine dialogue between adherents of different religious traditions.

The existence of multiple types of worldview within a single tradition is, then, significant in that it allows and indeed encourages self-conscious development and even modification of one's own commitments. The fact of pluralism within ostensibly unified traditions is, moreover, of further significance because it establishes the context for any systematic and at least potentially comprehensive evaluation of other communities. This context may be stated aphoristically: each of the various religious traditions includes different approaches leading to different goals. Perhaps the most facile response to the fact of religious pluralism is the assertion that the various perspectives and correlative practices are simply different paths or ways to the same ultimate destination. This response is in any case an artificial homogenization of the enormous diversity among the world's religious ideas and actions. But it is also an oversimplification of the situation even within a single tradition. The goal of the religious life as it is conceived or imaged in the various Christian Transactional perspectives is not, for instance, simply identical with God's ultimate purpose for man as the different Processive interpretations formulate it. Conversely, if one abstracts from the concrete images and conceptions and institutions and rituals, there may be greater commonality in systematic commitments or tendencies between some adherents of different traditions than among the full variety of perspectives within the same tradition. To be specific, there may be more systematic common ground between a Realist-Transactional position like that of Karl Barth and the Mahāyānist views of a D. T. Suzuki than between Suzuki and a Theravādin like U. Thittila or between Barth and a consistently Processive thinker like Wolfhart Pannenberg. Similarly, there may be a greater systematic contrast between a strongly Nominalist and Transactional perspective like that of Rudolf Bultmann and such a programmatically Processive and communitarian approach as that of Daniel Day Williams than there is between Williams and an at least incipiently process-oriented Mahāyānist like Susumu Yamaguchi or between Bultmann and a Theravādin who does not stress development over time like Walpola Rahula. Illustrations could of course be multiplied indefinitely, especially if one compared and contrasted positions from different historical periods instead of focusing on all contemporary figures. The central point is, however, simply that the question of similarities and differences between religious traditions can never be adequately analyzed unless one allows for the multiplicity of perspectives within the various traditions under scrutiny.

As is evident in the line of argument developed from the very beginning of this study, one approach which I finds useful in analyzing similarities and differences both within a single tradition and between traditions is the attempt to translate the positions under scrutiny into categories which allow comparison of the systematic implications of particular commitments. Although the total adequacy and therefore finality with which Hegel imbues the conception 'concept' (*'Begriff'*) is in principle inhospitable to the suggestion of comparative analysis, his attempt to translate religious images or representations (*Vorstellungen*) into concepts is in practice parallel to a typological analysis which abstracts from concrete images or ideas and practices in order to formulate the systematic structure of a particular position. In contrast to Hegel's apparent conviction, it must, however, be stated unambiguously that this analysis is a means for facilitating understanding and comparison, not an attempt to provide a strictly conceptual substitute for the affective and practical as well as theoretical or intellectual dimensions of religious systems. Also in contrast to at least some of Hegel's statements, the dependence of any such conceptual scheme on the tradition from which it is abstracted should not be obscured or overlooked. The attempt in this study to use a typology developed from Western history in order to illumine possible parallels among the multiple Christian and Buddhist perspectives is, therefore, defensible only if it is recognized as highly tentative and provisional. Ideally it would be refined or if need be fundamentally revised in collaboration with Buddhists and adherents of other traditions. But with those qualifications the elaboration of this and other typologies remains a potentially useful analytical tool for evaluating not only alternatives within one's own tradition but also the plurality of perspectives which other traditions exemplify.

In so far as a typology is genuinely instructive, it does not in itself determine the question of relative adequacy among the alternatives which it differentiates. Throughout this study I indicate my own judgment that a Processive interpretation which attends to the concerns of both the Realists and the Nominalists is the most promising of the positions which I systematize. This judgment reflects my view that the Realist-Nominalist-Processive position is most able adequately to interpret contemporary human experience and to foster what I consider a constructive response to that experience. In considering Hegel and in the chapters of Part Three, I attempt to support this judgment as to the adequacy of the position which I commend. Similarly, in evaluating other traditions my appraisal is most positive on perspectives which are wholistic as opposed to dualistic and which appreciate the temporal development not only of individuals and their communities but also of the whole of reality. This complex of interrelated judgments does not, however, follow from my typology itself. Others can and do choose other alternatives and argue for their greater adequacy. The continued advocacy of a Nominalist-Transactional existentialism and a Realist-Transactional orthodoxy illustrates this fact in the Christian case. And among Buddhists commitment to positions other than the one I commend is even much more pronounced because of a longer and more tenacious tradition of negative valuation of even the potential of phenomenal existence. The approach which I propose is not, then, one which unifies all possible perspectives.

Nor does it simply pronounce them all equally valid. Instead it analyzes similarities and differences and then makes choices which in turn entail criticism of the rejected alternatives.

It should perhaps be stated explicitly that decision in favor of one systematic alternative over others does not imply a judgment that the rejected positions are utterly devoid of value or, more particularly, that individuals subscribing to those positions cannot in their lives exhibit spirituality or virtue. The ideal of the religious life – the image of the saint – which a particular perspective espouses is, to be sure, correlative with the position as a whole. An ethic can, in short, be relatively more individualistic or relatively more communal (including community with the natural as well as the social order), relatively more contemplative and oriented toward a transcendent goal or relatively more activistic and focused on life in space and time. In this sense the choice of a metaphysics or of a religious worldview is not without definite practical consequences. Here again I find the wholistic, activistic, and this-wordly combination most congenial. Though that preference is no doubt in part matter of personal disposition, I think arguments for its greater adequacy in comparison to the alternatives can be advanced with particular reference to interpreting human experience in the distinctively modern period. Even if persuasive arguments to that effect are possible, they do not, however, imply a simply negative judgment on other ideals or images of the saint.

For the Christian perspective which I advocate in this and the two preceding chapters, appraisal of other approaches to Christian faith and history and of the various perspectives represented in other traditions assumes the specific form of asking about the extent to which any interpretation mediates a transformation of men from a self-centered preoccupation with their own concerns to an ultimate faithfulness and loyalty to that comprehensive spiritual process in which they are individual centers or moments. It asks, in short, whether those other perspectives promote realization of what I understand Christians to affirm in speaking of the kingdom or rule of God. I think the Realist-Nominalist-Processive position which I attempt to outline offers the most adequate approach to interpreting and supporting movement toward realizing that kingdom. There is, however, no Christological or ecclesiological or other doctrinal reason for this theological perspective to deny the realization of such faithfulness and loyalty through other traditions or through Christian images and practices and concepts interpreted differently. For one who knows Christians committed to different interpretations and believers or devotees of various perspectives in other traditions, it is, moreover, not only a theoretical possibility but also an empirical fact that those alternative approaches indeed mediate genuine spirituality and virtue. Hence it is fortunate that even a relativism which is critical and therefore engages in the process of evaluation nonetheless neither requires nor encourages any arrogation of exclusive or absolute validity to one perspective.

As a final indication of the coherence of this study, it is perhaps appropriate to reiterate and to amplify my comments in the introductory chapter about the double connection between the approach to religious pluralism which I advocate in the preceding pages and the Christological commitments which I outline in the eighth chapter. There is, on the one hand, the negative fact that the interpretation of the significance of Christ which I commend does not require or imply an exclusivism which makes all religious attainment or value dependent on or derivative from his work. But there is, on the other hand, also the positive suggestion that the vary process of interaction among traditions is itself significantly analogous to reconciliation or Atonement as it is interpeted in the Realist-Nominalist-Processive position. Indeed, in so far as the influence of the figure of Christ is understood as mediating a transformation through which loyalty to the ultimately all-encompassing rule or kingdom of God displaces preoccupation with the self's provincial concerns, the process of interaction between traditions may be viewed from within the Christian tradition as integral to the work of Christ itself. In this sense dialogue with adherents of other religious traditions is as much a Christian imperative as evangelizing with the aim of conversion to Christianity ever was. The paradigm for this development is the insistence of Pauline Christianity that the good news of the Gospel must embrace the gentile as well as the Jew. So too in the emerging world culture of today the Christian seeks commonality transcending traditional divisions toward the end of that ultimate community which is all in all. This search need not deny the profound facts of pluralism and disagreement even within a single tradition. But the end or ideal of unqualified comprehensiveness at the same time requires an interaction which calls into question every uncritically relativistic legitimation of the provincial. It may, to be sure, seem quaint to refer to this process of interaction as continuing the work of Christ. Yet for the Christian, liberation from bondage to the self and its tendency to social and cultural idolatry is central to that integration of the particular into the universal which the good news about the coming kingdom both announces and demands.

Index of Names